Funny You Should Ask

Funny You Should Ask

Oral Histories of
Classic Sitcom Storytellers

SCOTT LEWELLEN

McFarland & Company, Inc., Publishers
Jefferson, North Carolina, and London

LIBRARY OF CONGRESS CATALOGUING-IN-PUBLICATION DATA

Lewellen, Scott, 1964–
    Funny you should ask : oral histories of classic sitcom storytellers / Scott Lewellen.
       p.   cm.
    Includes index.

    ISBN 978-0-7864-7148-5
    softcover : acid free paper ∞

    1. Television comedies — United States — Authorship.
    2. Television comedy writers — United States — Interviews.
I. Title.
PN1992.8.C66L48 2013
08.2'523—dc23   2012051778

BRITISH LIBRARY CATALOGUING DATA ARE AVAILABLE

© 2013 Scott Lewellen. All rights reserved

No part of this book may be reproduced or transmitted in any form or by any means, electronic or mechanical, including photocopying or recording, or by any information storage and retrieval system, without permission in writing from the publisher.

On the cover: 1960s stylization of a man with typewriter (iStockphoto/Thinkstock)

Manufactured in the United States of America

McFarland & Company, Inc., Publishers
  Box 611, Jefferson, North Carolina 28640
    www.mcfarlandpub.com

Table of Contents

Acknowledgments   vi
Preface   1
The Writers   3

1. I'm Really a First Baseman: Getting the Job   17
2. Careening Into a Wall: Writing the Script   35
3. We Had to Cut the Laugh: Classic Series   64
4. A Spectacular Idea: Classic Episodes   87
5. This Is Good: More Hits   102
6. I'm Going to Acting School: Flops   132
7. Gold Is What You're Always Going to Get: Working with Actors   166
8. Like a Marriage: Collaborators   187
9. The End of It: Retiring   207

Index   211

Acknowledgments

Thank you to Bertha Garcia, Gwen Ecklund, Thomas Watson and Sam Bobrick for their assistance in arranging interviews, Christina Carroll, Sabrina Schiller, Abbie Schiller, Michael Q. Martin, Sharon Denoff, Arline Lloyd, Estelle Elinson and Douglas Denoff for providing permissions and photos, Keith Brown, Martin Gostanian and Mark Quigley for their help in gathering research, Mark Lunde, Gina Adam, Alice Lewellen, Kate Jordal, Wendy Gray, Brandon Klinge, Annie Fuhrman and Brian Sauer for their assistance with the manuscript and Sharon Henderson, Curt Lewellen, Mindy Toyne and Evelyn Lewellen for their support.

Special thanks to the writers who so generously offered their time and memories: Sam Denoff (June 22, 2001); Bob Schiller (August 18, 2001); Bob Carroll, Jr., and Madelyn Davis (September 8, 2001); Jack Elinson (October 31, 2005); David Lloyd (November 1, 2005); Paul Wayne (March 19, 2012); Sam Bobrick (March 19, 2012); Allan Burns (March 21, 2012); Jerry Mayer (March 22, 2012); Lila Garrett (March 23, 2012); Fred Freeman (March 26, 2012); Rick Mittleman (March 26, 2012); Elroy Schwartz (March 27, 2012); Austin Kalish and Irma Kalish (March 27, 2012); Carl Kleinschmitt (May 8, 2012); Saul Turteltaub (May 23, 2012); Arnold Margolin (May 25, 2012); Ed Scharlach (July 2, 2012); Bill Persky (July 10, 2012); Bernie Orenstein (July 18, 2012).

Preface

Imagine a job where you had to find a logical way to set Lucy Ricardo's putty nose on fire. Or get laughs from Chuckles the Clown — by killing him in the most bizarre fashion possible. Or carefully mix comedy and drama by causing Edith Bunker to nearly become a victim of sexual assault.

Although you are likely familiar with classic sitcom stars, the other "stars" of these shows are often overlooked. These series were written by a very talented group of men and women who toiled at their typewriters for decades. *Funny You Should Ask: Oral Histories of Classic Sitcom Storytellers* is about television sitcom writing from the perspective of 22 of television's best and most prolific early comedy writers. I interviewed many of them in 2012 (a few together, most separately) but some much earlier, in 2005 and 2001. Their anecdotes are presented here thematically interrupted by me only when necessary.

Television is a writer's medium. And sitcoms have been a major component of the industry since its infancy. Yet relatively little has been written about sitcom writers' contributions to our culture. Their memories are important. Generally, the subjects of this book are not the writers or creators or producers who became moguls. The focus is on writers who mostly worked in the trenches, turning out dozens, even hundreds, of scripts.

What is perhaps most striking about these writers is their endurance and versatility. Their careers extended from the innocent but often hilarious sitcoms of the '50s and '60s to the more realistic and relevant shows of the '70s and '80s. Yes, the Bob Schiller and Bob Weiskopf listed in the credits of *I Love Lucy* were the same men who wrote many of the best episodes of the later seasons of *All in the Family*. They were among a number of former radio writers thriving in television in the 1980s — including Bob Carroll, Jr., and Madelyn Davis; Jack Elinson; Austin Kalish; Milt Josefsberg; Howard Leeds; Fred Fox; Seaman Jacobs; Larry Rhine; Larry Gelbart; Aaron Ruben; Bill Davenport, and Arthur Julian. Likewise, many

Preface

of the writers who entered the comedy writing field in the '50s and '60s were still working many years into their career. Can we expect similar longevity and adaptability from more recent sitcom writers? In a business now fraught with ageism, it's highly unlikely.

Although today's sitcoms retain some of the structure and techniques of their predecessors, they are written much differently (mostly in large groups) than early sitcoms. While some of those changes may be for the better, others clearly are not. Fortunately, for the first 40 years of television, the writers chronicled in this book, along with their peers, dominated comedy. Their work still makes us laugh today. These are their experiences — told from their unique and humorous points of view.

The Writers

Bob Carroll, Jr., (d. 2007) **and Madelyn Pugh Davis** (d. 2011) Carroll and Davis were the epitome of a comedy-writing duo. For more than 35 years, they wrote hundreds of television sitcom scripts — always as a team. They even shared credit on Davis' 2005 autobiography. Their distinctive stamp — logically plotted farces with a dose of meticulously

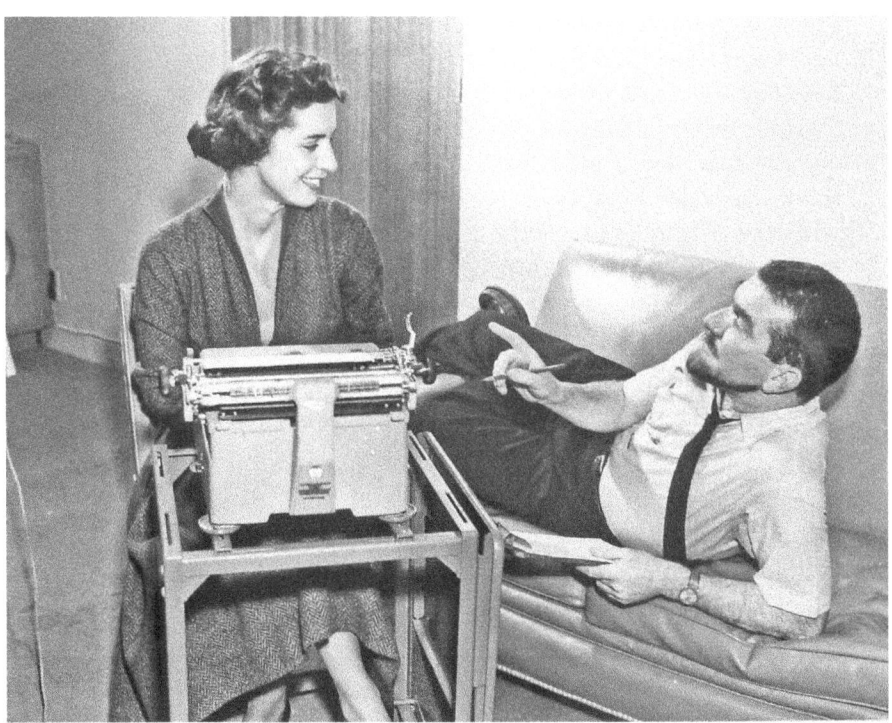

Madelyn Pugh Davis and Bob Carroll, Jr., during their radio days (courtesy Christina Carroll/Michael Quinn Martin Collection, used by permission, all rights reserved).

scripted physical comedy — marked most of their scripts and were often imitated by subsequent writers. Their style served them well in writing for the peerless Lucille Ball, beginning with Ball's radio series, *My Favorite Husband*. Contributing to every *I Love Lucy* script, the team established their credentials as pioneering sitcom writers, with Davis — nearly the only woman writing sitcoms in the early 1950s — also paving the way for future generations of female writers. They continued to work with Ball on *The Lucille Ball–Desi Arnaz Show* specials and the first two seasons of *The Lucy Show*. During a hiatus from Ball, they created and wrote more than half of the episodes of *The Mothers-in-Law*. Returning to Ball, they worked on *Here's Lucy* from 1970 to 1974. In 1977, Carroll and Davis were hired to produce *Alice*, which turned into an eight-year gig.

David Lloyd (d. 2009)   David Lloyd was skeptical that anyone would want to read about him because he was just a "hired gun" and not a famous creator or executive producer. When Lloyd died, he was the subject of numerous Internet posts from fans who knew the words "Written by David Lloyd" frequently preceded a superior sitcom episode. Even *Entertainment Weekly* and *Time* weighed in on the incredible talents of this "hired gun." While Lloyd gained immortality for writing the "Chuckles Bites the Dust" episode of *The Mary Tyler Moore Show*, many commentators focused on his prolific output. After a long stint as a writer for the top talk shows of the '60s and early '70s, Lloyd attempted his first script for *The Mary Tyler Moore Show*, a series he had never watched. Fulfilling his ambition to be a playwright through his television scripts, Lloyd wrote at a breakneck pace for

David Lloyd, 1976.

the next 30 years. The only writer to work on all four of the major ensemble sitcoms of the day (*The Mary Tyler Moore Show, Taxi, Cheers* and *Frasier*), Lloyd also distinguished himself by contributing to *Rhoda, The Bob Newhart Show, Lou Grant, Wings* and *Amen*.

Bob Schiller When I asked Bob Schiller to describe a Weiskopf and Schiller script, he simply said, "Funny." Schiller is rightfully proud that he and Bob Weiskopf were amazingly adaptable writers during their nearly 40-year partnership. Striking gold in the farcical comedies of the '50s and early '60s, the duo wrote for the final two seasons of *I Love Lucy,* all

Bob Weiskopf and Bob Schiller, late 1970s.

13 of *The Lucille Ball–Desi Arnaz Show* specials, *Make Room for Daddy, The Bob Cummings Show, The Ann Sothern Show* (which they also created), *Pete and Gladys* and *The Lucy Show*. Switching to variety shows in the mid-'60s and early '70s, they worked on three of the top shows of that genre — *The Red Skelton Show, The Carol Burnett Show* and *The Flip Wilson Show*. Returning to situation comedy in 1972, they began a long stint with Norman Lear's *Maude, All in the Family* and *Archie Bunker's Place*. The pair weren't just adaptable, they were good — and successful — picking up six Emmy nominations and two Emmy awards while working for six different top-five shows. Weiskopf died in 2001 and his good friend Schiller clearly missed him when we talked later that year.

Jack Elinson (d. 2011) Jack Elinson earned his first paycheck as a writer at age 16 by contributing a joke to Walter Winchell's column. After he worked in radio and early television variety series, his career really took off when he joined the staff of *The Danny Thomas Show*. Frequently partnered with Charles Stewart or Norman Paul, Elinson spent the next 30-plus years turning out an impressive number of consistently funny scripts for top series. His eight-year stint with Thomas coincided with his contributions to other series from Thomas' production company, including *The Real McCoys* and, most significantly, *The Andy Griffith Show*. Elinson's early scripts for Griffith established many of the hallmarks of that series. After the Thomas series ended, Elinson contributed to hit after hit as a writer and producer, including *Gomer Pyle, U.S.M.C., The Doris Day Show,* and *Good Times*. Elinson concluded his career serving as executive producer of still more hits—*One Day at a Time, The Facts of Life* and *227*.

Sam Denoff (d. 2011) **and Bill Persky** Sam Denoff aspired to be a songwriter and Bill Persky wanted to be an advertising copywriter. They used their words more successfully to make television audiences laugh.

Jack Elinson.

The team broke into sitcoms on *McHale's Navy* and *The Joey Bishop Show*. They soon made their mark during a three-year stint with *The Dick Van Dyke Show*. Their first script—"That's My Boy??"—was one of the series' best and best-remembered episodes and "Coast-to-Coast Big Mouth" in the fifth and final season won them their second Emmy award. Following their success with Van Dyke, they created and served as executive producers of the long-running *That Girl*. The duo also thrived in writing and producing variety specials for Julie Andrews, Goldie Hawn, Bill Cosby, Sid Caesar and Imogene Coca and Dick Van Dyke and Mary Tyler Moore. After Persky chose to concentrate on directing, Denoff continued as a writer, producer and consultant on *It's Garry Shandling's Show, Harry and the Hendersons* and *Life with Bonnie*. His sitcom career even gave him a few songwriting opportunities, including "Bupkis" for an episode of *The Dick Van Dyke Show* and the theme song for *That Girl*. Persky quickly became as highly respected as a director as he was as a writer, with assignments on *That Girl, The New Dick Van Dyke Show*

The Writers

(which he and Denoff also contributed to as writers), *Alice, Welcome Back, Kotter*, the pilot of *Who's the Boss?* and most notably as an Emmy winner on *Kate & Allie*, a series he also executive produced.

Allan Burns It took a few years for Allan Burns' comedy writing career to take off but it was worth the wait. A former page, screener, game show writer, cartoonist and greeting card writer, Burns got his first break with Jay Ward Productions as a writer for *The Bullwinkle Show* and creator of Captain Crunch. He teamed with Chris Hayward, and their idea for *The Munsters* was stolen and bastardized. But their luck began to turn when they won an Emmy for

Sam Denoff, ca. 1970.

Bill Persky.

The Writers

He & She, then joined the staff of *Get Smart*. Working solo, Burns wrote early episodes of *Love, American Style* and *Room 222*. He then formed a legendary comedy writing team with James L. Brooks. Co-creating and serving as executive producers of *The Mary Tyler Moore Show, Rhoda* and *Lou Grant*, they won five Emmys. A stint as a screenwriter earned Burns an Oscar nomination for *A Little Romance*. Returning to television, he provided crucial career breaks to Jim Carrey, Scott Bakula and Patricia Richardson.

Saul Turteltaub and Bernie Orenstein Saul Turteltaub and Bernie Orenstein loved show business. And it loved them back, rewarding them with a 40-year television career. Turteltaub wrote for Shari Lewis, Jackie Gleason, Carol Burnett, *Candid Camera* and *That Was the Week That Was*, while Orenstein succeeded him on *Candid Camera* and also worked on *The Hollywood Palace* and *The Monkees*. Forming a partnership, they wrote and produced *That Girl, The New Dick Van Dyke Show, Love, American Style, Sanford and Son, What's Happening!!* and *Kate & Allie*. They closed their careers as consultants on *Cosby*. While many scribes were writers first and producers later in their careers, Turteltaub and Orenstein

Allan Burns.

Saul Turteltaub, 1966.

The Writers

Bernie Orenstein (photograph by Robin Platzer/Twin Images).

spent nearly their entire sitcom careers serving simultaneously as producers and prolific writers.

Austin "Rocky" Kalish and Irma Kalish Austin and Irma Kalish formed two long-running partnerships — as a comedy writing team and as husband and wife for more than 60 years and counting. Austin followed Dean Martin and Jerry Lewis from radio to television as a writer for *The Colgate Comedy Hour*. After co-writing the pilot of *Gilligan's Island* with Elroy Schwartz, Austin partnered with Irma, leading them to become not only television's most prolific husband and wife comedy writing team but also one of the hardest working teams, period. They moved seamlessly from '60s hits *The Patty Duke Show, I Dream of Jeannie, My Favorite Martian, That Girl, F Troop, The Flying Nun, Family Affair* and *My Three Sons* to '70s and '80s successes *Maude, All in the Family, Good Times, The Bob Newhart Show* and *Too Close for Comfort*. Beginning with *Good Times*, Irma (co-producing with Austin) became one of the first female executive producers of a comedy series. Later she ran *The Facts of Life, 227* and *The Hogan Family*.

Irma Kalish and Austin Kalish.

The Writers

Paul Wayne As a young man, Paul Wayne studied French farce. The story of his first job in Hollywood is more fanciful than many a great farce. The play he had written for Canadian television about a Jewish leprechaun earned him a movie assignment — to write a pirate picture. Wayne soon moved to the relatively saner world of television comedy. He immediately applied his talent for farce on some of the best early episodes of *Bewitched*. Alternating between sitcoms (*The Andy Griffith Show, The Flying Nun, That Girl, All in the Family, Sanford and Son, Benson, Welcome Back, Kotter*) and staff jobs on variety series (*The Smothers Brothers Comedy Hour, The Sonny and Cher Comedy Hour*), Wayne kept busy working solo or with frequent partner George Burditt. Returning to his background in farce, Wayne teamed with Burditt to write prolifically for the first three seasons of *Three's Company*.

Paul Wayne.

Sam Bobrick The product of a small town, Sam Bobrick had a special touch with scripts about the denizens of Mayberry. In fact, his very first sitcom script, "The Shoplifters" episode of *The Andy Griffith Show*, won a Writers Guild Award. Working with former actor Bill Idelson, Bobrick continued to contribute to *Andy Griffith*

Sam Bobrick (courtesy Steven Stanley).

The Writers

along with *Gomer Pyle, U.S.M.C., Bewitched, The Flintstones* and *Get Smart* (for which they won another Writers Guild Award). After a successful stint on *The Smothers Brothers Comedy Hour*, Bobrick and his new partner, Ron Clark, alternated between writing plays and sitcom pilots. After Bobrick's creation, *Good Morning, Miss Bliss*, evolved into *Saved by the Bell*, he gained the financial security to write plays full-time. Samuel French has published more than 20 of his plays, four of which were produced on Broadway.

Jerry Mayer At the age of 35, Jerry Mayer packed up his family and left St. Louis to try his hand at comedy writing. His gamble more than paid off. He sold a story to *McHale's Navy*, then wrote a spec script about Leonardo da Vinci which earned him multiple assignments on *Bewitched*. Soon Mayer was alternating assignments for variety shows and specials for Don Knotts, Jonathan Winters, Bill Cosby and Mitzi Gaynor with multiple scripts for the four series that formed CBS' legendary Saturday night comedy block of the early 1970s—*All in the Family, M*A*S*H, The Mary Tyler Moore Show* and *The Bob Newhart Show*. Mayer also spent six years running *The Facts of Life* before becoming a successful playwright, which he is still doing full time.

Jerry Mayer.

Lila Garrett Lila Garrett had a message. Ask her about nearly any script she wrote and she can tell you the larger message behind it. One of the first women to write television comedy, she scripted episodes of *My Favorite Martian, The Lucy Show, The Addams Family, Petticoat Junction, Get Smart, The Courtship of Eddie's Father, Love, American Style* and *Bewitched*. Moving into an era when sitcoms had overt messages, she contributed to *Maude, All in the Family* and *Barney Miller*. Garrett occasionally worked alone but more often teamed with a partner, including Bernie Kahn, Joel Rapp, Michael Elias, Mickey Rose, Mort Lachman

The Writers

and Sandy Krinski. Continuing to break ground, Garrett successfully wrote, produced and directed several TV movies. She still has a message, as the host of the radio series *Connect the Dots*.

Fred Freeman Originally teaming with Garry Marshall, Fred Freeman broke into television comedy on *The Tonight Show with Jack Paar*. Switching to sitcoms, Freeman and Marshall wrote for *The Danny Thomas Show* and *The Joey Bishop Show*. After the pair amicably split, Freeman worked on *Jackie Gleason's American Scene Magazine* before he started a longstanding partnership with Lawrence J. Cohen. During their first two seasons as a team they had an incredible run, working on four top 20 shows at once — *The Dick Van Dyke Show, Gilligan's Island, The Andy Griffith Show* and *Bewitched*. Their talents were soon in demand for pilot and movie scripts. They sold several pilots — *The Pruitts of Southampton, Occasional Wife, The Good Life, Apple Pie, Empire* and *First Impressions* — but had greater success with their screenplay for *Start the Revolution Without Me*. Free-

Lila Garrett.

Fred Freeman (photograph by Lisa Angle).

man and Cohen ended their television careers with a stint as executive producers of *Empty Nest*.

Rick Mittleman It might be easier to just list the series Rick Mittleman *didn't* write. Although he occasionally took staff jobs on series such as *The Red Skelton Show, McHale's Navy, Arnie,* and *What's Happening!!*, Mittleman thrived as a freelancer. His assignments included *The Dick Van Dyke Show, The Donna Reed Show, The Flintstones, Petticoat Junction, Get Smart, Gomer Pyle, U.S.M.C., I Spy, The Courtship of Eddie's Father, Bewitched, That Girl, The Mary Tyler Moore Show, The Doris Day Show, The Odd Couple, Welcome Back, Kotter, M*A*S*H, Sanford and Son, Alice, One Day at a Time* and *The Love Boat*. When sitcoms went through a brief dry spell, Mittleman switched to light dramas, adding *Emergency, CHiPs, Remington Steele, Simon & Simon, Matlock, Jake and the Fatman, MacGyver* and *Murder, She Wrote* to his credits.

Rick Mittleman.

Elroy Schwartz Following his brothers Al and Sherwood into comedy writing, Elroy Schwartz soon made a name for himself in radio. He spent television's early years writing for game shows before switching to comedy series. The versatile Schwartz alternated between sweet episodes for soft series like *Bachelor Father, My Three Sons, Family Affair, The Flying Nun, The Brady Bunch* and *Mayberry R.F.D.* and wacky episodes of wild comedies such as *My Favorite Martian, Gilligan's Island, The Addams Family, McHale's Navy, The Lucy Show, Green Acres* and *Get Smart*. Switching to hour dramas, Schwartz continued to prove his versatility with scripts for *It Takes a Thief, The Virginian, The Mod Squad, Police Woman* and *The Six*

Elroy Schwartz.

Million Dollar Man, while still writing the occasional sitcom script for *Good Times* and *The Munsters Today*.

Carl Kleinschmitt   Still in his twenties when he broke into sitcom writing, Carl Kleinschmitt, along with his partner, Dale McRaven, hit the ground running by writing more than half the episodes of the final season of *The Joey Bishop Show*. As that series wound down, Kleinschmitt and McRaven contributed an episode of *The Dick Van Dyke Show* that won a Writers Guild Award, which led to them writing eight additional segments during that series' last season. Working mostly solo for the rest of his career, Kleinschmitt contributed to *That Girl, Gomer Pyle, U.S.M.C., The Doris Day Show, The Courtship of Eddie's Father, Love, American Style, The Odd Couple, Welcome Back, Kotter* and *The Love Boat,* in addition to creating the early HBO comedy *1st & Ten*. The landmark first season episode of *M*A*S*H*, "Sometimes You Hear the Bullet," is Kleinschmitt's best-known script.

Arnold Margolin   For someone who had never previously considered writing comedy, Arnold Margolin found fast and lasting success.

Counter clockwise from bottom right: Arnold Margolin, Carl Kleinschmitt, Garry Marshall, Jerry Belson, Dale McRaven and Jim Parker, 1970 (courtesy Arnold Margolin).

Entering the field in 1965 at the height of the high concept sitcom era, he and his partner, Jim Parker, became very busy on multiple fantasy comedy series. Fortunately, they soon earned assignments on more realistic and, in most cases, more successful series like *The Andy Griffith Show*, *That Girl*,

The Writers

He & She and *The Mary Tyler Moore Show*. Margolin and Parker graduated to executive producer status with a three-year run on the innovative *Love, American Style*. Working solo, Margolin continued to keep busy writing pilots, movies and TV movies and serving as a producer and writer on *Private Benjamin, Growing Pains* and the drama *Promised Land*.

Ed Scharlach Ed Scharlach wrote his first sitcom episode when he was just 23. Teaming mostly with Peggy Elliott and later with Tom Tenowich, Scharlach moved from one hit to the next, quickly racking up credits that include *Love, American Style, The Doris Day Show, The Dean Martin Show, Room 222, That Girl, The New Dick Van Dyke Show, The Odd Couple, Happy Days, Chico and the Man, Mork & Mindy* and Bob Hope specials. He proved his versatility by continuing his career in dramas (*Quantum Leap*), comedies (*Empty Nest*) and cartoons (*Duckman* and *Pinky and the Brain*).

Ed Scharlach.

1

I'm Really a First Baseman: Getting the Job

The first question an aspiring television comedy writer is likely to ask is "How do I break into the business?" Today, young writers can get started with the help of college classes, internship programs, how-to books, web sites, software programs or simply studying the form. When many early TV sitcom writers broke into comedy writing, the television comedy business didn't even exist.

Jack Elinson I had a brother who was a writer—Izzy. Without him, I never would have become a comedy writer. In those days, he was a big hit. Most people didn't know there was such a thing as a comedy writer. The comedians make 'em up as they roll along, right? He was terrific. He got his start writing jokes for Walter Winchell's column. I went to him and said, "Can I do what you're doing, Iz?" I was so jealous reading in the paper "Iz Elinson says." I was so proud of him. He said, "Go do what I do. Send some jokes to Walter Winchell." Sure enough, I got my first joke in Walter Winchell's column. I was 16.

For the record, here's the joke that started Elinson's career: A famous Hollywood show biz couple had a violent argument and shot each other to death. Their last words were "But we're still very good friends." Still funny 75 years later.

Bob Schiller I found out that a very popular radio show, called *Duffy's Tavern*, would hire anybody that showed any propensity for comedy for a week for 50 bucks. I had never written jokes before. It's a totally different way of writing. Before, I was writing whimsy. And whimsy, you don't laugh out loud at; you smile. If you're writing stuff that people are smiling at on radio, you're out of work as a writer. So it needed what they call muscle, a joke. And that was very, very hard. Not many people can write jokes. It takes a warped mind and a person that thinks crooked. The head writer said, "We go out to [*Duffy's Tavern* star Ed] Gardner's house in Bel Air every Sunday. How are you at pitching?" I said, "I'm really a first baseman." Pitching jokes is what he meant. I had never heard that expression. That's how green I was. Ed Gardner was a brute to work for. He'd fire you purposely to keep your money down. So you wouldn't ask for more money. You were grateful to get back on the show. It was a brilliant show. They had brilliant jokes. Like, I went to the ballet last night. I don't get it. They had a bunch of dames dancing around on their tippy toes. Why don't they just get taller dames? It's become a standard joke. Brilliant. They had the best jokes in radio. That's where I cut my teeth.

Madelyn Davis We were working for Steve Allen on radio and we did a spec script for Lucy's radio show, *My Favorite Husband*. It was the episode with Richard Crenna that we redid for *I Love Lucy* called "The Young Fans."

Elroy Schwartz My brother, Al, had been writing jokes for Leonard Lyons and Walter Winchell and other people with columns. And they were buying them. Then Bob Hope came along and wanted Al to write for him. He and Abe Burrows were the two top writers in comedy at that time. I was going to school in New York and I never contemplated being a writer at that time. Then my brother, Sherwood, got involved and Al got him on the Bob Hope radio show. I came to visit Al after I got out of high school. I was playing tennis with Artie Stander, who was a nephew of Lionel Stander, and he said to me, "Did you ever try writing?" And I said, "No, I never thought of it." He was working on a thing called *The Ransom Sherman Show* on radio out of Chicago. He said that they needed another writer and I should try writing a script. So I listened to the show and sat down and wrote a script. I gave it to the producer of the show. He read it, called me and said they accepted it. He gave me a 13-week contract for $100 a week. In those days, $100 a week was a lot of money and I was 18 years old. The next thing I knew, I was fired but they couldn't tell me why. They said they'd pay me for the whole contract. Stupid me. I said, "If I'm not working, I don't want the money." I wouldn't say that today. It turned out that the producer was Bob Hope's agent. Bob Hope heard that I was working on *The Ransom Sherman Show* and Bob Hope did not want Al or Sherwood taking any time off from him to help me. Well, they hadn't helped me. But his word was law with his agent, so I ended up getting fired. Al said, "Once Bob has his mind set on something, you're not going to change it." He suggested what I should do is write some jokes for Bob

1. I'm Really a First Baseman

Hope's monologue. I sat down and wrote 25 jokes for the monologue, Al sorted it down to 15 and Hope didn't use any. That went on for about six weeks. Didn't use any of my jokes. Al said, "It's your name on them. He just doesn't want to deal with you. Give me some more jokes and I'll put them under my name." Which happened. Fifteen jokes, he used like eight of them. World War II came along and I left to go back to New York to enlist in the Air Force. During the interim, I started selling jokes to Milton Berle, Henny Youngman and Herb Shriner. Herb Shriner was booked on *The Kate Smith Hour*. I'd been working and waiting to be called to active duty. I went backstage with Herb when he was a guest. I was waiting in the wings when Bob Hope walked in. He came over to me and said, "Hi, Elroy. How are you?" He put his hand out. I did not shake his hand. He said, "Are you waiting to see me?" I said, "No. I'm working for Herb Shriner. You can't get me fired."

Irma Kalish   I always wanted to be a writer since I was this high. And I'm only a little taller than that now.

Austin Kalish   We measure you regularly on the wall.

Irma Kalish   When I graduated college, I aimed straight for a publishing company where I could write short stories. They gave me a job for $30 a week. I was an assistant to the editor and proofread copy and I figured I could write this stuff myself. I asked if I could write some, which I did, and they bought from me at one cent a word. When you get paid by the word, as anyone would, you throw in a lot of adjectives and adverbs to pad your paycheck. You're by no means a Hemingway. You're not going to write crisp and to the point.

Austin Kalish   I was writing material for acts and I'd get 10 percent of what they got on the road. None of the acts were big. I wrote for radio. I wrote for Martin and Lewis. I wrote some fill-in things for *Duffy's Tavern*. I didn't have a big radio career but I worked for Martin and Lewis on radio for three years.

Many early television sitcom hits were based on successful radio series, including The George Burns and Gracie Allen Show, Our Miss Brooks, Amos 'n' Andy, The Life of Riley *and* December Bride. *These series, along with new comedies created for television, and television variety shows relied mostly on a ready stable of writers crossing over from the heyday of radio comedy.*

Austin Kalish   When Martin and Lewis did TV, I got into that mix on *The Colgate Comedy Hour*. In the early days, Jerry was very open. He was also an ad lib kind of a guy. Dean was in my corner. He protected me. I liked Dean and ended up finding Jerry not to be the charming person he was in the beginning.

Madelyn Davis   Lucy said when she went into television to CBS, bless her heart, she said, "I'll go but I want the same writers." She wanted Jess Oppenheimer and Bob and me. So she took us with her.

Jack Elinson   Whoever was writing the monologue for Garry Moore got pissed off and walked off the show. They were really going crazy because they needed someone to write that piece. This is where my brother came in. Talk about a good idea, having a brother. Iz said, "My kid brother is a writer and he's pretty good. Maybe you'd want to try him." I went on that show. You could talk about anything you wanted. It was easier than writing a story with a beginning and end.

Bob Schiller   When radio started sinking, I had just had a child and I figured I'd better get the hell out of the business because I wasn't making a living. I was going to be a salesman. They were gonna put me on the road nine months of the year. It was housecoats. They were gonna pay me $75 a week. William Morris pretty much controlled most of television in New York. And they would be having problems and my agent, Harvey Orkin, would say, "If we could only get Schiller." They'd ask, "Why can't we get Schiller?" He says, "Haven't you heard? He's getting out of the business." They'd never heard my name before. They said, "You call yourself an agent? Get him. We need him." So that was the beginning of my television career. The next day I had three shows. I was on *The Ed Wynn Show*, *The Danny Thomas Show* and *The Garry Moore Show*.

After a fairly successful first decade, television sitcoms overcame Westerns and variety series to become the medium's most popular format. Viewers' voracious appetite for television comedy in the early 1960s created openings in the field. The second wave of sitcom writers often held other jobs in the new industry first. Others simply caught the right break.

Sam Bobrick   It just happened through a series of lucky events. Because I really had no idea what I wanted to do. I got at job at ABC in the mailroom, delivering mail. Somebody told me they were looking for an office boy on a Ray Bolger show. The guy who hired me is my best friend to this very day—George Shapiro. He became an agent and he would get me jobs on game shows, writing interviews. All made-up stuff but that's what you needed on a game show, so I'd write interesting back-

1. I'm Really a First Baseman

grounds for people. I got to write *Captain Kangaroo*. That was fun. That was nice. It was such an easy job and they were so nice and it was like a job I could almost have for the rest of my life. And I didn't want it. Most of the TV was out on the West Coast. George Shapiro wanted me to come to Los Angeles. Even though I was in the Air Force, I was scared to death of flying, so he came and he got me.

Allan Burns   I had never thought about being a comedy writer, or a writer at all. I interviewed to be an NBC page. About two weeks later they called and told me to come in and get fitted for a uniform. It turned out I got the job because I was a size 42 Long and that was the only size they had left. That's why I am now a comedy writer, because I fit the uniform. I was there for two and a half years as a page and a supervisor of pages. I was making $1.10 an hour. The first show I worked on was the old *Tonight Show* with Steve Allen. Steve was out here making a movie, *The Benny Goodman Story,* and *The Tonight Show* was done at 8 or 8:30 here. It was a revelation to me. To be associated with something that was that funny or that good. The singers on that show were Steve Lawrence, Eydie Gorme and Andy Williams. They had people like Louie Nye and Tom Poston, all these top comics. And Steve was no slouch. I would go stand in the back and hang around and watch. It was also the year that George Gobel's show hit like a rocket. It was the hottest show going. People would come back from their dates on Saturday night to watch Gobel and then go back out again. I wanted so badly to be part of it. I bought this ancient typewriter and would go back to my little apartment and peck out monologues for George Gobel and hope that one day I would get some stuff to him. I never could. Hal Kanter and Norman Lear were among the writers. The writing staff on that show was unbelievable. I just kept trying.

Saul Turteltaub   I just loved watching Jerry Lewis when he was young, and Frankie Fontaine, and I always wanted to be that. In college, I met a friend who, like me, wanted to be a performer. We put together a terrible comedy act and worked in the Catskill Mountains in New York. While we were working there, a comedy team — Marty Allen and Mitch DeWood — needed some material, so we sold them our act. We made more money selling the act than we ever did performing it. So we decided maybe it would be good to be writers. After I got out of the Army, I turned on television on Saturday morning and saw Shari Lewis, who I had known as Phyllis Hurwitz from a summer camp. We had been boyfriend and girlfriend that summer. So I called her up and said, "Remember me?" She said, "Yes." I said, "I saw your show. You're wonderful. I'm a writer." She said, "Good. I don't need one. But you can come in and talk to my writer." I wrote a sketch for Lamb Chop. And I sent it to her. She called up the following day and said, "You're hired." Just like that. I did her show from 1958 to 1963.

Lila Garrett   I began to write for the news on television. I found that writing jobs were much easier for me to get than acting. I was just a natural writer and there weren't that many women writing, and instead of finding resistance, I instead found really a willingness to take on a woman because it made them look good. I went on to a quiz show called *Who Do You Trust?* with Johnny Carson. This was before Johnny took over *The Tonight Show*. I became first a question writer and I wrote funny questions just to amuse myself. For some reason, somebody at King Features found me and said, "You know your questions are awfully funny and we do these five-minute cartoons—*Beetle Bailey, Krazy Kat* and *Snuffy Smith*. We'd like you to try your hand at writing some of these five-minute cartoons for us." They paid $400 a cartoon. That's like nothing now but I was glad to get the money. So I moonlighted and did about 11 or 12 of them. Someone reminded me of them and I saw some of them online. One of them was called "There's No Feud Like an Old Feud." Snuffy Smith was a mountaineer. I was always anti-war but even then I had that message in mind and so it turned out to be a very enjoyable job.

Elroy Schwartz   Television was in New York in the early days, so I moved back to New York and I started working in television on game shows, doing interview comedy. I wrote the pilot for *The $64,000 Question*. The odd thing is I got fired after the second week. And again, I had a contract but they paid me. I did comedy interviews and by the second week on the air, it turned out to be the most dramatic show on the air. They didn't need a comedy writer. So they hired a guy to write straight. I stayed writing daytime comedy interview shows for about nine years. I did all those shows that came out of New York, like *Double or Nothing*. I worked with Bill Cullen. Alan Alda did a show back then. Then I came back to California and started writing half-hour situation comedies.

Fred Freeman   I went to Northwestern University, where I met Garry Marshall. After college, we decided to meet in New York. We roomed together for three or four years. We used to take an ad out in *Show Business*, which was a daily paper in New York and we thought we were

1. I'm Really a First Baseman

so clever when we said the virgin material of Freeman-Marshall. We wrote for a lot of comics you've never heard of. Like a half-hour monologue for $50 or something. Shari Lewis was one of the people we wrote for a little bit. We were in her apartment. I remember sitting on the floor and she was on the couch. And she had Lamb Chop, which was on her hand, and she was talking to us as Lamb Chop. We didn't know if we should look at her hand or at her. It was a weird, weird experience. But she was very nice. Then Phil Foster was one of the first to help us a lot, to get a manager. The big break Garry and I got was when we were writing for Phil Foster and Joey Bishop. We were writing for Joey when he did guest appearances on *The Jack Paar Show*. Jack Paar needed writers. Somehow we got connected and we got hired and that was our first big professional job. We mostly wrote monologues. Sometimes ad libs for certain guests. Paar was terrific at making the monologue seem spontaneous because he fumbled through it a lot. He was very, very good at that.

Bernie Orenstein   I'm Canadian, so in Toronto in the '50s I was an actor and I did some stand-up and I was terrible in both of those professions. I was on a television show as the funny office boy. The producer was Norman Jewison and I went up to him and said, "I can't do this any more. I'm no good. I'd like to be a writer." He said, "Okay, come in Monday, you'll be a writer." That's how I became a writer. It was easy in those days. Eventually I moved to New York to see if I could get some work as a writer. The luckiest thing there was that I met my future partner, Saul Turteltaub. I got a job on *Candid Camera*, which was a pretty popular show at the time. But it was like a factory. Allen Funt hired a bunch of young people to write the situations and sometimes perform in them. He paired us off with partners and I worked with Joan Rivers. We both lasted just a few weeks. It was not a pleasant experience but it was a job.

Rick Mittleman   Some people do crossword puzzles in their spare time, I wrote comedy material. Sam Denoff and I were pals and always interested in the entertainment business. I had a cousin living out here and flew out and came to Hollywood looking for work. I ended up writing for *You Asked for It*. It was the granddaddy of all the reality shows. Camera crews went all over the world. I became an associate producer, traveling with my own film crew all over the country. And I was writing the segments. Eventually I showed my comedy material that I did for fun to the head writer on *The Red Skelton Show*, Ed Simmons. He liked it enough and he hired me as a junior writer. And lo and behold, I got an Emmy nomination that first year and I thought, boy, is this going to be easy. Little did I know. Things changed and I left the show. Then I became basically a freelance writer. I think the first half-hour sitcom I wrote was *The Donna Reed Show*.

David Lloyd I wrote shows in high school, in college, in officer candidate's school in the Navy. When I wrote shows at Yale, Dick Cavett was in a couple of shows and I became friends with him. When I was looking for a job, I wrote to Jack Paar, whom I knew socially. At that point, Cavett was working for him. When one of his writers left, he was able to hire me but could only promise me 13 weeks. So I went. And I worked on talk shows for 12 or 13 years in the East. I wrote monologues for Johnny Carson for five years. It certainly prepared me for turning out jokes. With Carson, I had to give four pages of jokes every day, five days a week. And I was so brilliant at negotiating my own contract for the first three years, I had no vacation. So it was 52 weeks a year. And *The Tonight Show* did all the holidays if they fell on weekdays, except Christmas. And that was because we were preempted on Christmas Eve. And so on Christmas Eve we would tape the Christmas show and get an actual day off. Johnny Carson, when I was writing his monologue, once in a while we'd be preempted, something would come up — a national news story or something or the New York City blackout or something would come up *after* we'd given him the monologue material for the day's show. He'd had it. He'd read it. And something would come up to preempt that show. The next day, he would never do one joke left over from the day before because he'd seen it, it was old. That used to make us a little crazy.

Sam Denoff I met Billy Persky in 1954 at WNEW, which was the number-one pop radio station in New York. Persky wanted to work in advertising. My aspirations were to be a songwriter. We were just happy to have jobs to pay our rent. We started writing for William B. Williams, who was a legendary disc jockey. Our material helped us build a reputation and pretty soon we had an agent. The management at the station was really supportive. They let us try some crazy ideas. We idolized Steve Allen and he was starting a new show in California. We got together some of our material we did for WNEW and it got us the job. We got an offer for three weeks on this new Steve Allen show. Steve Allen gave a lot of people their start. It was like coming out to heaven.

Bill Persky I just wanted to earn a hundred dollars a week. I wanted to be a writer. The truth is, I wanted it to be in advertising. I wanted to

1. I'm Really a First Baseman

be a copywriter. I never thought about anything else but advertising because that's what I studied in school. Sam and I started writing jokes for the disc jockeys for them to enjoy and they started to read them on the air. The head of the station wanted us to do more of that. WNEW had a Christmas party and Sam and I did a musical variety show about the station and there was this young guy came up to us and said, "I would like to represent you. I'm with William Morris." He didn't have a card because he had just come out of the mailroom. That turned out to be George Shapiro, who is a legend at this point in terms of finding Andy Kaufman and Jerry Seinfeld both. He got us started writing for nightclub comedians. Then George moved to Los Angeles and got us a job on *The Steve Allen Show*.

Jerry Mayer   I never really thought I'd go into show business. For about ten years I was working in my father's construction business in St. Louis but I was doing cartoons for magazines and I finally got into *Playboy*, doing cartoons for them. So that was keeping me in touch with comedy. I had written jokes for Phyllis Diller who lived in St. Louis for a while with Fang, her husband, and she was paying me $15 a joke. So I get a call that Jerry Lester was in town. He did *Broadway Open House* before there was a *Tonight Show*. I gave him a ride to rent a car and he was very friendly and I told him that I would love to be in comedy writing. When I told Jerry that, he said they were giving a going away party for Joe Garagiola, who was moving from St. Louis and he needed to do ten or fifteen minutes. He asked me if I'd write it for him. I said, "Sure." So I went home and worked on it and he thought it was good stuff. He told me I should come see him perform. I went there and saw him do my material and it was getting nice laughs. He knew the producer of *McHale's Navy* and he told me if I wanted to write a spec script, he'd tell him to read it. So I wrote a spec script and sent it in. They bought the story. They wanted one of their regular writers to do the writing. I think I got $500 for writing the story. The night the show went on and we were watching it and I had one of those Polaroid cameras and here it came on "Story by Jerry Mayer" and I took a picture. I still have it in my office. I decided I wanted to go out and try to make it. I thought it was a good foot in the door. We took our three kids out here. I wrote a *Bewitched* on spec with a friend of mine who was in a comedy workshop with me. They liked it and bought it.

Arnold Margolin   In 1962, I moved to California. I went out there without a job. I did end up in a job as a literary agent for less than a year.

But during that time I met people that later became lifelong friends. They helped me get started writing. I loved finding new writers and I did find a number of them but I hated the business of selling people. I wasn't very good at that. Several of these writers who I had represented or teamed up became successful comedy writers. There were two teams — Carl Kleinschmitt and Dale McRaven were one team and also Garry Marshall and Jerry Belson. I was unemployed at the beginning of 1965 and they invited me to come and use their office on the Strip and take my calls from there. I was hanging out there and one day Dale McRaven, on a Friday afternoon after everybody had gone away for the weekend, asked me if I could write some jokes. I had never written a joke in my life. They were in a bind because they had to finish a script for *The Joey Bishop Show* and also had to write some jokes for someone who was performing at a roast. I didn't have anything else to do and I could use the money so I sat at a typewriter for a couple of hours. If you've never written a joke before, you don't know where to start exactly. I filled up a page and I almost tore it up. I thought it was so bad. I took a copy home and showed it to my wife and she read it and said, "Well, we know one thing. You're not a comedy writer." I forgot about it but when I came in the office I found a note from Dale that said, "We loved your jokes. We'll pay you when we see you." Then Garry started getting me work ghostwriting jokes for a comedy writer named Harry Crane. I was writing for Sinatra and the Rat Pack's nightclub acts. I was getting paid in ice cream coupons and sweaters and all kinds of stuff but not much money. I wanted to get into variety writing because variety shows were still very big in those days. Jerry and Garry said that I needed a partner. Jerry had a high school friend who was moving to town and he wanted to be a comedy writer. He came over to the office and they introduced us. His name was Jim Parker. We went off and wrote five minutes after we met. We tried to figure out how to write together. Neither of us knew how to write individually so we didn't know how to write together. Desperation solves a lot of problems. We actually wrote some sketches for *The Danny Kaye Show* as a sample of work to try to get on there. We were also writing jokes. I don't think we ever did get the sketches to *The Danny Kaye Show* but we did get it to Dave Davis who was on *My Mother the Car* and he liked it and his boss liked it and they had us in and we pitched them an idea for a script that they liked and we were off and running.

Ed Scharlach   I went to the University of California and I wrote college shows. We were in a competition with an audience of 3,000 people.

1. I'm Really a First Baseman

The little play that I wrote and directed came in first and we got the big trophy and my cast carried me on their shoulders onto the stage at the end. That was the night that based on that huge success that I announced I wasn't going to law school. Once I graduated, my stepfather, Harry Crane, helped me find a writing partner because I saw that most TV writers worked in pairs and that appealed to me. He was working with someone he had mentored, Garry Marshall, and at the time Garry knew a lot of young writers so he put me together with this woman, Peggy Elliott. We clicked immediately. We were an anomaly at that time. We were both in our early twenties. We were a male-female team. It made us unusual. When we first got together, we wrote sketches just to see if we wrote well together. These days I tell young writers when they write a spec script to think of the smartest, funniest, classiest show on television and try to do the best version of that show that you can. When we started out we decided to just pick a nice show that when we watched it, it was not intimidating to try to write it. So we picked *Green Acres*. It was not *The Dick Van Dyke Show*. We just picked the show that we thought would be easy to write. We wrote a spec script and it was a good one. Based on that and the sketches, we got a really good agent. We started writing based on that. It was fun. The mid–'60s were a highly electric time in our culture and it resonated in even TV comedy writing. A lot of people my age were still struggling with where they wanted to be in life and I was fortunate enough to have a career and having my scripts performed by wonderful actors.

Paul Wayne Bernard Slade and I are both from Toronto, Canada, and we met as actors. I was 19 and he was 20. And we became fast friends. Later Bern was the head writer on *Bewitched* and I was writing plays for television in Canada. He said, "You've got to come because there's a heavy demand for writers." So I just trailed in Bern's shadow. My first two seasons here were writing *Bewitched*.

Carl Kleinschmitt It was a fluke. I was 24 or 25 years old, working at a wholesale grocery company as an industrial editor, putting out company magazines. I had been playing around with writing on the side, getting nowhere. I met a guy in my Air Force Reserve unit. He said, "You're kind of an amusing guy, you should meet my roommate, Garry Marshall." I met Garry, who was then working for Joey Bishop. He started feeding me little tidbits, ghostwriting for him. Jokes for various comedians, like Vaughn Meader, who did the JFK impersonation. Garry and I worked on those together and had the misfortune of sending him a whole batch of material on the night of Thursday, November 21, 1963. We never got paid for it. On my own, I did a silly little parody for Steve Allen. They bought it for something like $45. I quit my job and tried to be a writer. I met my one-time writing partner, Dale McRaven, and wound up working for Joey Bishop on a situation comedy show in 1964.

In some cases, writers made their own breaks thanks to a little chutzpah.

Jerry Mayer   I was visiting for two weeks over the summer and I'm trying to make contacts and see how it would be to live in Los Angeles instead of St. Louis. I went to a comedy seminar at UCLA. Garry Marshall was a guest speaker. It was very exciting. One day, I'm driving on Sunset Boulevard by the Beverly Hills Hotel. All of a sudden I see Buddy Hackett driving west and I was driving east. So I make a u-turn and he took a left toward the Beverly Hilton Hotel and I'm following him. I had two or three pages of jokes in my pocket that I always carried in case I would run into someone. They have a big parking garage and he goes in. I drive in and follow him and get up to the level where he is and he's parking his car and getting out of it. And I think I can't look for a parking space, I'll have to stop right in the middle of the aisle. I get out of the car and walk over to him and I say, "Mr. Hackett." And he says, "Yes?" And I'm reaching in my pocket for the jokes and he didn't know if it was a hit or what. And I pull out the jokes and he's relieved. He says, "What can I do for you?" And I said, "I'm a comedy writer and I've written some stuff here. I'm trying to get started and I wonder if you'd look at it and maybe you'd be interested." He said, "Sure." And he takes a minute or two and reads it and says, "I don't do other people's material. I do my own. But I think this is good stuff and Jack E. Leonard is in Vegas. You should show it to him." I thanked him and he thanked me for not being a hit man. So I went to Vegas and went backstage and said Buddy Hackett told me to see him. He said, "Yeah. I think I can use that." The next year, we came out to Los Angeles.

Allan Burns   I'm working at home one day and I'm watching television in the afternoon and there was this cartoon show on called *Rocky & His Friends*. I got fascinated by it. I thought it was the funniest stuff. Just wonderful. Who are these people? And I watched the end of it and the credits go by really fast. But it says Jay Ward Productions. So I look them up in the phone book and there it is. It was on Sunset Boulevard. By that time I've got three or four years worth of greeting cards with my

1. I'm Really a First Baseman

drawings on them and my gags in my portfolio. I just went over there and walked in the front door. I didn't call or anything. And there's a sort of battle axe of a receptionist at the front door. And I said, "I'd like to see Mr. Ward." I got nowhere with her. I'm standing there with my portfolio on her desk and she's wanting to get rid of it when a guy walks in and starts shuffling through mail. And he says, "What have you got there?" And I said, "This is some work I've done — cartoon drawings, gags." He said, "Mind if I look at it?" I said, "No." He starts looking at it and laughing. It turns out it's Jay Ward. I didn't know it. He said, "This is funny. Wait a second. Come here." We go into an office that's just cluttered and he yells down the hall. And Bill Scott comes in. He was Jay's writer. And Bill starts laughing at the stuff. I close up my book and Jay says, "When do you want to start?" Those things do happen.

As sitcoms became dominant, writers who started in other television jobs made the transition from variety series, game shows and talk shows to situation comedy.

Jack Elinson   Sheldon Leonard, who was the boss of that whole place, was the director of *The Danny Thomas Show* and after that he became the producer so he needed to get some writers. Now he had to pick writers and I was lucky enough to be one of the writers. One script turned out to be eight years. I felt really comfortable on *The Danny Thomas Show*. I thought it was a lot like me. I'm a New York guy. I was doing me, in a way. I got a good start there.

Bob Schiller   Bob Weiskopf was married to a Japanese woman. After Pearl Harbor, she had to either go to Chicago or go to a relocation center. She went back to Chicago and Bob moved in with Jess Oppenheimer. So years later when Jess needed some relief on *I Love Lucy*, he called Bob and I came along.

Sam Bobrick   I always did spec writing. I always did sketches. I liked that. I liked comedy. Then they teamed me up with Bill Idelson, who was an actor. We got an assignment to write *The Andy Griffith Show* — which was a fun show because of Don Knotts and Andy Griffith. And the first one we wrote won the Writers Guild Award. We were shocked that it won the Writers Guild Award. It was a great surprise for us. From then on people hired us. It was a very small industry. Everybody knew everybody.

Bernie Orenstein   I went on the staff of *The Monkees* with a lot of bright, young people. The kids were very appealing. I was always good at writing physical comedy stuff, which was very important to *The Monkees*. We did make suggestions of what could happen, what the visuals could be when we gave them a song to do. The problem with that show for me as a writer was that it was about 10 writers sitting around a table figuring out what kind of story we could do and then we broke off and wrote the script that was designed by all of us. It was a very strange writing assignment. It was more factory-like.

David Lloyd A guy who had written on Carson, Ed. Weinberger, came and stopped in at *The Dick Cavett Show* to say hello because he knew Cavett and he knew me and he said, "You should be writing for *The Mary Tyler Moore Show*." Which is what he was working on then. And I said, "Well, I don't have any idea how to go about it." And he said, "Well, write a script, send it to me." My then–12- or 13-year-old daughter said everybody watched *The Mary Tyler Moore Show*. I had never even seen it. Somewhere I have it still, she made me a little cheat sheet — who the characters were on *The Mary Tyler Moore Show*, what their relationship to each other was, their attitudes. And I, of course, immediately started watching it. And I wrote something that was completely wrong and sent it to Ed. And I guess they found something in it to like because he called me on the phone and said, "Okay, we'll give you a story. Here's what we want you to write." And they gave me a story. It was Ted Baxter running for city council with Cloris Leachman, Phyllis, as his campaign manager. They hired me. They wanted me to replace Treva Silverman, who was the story editor on the show at that point. I said, "I don't know what a story editor does." I took the job and I have been doing it pretty much ever since.

Sam Denoff We thought there was more security in sitcoms. We got some assignments on *McHale's Navy* and *The Joey Bishop Show*. We even had a chance to do *The Judy Garland Show* but we turned it down.

Saul Turteltaub I was writing for Pat Boone and Bernie Orenstein was writing for *The Hollywood Palace*. At night we would work on writing sitcoms for a whole bunch of shows because that was where the future was. We got an offer to produce *That Girl* and we went into sitcoms full force.

Lila Garrett I moved with my husband at the time to Los Angeles. We came out here and we became a team. We were one of the first husband-and-wife teams. We presented like eight storylines to various shows and one of them picked us up. I think it was *My Favorite Martian*. We worked as comedy writers constantly. Once we got going, we were a very desirable team. Also, because we were a husband-and-wife team. In this town, anything that's a little quirky or a little different is fun for a while. That was a good thing.

Fred Freeman Joey Bishop was given a half-hour comedy show and quite honestly, I didn't like Joey. He was not a very pleasant man. He was miserable, therefore he would make everyone around him miserable. But he wanted some rewrite people on his TV series. Garry Marshall wanted to stay in New York but there was nothing left there any more. So we came out here as rewrite men for Joey. We also wrote for *The Danny Thomas Show*.

Unfortunately, it was the 1970s before many minorities were given the chance to break into sitcom writing. While some opportunities existed for women, they were few. Madelyn Davis was one of the only women to write television comedy in the 1950s. A handful of additional opportunities opened up in the mid–1960s before women made major inroads in the field in the 1970s.

Madelyn Davis Because I had a male partner, it didn't seem to be an issue. I never said I'm going to break ground here. I just wanted to get on a show. And I'm sure the fact that I worked with a man, and then to get on *I Love Lucy,* which is the first big thing we did, it's silly to say you can't work with her because you're a woman, because she was a woman. It wasn't a big deal. Now that I look back, I think I had more nerve than I knew.

Bob Carroll, Jr. Before we teamed up, she was rejected from one show, a radio show, because she was a woman.

Madelyn Davis They said, "You wouldn't fit in. You're a girl."

Austin Kalish Irma had the children to take care of so I wrote with Elroy Schwartz. We were pretty effective. We were working together the morning when we heard Kennedy had been killed. It was such a shock to us. We were doing a pilot for *Gilligan's Island* at the time.

Irma Kalish Rocky was writing with Elroy and they decided to break up. I used to call Elroy Rocky's ex-wife. They went their separate ways but they still had a couple of assignments that they had to do. They divided them up. Rocky took a couple of *My Three Sons* assignments. Ed Hartmann was a great guy. A wonderful man. He was the producer of *My Three Sons*. Rocky told him he couldn't do the assignments with Elroy and asked if he could do them with me. He told him I was a writer and had a few credits. And Ed agreed to give me a chance. We did a script together and didn't even have to do a second draft. The first draft was accepted. After that we were off and running. We never looked back. We just never stopped. We had assignments every year. We always got another job.

I was regarded as a pioneering woman writer. You'll excuse me if I don't put on my bonnet. It's a little warm today. But I was with Rocky so most people assumed that Rocky did the writing and I did the typing. In fact, Sherwood Schwartz thought that.

Austin Kalish   They thought that women did not do comedy.

Irma Kalish   They thought women couldn't be funny. We didn't face resistance from Ed Hartmann but along the way there were some people.

Austin Kalish   I had a chance to write for Jackie Gleason.

Irma Kalish   When he said he wanted his wife to write with him...

Austin Kalish   That stopped it. There was a lot of resistance.

Irma Kalish   Before we did *The Brian Keith Show*, it was called *The Little People*. Brian wanted a new producer. He didn't want Garry Marshall. We got to do the show, which was nice because we got to get over to Hawaii a couple of times. Brian was very reclusive. He was a man's man. He'd talk to Rocky but not to me. Once I was on the set in Hawaii and Rocky had gone off somewhere and when Brian came off the set, he headed straight for me and I thought he was going to talk to me and he came up to me and said, "Where's Rocky?" He was nice and he appreciated me, I believe, but that's the way he was.

Lila Garrett   I think I faced some resistance as a woman. When I tried to write adventure shows, I faced some resistance because everything was stereotypical. When I tried to produce, I faced tremendous resistance. When I tried to direct, the resistance was almost impossible. Directing is a very desirable job and there is always resistance to a new group coming in to a desirable job. Good jobs are hard to get in our industry. That's what I really felt was at the bottom of it. That's why it's hard being a pioneer. Being a pioneer is overrated. The writing was different. The writing was easy. It's very hard to find good writers. When they found a good writer, they were going to take her. And also I had a male partner at that time. So I was half all right. Eventually they all accepted women. Producing and directing was different. I was a woman alone, telling men what to do. It was terrible.

Bob Carroll, Jr.   Madelyn's a great producer.

Madelyn Davis   It's just that when you're a woman in charge, this becomes a little, I assume, a little threatening. I kind of had to work my way around. I just convinced them I wasn't out to be anything grand, I was just trying to get a show together here. It was okay. But it was a little more than I realized.

Irma Kalish I didn't face resistance to running a show. Things had changed. I did some of them by myself. I guess they didn't mind taking orders from their mother.

Bob Carroll, Jr. Didn't some actor say, "Who's that talky broad at the end of the table?"

Madelyn Davis I was going through the script and he said to the person next to him, "Who's the gabby broad at the end of the table?"

Irma Kalish It was Rocky's idea that what I needed to do was go off on my own and do things because that way they would realize that I wasn't just an appendage of Rocky. Eventually I became a board member and then vice president of the Writers Guild. And I became president of Women in Film.

Austin Kalish As a matter of fact, I dropped back when we had a job. I made Irma be the talkative one. In the early days, I did all of the talking. I was the force. I changed that deliberately. She did the presentations and I would sit back and add to it. I felt very strongly about her. She had the ideas but there was a timid aspect to her. Maybe because she was feeling the pressure of women in general. Because women in general, they walked behind you. I didn't feel that was a proper way because I knew her skills, her intelligence and I knew her talent. I wasn't going to hold her back. So she became much more forceful. She became the woman who ran for president of the Writers Guild.

Irma Kalish Eventually I learned you have to be one of the boys. You can't be "Oh, my goodness, you can't talk four letter words in front of me." You had to be one of the boys. To the extent that one time I was in a room with the writers and the usual off-color jokes were going around the room and four letter words and there was a knock at the door and someone, another woman, stuck her head in and one of the guys said, "Okay, guys. Can it. There's a woman in the room." I wasn't "a woman." I was another writer. Which was fine. As long as I could write, I was one of the boys.

Austin Kalish That has extended into three or four months ago when I got a call from a writer that we had never worked with. He said, "Would you come to a writer's luncheon?" They have a luncheon every week for writers in Palm Springs. I said, "That would be a great idea. That's wonderful. Irma and I will go." A few days later I get a call and he said, "I've got some bad news. Irma can't come with you. We tell naughty jokes and sometimes the language isn't good."

Irma Kalish   I hadn't run into that for so many years and there it was again.

Lila Garrett   Younger writers have acknowledged my contribution. The woman who did *Designing Women*, Linda Bloodworth-Thomason, said to me, "Lila, you were a little too early. Just a little too early." I was a little too early not to be knocked about.

Madelyn Davis   They just carry on. They are very, very flattering and cute about it. I'm always so surprised. People say, "Did you know you were writing a classic when you did *I Love Lucy*?" Well, of course not. And, "Did I know I was breaking ground?" I didn't know. We were just trying to get jobs and write a script, get the show on. You don't realize what you're doing at the time.

2

Careening into a Wall: Writing the Script

Every classic sitcom script began with a blank sheet of paper. In 1951, Bob Carroll, Jr., and Madelyn Davis faced an even more daunting task. Not only were they—along with producer and head writer Jess Oppenheimer—expected to turn out script after script for the new comedy I Love Lucy, *they had to do so without much precedent. While* I Love Lucy *had a few television comedy predecessors, most were warm family shows light on comedy such as* Mama, The Goldbergs *and* The Aldrich Family. *In addition, the duo had to start scripts before sets were built or the supporting cast was hired. In fact, Carroll didn't even own a television. "I just bought one last week," he quipped at a 2005 book signing.*

At least the duo had their radio sitcom writing experience to lean on. They had spent the previous three years writing for Ball's radio series, My Favorite Husband. *While some* I Love Lucy *episodes were based on old radio scripts from* My Favorite Husband, *the new series was a different animal, as Ball's gift for physical comedy could now be fully exploited. As a result, the writers were free to make Lucy Ricardo even wackier than her radio counterpart, Liz Cooper. However, Carroll and Davis had never worked with Desi Arnaz, who was not part of the radio series, and they didn't know if he had the capacity to do comedy. He soon proved to be a major asset, as both a performer and executive. Although some of the early episodes proved that the series was still a work in progress, several first season episodes capture Ball's brilliance by seamlessly integrating hilarious slapstick scenes into the stories. Soon Carroll, Davis and Oppenheimer were on a roll, scripting first season classics—"The Ballet," "The Freezer" and most notably "Lucy Does a TV Commercial"— that audiences are still laughing at more than 60 years later.*

Madelyn Davis We didn't know how to do it. We had written for Lucy in radio on *My Favorite Husband.*

Bob Carroll, Jr.   And also that show was done before a live audience so we and she were used to reacting to an audience.

Bob Schiller   It wasn't too difficult to write sitcoms. They were already laid out pretty much. There were a lot of sitcoms on radio.

Rick Mittleman   None of us had any formal training. It was more of a gut-level type of thing. It was more watching what was on the air and saying, "I could do that." And we all did. I never met anyone in my first 20 years in the business who graduated college with a degree in Communications. Now the competition is just tremendous.

Ed Scharlach   We learned just by doing it. I always tell people that if you want to write you can take every class in the world and read every book that you want to read but the way to teach yourself writing is by writing. That's what we did. We wrote.

Some classic sitcom writers worked for 20, 30, even 40 years in television — turning out, in some cases, hundreds of scripts. In constant search of story ideas, they not only tapped their fertile imaginations, they also looked to their own lives for inspiration.

Bob Carroll, Jr.   The storyline was the most challenging part.

Madelyn Davis   I kept a loose leaf, one of those little steno notebooks, and whenever something came up or we'd think about it, like when something funny happens when you're out at a restaurant, I'd go home and put it in the book. I'd make a note and then sometimes six months later we'd use it. We'd go over the little notebook and say, "Oh. We were going to have her do this." We'd see something funny happening. A lot of things happened to us and our friends. They were the germ of the idea. Or we'd see something in the paper.

Bob Carroll, Jr.   When we saw a guy twirling a pizza in a window, we built a story around Lucy doing that.

Bill Persky   Stories are the toughest part of writing situation comedy. They just take forever to work out. Jokes are easy. But stories are extremely, extremely hard.

David Lloyd   It's groupthink. You sit in a room. Even my best-known *Mary Tyler Moore* script, which is "Chuckles Bites the Dust." We had had a funeral, our set designer Lew Hurst had died and we went there, all of us on the staff were at the funeral. And there was a minister there who was kind of stage struck and was sort of playing to the actors and celebrities in the crowd. And it pissed off Jim Brooks and Ed. Weinberger.

2. Careening Into a Wall

And coming back, Jim said, "We should do a show about a funeral. We've got to do something about a funeral." And that was the genesis there. And then we sat in a room and we pitched various elements of it. And then Ed. Weinberger said, "David loves death jokes. He'll be a natural for this." And I went off and did it.

Bob Schiller My wife ran for senate. That's how we got the idea. I came in one day and said, "Sabrina is running for the state senate." And one of the guys on the *Maude* staff said, "If my wife did that, I'd divorce her." So Norman Lear very astutely said, "Wait a minute. Hold it." We used to plot around a table with a tape recorder in the middle and we'd tell about all the problems we had at home and we'd get stories out of them. He said, "We've been looking for a way to split them."

Fred Freeman What makes something seem credible is if it's a part of you. It will be honest and real. That's where I got a lot of it. Sometimes you'd see something in the newspaper. A lot of it was just me looking at my own insecurities or fantasies. I did a *Dick Van Dyke Show* where what I wrote was about him writing a children's book. What would I be afraid of writing? A children's book.

Carl Kleinschmitt I don't remember another show where we were encouraged to bring in real life things the way Carl Reiner did it. We did a two-part show about Rob running for the city council and that was based on that fact that several years before I had actually been stupid enough to run for the California State Assembly. I was as unprepared for that as I was for show business. That was another thing that came from real life. A little more complicated was the "Obnoxious, Offensive Egomaniac, Etc." script where Rob is trying to break into Alan Brady's office to retrieve a script on which the writers have written in bad things about Alan Brady, based on something Dale and I did when we were working for Joey Bishop. We were very tired one night about 4 o'clock so we wrote things in the script like "The moronic man from Philadelphia enters." We were saved by the producer, Chuck Stewart. He saw it and took all that out before it got printed. I don't remember any producers besides Carl asking for my real-life stories. When I pitched on my own, I would try to make it fit the show but try to find something they hadn't done. I thought of myself as a tailor. If they needed a 42 Long, I would write a 42 Long.

Sam Bobrick I had an uncle who punched several people in the nose. And I had another uncle who sold salve and things like that. I turned both of those ideas into scripts for *The Andy Griffith Show*.

Jack Elinson I don't think anything exciting ever happened in my life that I put in a story.

Rick Mittleman The stuff I wrote had bits and pieces from my own life or my own take on life.

Ed Scharlach It depends on the show. You'd come in with five or ten story ideas and see if any of them click with the producer of the show. I think the best stories come out of real life. We'd search for things that had happened to us and try to adapt them into what the show's characters would do.

Lila Garrett Everything that a writer writes is part of his life. You can only write from your experience, either your vicarious experience like something you've read about or your life. You can't put things in a world of your imagination that your imagination can't depend on. You have to know that there is a tree before you can image a new tree. My life experience is in everything I write and every character that I ever wrote is a part of me, whether it's a man, woman or child. They're all a part of the writer. My writing is very personal, even when it's fictional. And even when it follows a list of rules that are not my own that have been created for any given series. I always try to put myself in there somewhere.

Paul Wayne Stories would come from everywhere. I used to do an awful lot of reading and stories would come from ideas from *The Three Musketeers* or an opera. As a kid I was just crazy, I would read everything— toothpaste labels, cans of salmon. Everything that would come into my hands I would read. When I was just a teenager I would make a point of going to Broadway plays and spend a week in New York and see ten plays. That was my nerdy life. So there was so much material packed in my head. Any time I would think of an idea I would think of all that stuff in my head. Two or three things mixed together plus all that stuff in my life that I'd gone through. Ideas come from reading, from having experience with life and just applying one thing to the other and try to make them great. There are a tremendous amount of things from my life that I've used. Most of my stories have had me in them somehow.

Rick Mittleman You sit in your office and you just think of situations that may be very funny if it's situation comedy or may have some touching universality. You try to do a show about something people can relate to. A *Dick Van Dyke Show* I did revolved around summer hiatus, which I went through. You did thirty-some shows a year and when the summer would come, everybody was off. They did repeats. And I had a

2. Careening Into a Wall

show about Dick Van Dyke newly on staff on the show and it's summer hiatus time. He's got a new house, he's got mortgage obligations and no furniture so he goes down to the unemployment insurance office. It turned out, I think, to be a pretty funny show. The clerks see that he's in the television business so they gave him a job writing a manual for a company that manufactured television tubes. And the first day on the job, they go on strike. There's a universal feeling of suddenly having a tremendous financial obligation. What are you going to do to get through the hard times when you have fifteen weeks off?

Sam Bobrick We made stories up. That's what writers do. We made up things. I loved it. You had the characters, you just put them in a situation. That comes from doing it over and over.

Elroy Schwartz If I could tell you how my brain works, that would be amazing because I don't know. It's just something I do. I got stories from my head.

Jerry Mayer A lot of it has to do with not going with the first idea if it isn't strong enough. Don't settle too easily.

Saul Turteltaub We just sat around and thought of an idea that would be good for the situation of the characters. You had to start with the problem they faced this week. Just think about what life is. It would just be based on the reality that people faced.

Bernie Orenstein It starts with the germ of an idea — maybe something that happened to you or something you observed or something you saw in a newspaper or something suggested to you by another writer or even by the performers. The characters are already established so it's a lot different than writing a play.

Bob Carroll, Jr. When we were doing *I Love Lucy*, Madelyn and I would meet at Schwab's Drug Store to get our ideas ready. Then once a week we'd meet with Jess Oppenheimer and spend the day plotting.

Madelyn Davis We would have four or five ideas and tell Jess. Jess would call about Wednesday and ask what page we were on and we'd say, "Twenty-nine." And we were on page four. And he never knew that.

Bob Carroll, Jr. Then we'd work all night.

Madelyn Davis There were a lot of weekends.

Jack Elinson We'd finish the season and instead of just dispersing, Sheldon Leonard came up with the idea of going to Las Vegas and go with Danny Thomas and get our stories. It was a delightful week and we'd pitch things. Not long days, because he had to work at night. Then we would take a whole month off. It worked. The thing that was nice was that after a long season, we got it all set. It was nice not to come off of vacation and now we have to sit down and start from scratch.

Paul Wayne   When people would ask you to add more jokes, you'd have to say, "The jokes won't help it. It has to be the idea that's funny." You have to have Archie in the lockup with a bunch of hippies on *All in the Family*. That's funny. That's not a joke. That's a funny image. There can't be a bigger contrast than being locked in with something he despises. You start writing and then the jokes come. It just comes out of your typewriter. It's that simple.

Rick Mittleman   It was hard work. I worked primarily by myself when I wasn't on staff and I'd sit there in my little office in Studio City and it was tough working on stories. And then getting it right once you got the go ahead from the producer. Sometimes you'd get stuck on something and you couldn't solve something. At Studio City when you'd get stuck, you'd go across the street to Sav-On Drug Store and you'd see a bunch of writers walking around, loading up on toilet paper or toothpaste because they had to get out of their offices. It was never easy. It just didn't flow. It was always a challenge. It was a pleasant experience but it was at the same time difficult. Sometimes more difficult than others.

Sam Denoff   What does every kid say? "Tell me a story." People want a good story.

Fred Freeman   Even if you have a good story, the script can be screwed up.

Rick Mittleman   Story construction was very important. Even with sitcoms. A lot of teams would have one writer that was really quick with jokes and the other was an expert with story construction. When you write alone, you have to be both. I think I did pretty well in paying attention to construction and making things work. I see things in movies that get by in terms of writing that we never would have let go by in a half-hour television show, in terms of logic or making the audience accept things that really don't make sense. It's always intrigued me that for some reason television producers and script consultants are more fastidious when it comes to making sure that there's a logic in flow from scene to scene to scene. That's my impression.

Paul Wayne   One of the stories I remember using in almost every situation comedy I ever wrote—I used it in the *Flying Nun* and it was very sweet and in *Three's Company*—it was the *Cyrano de Bergerac* story. I used that three or four times. There was a *Bewitched* that I used a Mozart opera. I'm a thief. It stimulates you.

Rick Mittleman   There was a story that was written in *The New Yorker* by Alexander Woollcott. He was invited to speak at a nudist colony and he didn't know how to go down to dinner but he finally figured what the hell, it's summer and it was warm, with no air conditioning, so he comes down the stairs naked. And everybody's sitting around the table fully dressed. So I used that as the inspiration for a story where the disc jockeys on *Good Morning, World*—Ronnie Schell and Joby Baker—are invited to what they think is the Sunshine Dude Ranch and it turns out to be the Sunshine Nude Ranch. They come down to dinner early to be seated first. That was considered really off the wall in those days. The network was okay with it as long as they were seated. The problem was at Desilu Cahuenga we had to ship in audiences and for that particular show the people we handed out tickets to on Hollywood and Vine to get an audience to, in a location off the beaten path, happened to be full of people from a Seventh-day Adventist Church. So they pretty much sat on their hands. We had to do a little adjusting with the laugh machine on that one. It's funny what was risqué then.

Jerry Mayer   You should be able to tell it in two or three sentences to see if it's interesting. Like "The Ringbanger" episode of *M*A*S*H*. It's a guy who thinks too much of himself and they can sometimes get people killed because they're giving the orders. That's all I had to say. It said in the article I read that sometimes these people are in way over the heads as far as being authorities. You realize the importance of that. The laughs will come.

David Lloyd   Very seldom did I come in with a story idea that was the whole thing. I might come in with a little plot or subplot or what about something in the general area of this. And then four of us sitting in the room, or five of us, and toward the last couple years of the show, six of us sitting in a room would kick it around and find the form of it. Where's the act break? Where's the end?

Jerry Mayer   You look for something really different that the audience gets a kick out of it because they didn't expect it. That's what you're looking for—a surprise that's not expected, furthers the story but is amusing. It's a funny little island. Part of good writing is to do the unexpected. But not out of the blue like it doesn't belong in the story. It's creative and they don't expect it and they feel satisfied at the end.

Irma Kalish What was so effective in the script we did for *All in the Family* where Gloria got molested and Archie, all of a sudden, wanted to do nothing about it, and Mike, who usually never wanted anything to do with law and order — the cops especially — was just the opposite. It was reversing an idea.

Austin Kalish We wrote looking for the unusual.

Jack Elinson It all starts from the storylines, it starts out as the germ of an idea. We can do something with that. Once we feel we've got it, we started with a blank piece of paper and went away.

Irma Kalish We always had ideas. I don't know why. We didn't come in with just two ideas and say, "Which do you like?"

Elroy Schwartz Until about three years ago, I had another career as a certified master hypnotherapist. Working with people in therapy and their subconscious made me understand character more. I was able to bring that into what I write.

Jerry Mayer You watch shows and you get the idea if you're meant to be in the business. You end the first act on a high note or a scary note. There's a structure. You can feel it without even talking about it. If you're meant to be in the business, the ideas come. Sometimes they're real good and sometimes they don't realize their potential or their humor. You always keep your fingers crossed.

Fred Freeman We had done sketches before. A half-hour sitcom was ideally an elongated sketch, in a way, with an act break.

Because most writers worked in teams, some of their most important decisions involved how to write together. Who does the typing? Do they work together on every single line? Should they split up scenes? Who wins when there's an argument?

Fred Freeman For a number of years, Larry Cohen and I would work together in the same room, tossing things back and forth. Sometimes I would go off and do some by myself and bring it in the next morning. Eventually, we started writing scenes separately. Then I enjoyed writing separately.

Irma Kalish Of course we argued when we disagreed. I cried a lot. But whenever we had an impasse and couldn't decide which was a better idea — a better joke or a better storyline — we dumped them both and came up with a third.

Austin Kalish We'd declare a truce and go to the third one. The third one was always better than the other two. Not that the other two were bad. They just weren't as good as we thought. And I couldn't stand her crying.

Irma Kalish   That worked. And it was funny because when we produced we could watch other teams who were on staffs and the way they did it. One of them said they took turns if they had an argument. They'd take turns who won. Still another team, I'll always remember that picture, looking out from our office into the hallway and the door opens and the two of them came out locked in battle.

Austin Kalish   On the floor.

Irma Kalish   They were fighting because they had a problem.

Austin Kalish   And they weren't doing it as a joke.

Paul Wayne   I thought George Burditt was a bright guy. The two of us just clicked. We split up the first and second act. I was a little more experienced and the first act was a lot more difficult to write. Then we would go over it together. We also did the outline together.

Elroy Schwartz   Rocky Kalish and I went line by line sitting in a room.

Sam Bobrick   I did a lot of spec writing. So I was always on top of writing. Billy Idelson worked on shows as an actor, so he was more used to the half-hours. So when we started writing, Billy kind of helped me get my legs for the half-hour shows. After about five or six shows, they became very easy because they all had a feel to them. I knew writers where one would write one act and the other would write the second act. I could never do that. I always need to know. We did it line by line. I would be at the typewriter. Billy would be pacing and smoking a cigar. It was a nice time. It got fairly easy for me to write the half-hours. It depended on if you had a good producer who knew what he wanted, the writing was easy. If you had a bad producer who didn't know what he wanted, and a lot of them did not know, it just took a longer time and was more frustrating. Fortunately, with the Writers Guild, you only owed them one or two rewrites.

Irma Kalish   One nice thing about being married, when we went on vacation we could still write.

Austin Kalish   One time when we were driving into work from Thousand Oaks, we wrote a story and had half the dialogue.

Allan Burns   Chris Hayward and I would work the story out together. One of the things we used to do, we would work out a story and work out alternate scenes. We'd write alone after having worked the story out together. Then we'd rewrite each other's stuff. Then together, we'd do the final draft. That worked for us. Sometimes we wrote head to head, but usually the third time through. I would read stuff he wrote and just laugh my ass off. What he'd come up with from our rough outline would make me laugh very hard. He was a marvelously funny man.

Arnold Margolin   It was difficult to learn to write together. We were doing it head to head. In other words, we weren't each taking an act and coming back with it. We were sitting there writing each line together. And until you learn to trust your partner, at the beginning we were arguing over commas and everything else. But eventually we got the drift of it and we made each other laugh and we began to have a rhythm together. We established who was going to be the guy at the typewriter and who's the guy that's just sitting there. That takes some time to figure out that role in the hierarchy. Finally we ended up that I was doing the typing and Jim Parker would lie on the couch.

Ed Scharlach   We went word by word. Punctuation point by punctuation point. That's the way I've always worked with my partners. You don't know where one person starts and where the other person leaves off. You have to have a pretty mutual sensibility and sense of humor and enjoy each other. You have to be a cheerleader for the other person and also stick up for your opinion when something doesn't work. Often, our biggest arguments led to idea number three, which was always the one that worked the best. Peggy Elliott and I had a very close sensibility. She didn't mind typing. I thought best when I was pacing. She had two Siamese cats. One would sit with her at the typewriter and the other one would pace with me.

Austin Kalish   We had our own little process. We would discuss the story idea and break the story down into scenes and where it would go. Irma would start on it.

Irma Kalish   I would do what was in effect a first draft because I was used to writing by myself. And then I would give it to Rocky.

Austin Kalish   And I would write the second draft.

Irma Kalish   And he would make it funnier and add some differences.

Austin Kalish   Then together, we'd write the third draft. So when they thought they were getting a first draft, they were getting a third draft.

Bernie Orenstein   I was more plot-oriented and Saul was more joke-

2. Careening Into a Wall

oriented and, as a result, it turned out pretty well. Saul is one of the great comedy writers of all time. We still email ideas to one another. He's a fabulous, wonderful person and very, very funny and very, very talented.

Saul Turteltaub We would talk out an idea, then Bernie would sketch out the show alone. After we talked what it was about, he would go and outline it. Then he'd hand me the outline and I'd touch it or not. Most of the times it was perfect. He's a wonderful story writer. I would take one act and he would take the other act and we'd hand each other the pages back and forth. Then I'd put them together.

Bill Persky I never wrote a joke in all of the years I have been a writer. I've written jokes for people making speeches or in sketches. But I wrote what had to happen in terms of the story and something funny would come out of that. I never approached it like something would be a good joke and I needed to find a way to fit it into the script. I'd put something in the script and ask what would be funny because of that. Then we'd find a joke. Sam, on the other hand, would love jokes and we would find a way to make it work in the script.

Sam Denoff There was a different dynamic when Billy Persky and I wrote together. It was like there was a third guy in the room. We always wrote together. Never broke up scenes and wrote separately. We had this office that was this little room and a toilet. In the room with the desk there was only room for one chair so one of us literally had to sit on the toilet when we were working on a script.

Bill Persky Sometimes I'd sit in the hall while Sam typed.

Carl Kleinschmitt When the six of us, Jerry Belson, Garry Marshall, Arnold Margolin and Jim Parker and Dale and I, all shared an office space on Sunset Boulevard, it had a pool. After lunch we'd go out and play water volleyball. We spent a lot of time fooling around. Jerry Belson and Garry Marshall split up scenes and each one would write a scene and then switch and work on each other's material. Dale and I, because we didn't trust each other to do that, sat side by side at a typewriter and I would type and we would talk and we would work it out that way.

Arnold Margolin Jim and I hadn't sold anything yet, so our office was in the hallway between Garry Marshall and Jerry Belson and Carl Kleinschmitt and Dale McRaven. We didn't get much work done. There was a swimming pool. It was the '60s and there were girls in bikinis all over the place. In the offices, we had a ping pong table. I think we had a pinball machine. Writers are always looking for an excuse not to write and we had them all over the place. Getting any work done there for a while was impossible. We took a picture there in front of that building in 1965 and we've gone back every five years to take another picture. There were six of us to begin with. We're down to five. Jerry Belson passed away. Ironically, he was the one who wanted to start a pool and each of us would put in a hundred dollars every year and the one who was left at the end would get the money.

Bob Carroll, Jr. We think pretty much alike. I never wrote a whole script in my life.

Madelyn Davis We just went line to line.

Those who wrote mostly solo faced other pressures, such as working out script problems on their own.

Rick Mittleman I had a technique of writing that worked for me. I don't necessarily recommend it. I find if you work with a yellow pad and a pencil or pen, you don't have the sense of angst that you have looking at a blank white page. Don't forget, I started when you were working with typewriters. You'd roll that blank page in there and I found that writing a scene on a yellow pad and making notes in the margin took the pressure off. It wasn't finalized but it was a good way to start into a script. I always worked that way.

Elroy Schwartz When I got stuck, I took a drive. It's amazing how many story problems I worked out while I was driving.

Jerry Mayer Susan Harris had her way of writing. I remember she used to say, "I go right to the scene that excites me when I start a script. It doesn't have to be page one. It can be in the middle or at the end." Which I thought was interesting. I've tried it myself sometimes.

To see if their ideas worked, writers sometimes acted out the scenes in their offices. Bob Carroll, Jr., and Madelyn Davis found additional ideas by trying out the physical stunts they wrote for Lucy, with the theory that if Madelyn could perform something, Lucy would be able to do it.

Bob Carroll, Jr. We wanted to be sure it worked and we would find better things acting something out than just writing it. There was one where we had Lucy and Ricky handcuffed. She handcuffed him to keep him home, borrowed some handcuffs from Fred Mertz and then couldn't get them off. They had to go to bed and take their clothes off. So Madelyn and I tied our left and right hands together and we found out that once you have that you can't take your coat off. It won't go past the sleeve. We wouldn't have thought of that unless we had actually done it.

Madelyn Davis A lot of times we'd find funnier things that way. You don't want to have a stunt and you go down there and have 60 people all ready to go and the stunt doesn't work. That's a little embarrassing.

Bob Carroll, Jr. Because they look down the table at you-know-whom.

Madelyn Davis One time we thought it would be funny to put Lucy on a unicycle. Sometimes we'd just try out stuff and then we'd think of a way to get her in it, we'd work backwards. I tried riding it. It's very tricky. She was very coordinated, more so than I am. But I think I went careening into a wall and we said, "Maybe not." We were very careful. If we worried about it, we'd ask her. She'd never turn anything down. Never. She'd say, "Is it funny?" And we'd say, "Yeah, we think so." Well, okay.

Irma Kalish If I would say, "How is this scene going to work?" Rocky would, in effect, direct it.

Austin Kalish In a room.

Irma Kalish That was a help in working it out.

Austin Kalish I became all the characters and showed the humor of a show. I wasn't putting jokes in it but there was big fun in it. Things that didn't seem like jokes were jokes.

Carl Kleinschmitt We tried to imagine what it would be like. Having Rob Petrie boxing was fairly easy. We concocted bits where the referee would say, "One!" And Rob would spring up and fall again. It was silly stuff but we carefully wrote each movement down. That was a lot of fun and fun to watch.

Although sitcom fans easily recall classic episodes, unfortunately not every segment can be a classic. In a carryover from radio, early television series produced as many as 39 episodes per season. By the 1970s, episode orders were smaller, but it was still a tremendous burden just to get a show on the air, much less produce an episode that turns into a classic.

David Lloyd Once in a while, the idea maybe wasn't quite as good as we thought it was. You can't do 24 winners a year. If you can get 10 that are really terrific shows, you're way ahead.

Bernie Orenstein We've done dozens of shows. We've written hundreds of scripts. They're not all great, unfortunately.

Madelyn Davis By the time it turned out to be a classic, you'd already written three more shows. You feel good. That went well. Then you go back to the office and start.

David Lloyd   Two years running I did 17 scripts—10 *Mary*s and then six others and then a pilot. So that was fun. I was also getting paid by the script, so the more I wrote, the more I made. But I also thought it was so neat, as a frustrated playwright, to suddenly have terrific actors doing my words. Okay, here's another terrific cast, let me see if I can have them do my words. I loved it, doing *Rhoda,* doing *Tony Randall,* doing *Phyllis,* doing *Doc,* doing *Lou Grant.*

Bob Schiller   I was on a deadline for damn near 50 years. It takes a lot out of you.

Fred Freeman   When you would sit pitching stories—like with *Andy Griffith*—we'd pitch four to five storylines. Sometimes it would take weeks to get the story right. Then the first draft. We figured we were making about $1.75 an hour. But it was really a good experience.

Madelyn Davis   The people who did the old *Your Show of Shows* were fantastic. You think we worked? They did an hour and a half a week! I don't know how they did it. It was so funny.

Jack Elinson   Whenever a new show popped up, Sheldon would push us to do a few scripts. We stayed with *The Danny Thomas Show.* Some shows we stayed a few years. It was hard work. We would do half of our scripts for *Andy Griffith* and half of them for *Danny Thomas.* And that was really quite a thrill to have both of those shows on the air back-to-back on Monday night. What a blockbuster of comedy shows!

Elroy Schwartz   I was busy all the time. If my family didn't have something to do on Saturdays and Sundays, I worked. Shows would be flipping in and flipping out. It was another piece of paper in the typewriter. One week, I was working on four different shows.

Fred Freeman   I used to be in the freelance business where you'd do a *Gilligan's Island* and a *Dick Van Dyke* and an *Andy Griffith* and a *Bewitched.* And I liked it because when you started doing the same show over and over, we'd start to get a little bored with it. Even though we should all be in church praying that we have a job. It was fun. It was a challenge. You wanted to do really good so you'd get more assignments. Sometimes they'd give you one more or three more. To be writing for *Andy Griffith,* that was a thrill getting reassigned on that show.

Rick Mittleman   There was a lot of insecurity when you were free-lancing.

2. Careening Into a Wall

David Lloyd I'd come off of sitting around a room every day writing jokes for talk show monologues and here suddenly I was writing scripts and my thought was just let me at them. I couldn't get to the typewriter fast enough to start another one. Somebody who wanted to be a playwright and here you've got good actors doing your lines, once a week, almost that often.

Allan Burns I think David Lloyd took a tremendous amount of pressure off of the rest of us. You knew every third episode or so, David was going to be in there writing the script. And he usually gave you a first draft you could use. We didn't, because we had a habit of rewriting stuff. He had the most unusual mind.

Madelyn Davis Somebody said once, "Why don't you write down everything you and Bob did, just to have it?" I couldn't believe it. And also, we had such nerve. We would tackle anything. They said, "Would you come back to Broadway and rewrite this show?" We said, "Sure." What nerve. And we did a lot of pilots that didn't go anywhere. It was a lot of pressure but we enjoyed it. We did nightclub material and a rewrite on a musical that bombed anyway. And movies. I think what nerve we had but we were young and didn't know any better.

Bob Schiller I pay homage to Jess Oppenheimer, Bob Carroll, Jr., and Madelyn Pugh. They did every single *I Love Lucy* show for four years. A remarkable job. It's not done anymore. A truly Herculean effort. They are really responsible for the success of the show. I'm not. They were a hit when we were on. They did a remarkable job.

Bob Carroll, Jr. Weiskopf and Schiller gave us great relief. It was good to have some other little fingers pounding down the hall.

Madelyn Davis They were experienced and had done a lot of stuff. When we put the show in Connecticut, Weiskopf had lived there.

Austin Kalish We were never hurting for work. We had to drive it away.

Irma Kalish Well past the cutoff age.

Austin Kalish We had writers coming to us for work. So we know other writers didn't have the access we did.

David Lloyd Looking back, I think I should have my head examined.

Most very early sitcoms had a small staff of just a few writers that were responsible for turning out every single script. By the 1960s, most series split scripts between their small staffs and freelance writers. Those staffs grew in the 1970s and '80s. Eventually, there were few freelance writers, and scripts were written with a large group scrutinizing every line.

Carl Kleinschmitt In those days, freelance writers would come in and pitch ideas and you would buy the idea, they would write it and either a producer or a couple of script consultants like us would work on it. Then you'd film it and that was it.

Madelyn Davis Now they have so many writers, it's hysterical.

Rick Mittleman There was the time when you just sat with the producer, you didn't sit with a whole room full of people.

Paul Wayne You landed there by yourself or with a partner and then you wrote. Now it's staff. I'm not quite sure how it's done because staff writing is just very peculiar to me. The way I think it goes now is it's writing in groups. It sounds terribly difficult to me because everybody has a vote about what line goes in. Working on anything in a group of 12 seems like a nightmare to me. I've never experienced it but I hear that's the way it's done now.

Arnold Margolin There got to be too many people on the staff. And the staffs got bigger and bigger. The network insisted you have huge staffs and it's counterproductive. It takes so much time to deal with all these people and find jobs for them.

Saul Turteltaub It changed a lot. All the shows we did, we never had staffs sitting around a table. They would write it, do the rewrite and we would touch it up. That was it. We would go home to be with our family. On *Cosby*, which was the first show we didn't produce, we were consultants; they would sit around the table —15 writers — and go over the script. It would be up on a monitor and go over it line by line. One person wrote it and would sit there and hear 14 other guys change every line. It was like a contest to make it funnier. Bill Persky used to say that the changes were all horizontal, they weren't vertical. It wasn't funnier. It wasn't less funny. It was just different. We had never worked that way.

Bernie Orenstein It's unnecessary. There are showrunners who need all those people. And those that don't. I am not comfortable sitting in a room with 14 people all pitching lines. I think that detracts from the development of characters and the consistency of the writing. That's how it's done and obviously some shows do it great. Others don't and are probably hurt by an overabundance of writers.

2. Careening Into a Wall

Ed Scharlach There are some shows I highly respect but for the most part it's a bunch of 25-year-olds crowded in a room trying to outshout each other with lines. There's no depth and great interest in developing stories, which I think is the basis of good scripts. They're there until three or four in the morning. What comes out of that is not the quality that I enjoy. There are others that are run really well and interested in story and character. The writing process for many of these shows, I couldn't do.

Arnold Margolin The last 10, even 20 years that I worked in Hollywood, you'd be up until two or three in the morning on shows. We never did that before. We were home by 7 o'clock every night and I lived in Malibu.

Bernie Orenstein We had families to go home to. There was sort of a rule to never work on a show where the showrunner is divorced because he's got no place to go and he'll keep you there all night.

Carl Kleinschmitt Today, and in many ways I think it's a better system today, someone on the staff writes a skeleton script and a bunch of people in a room yell jokes.

Today, writers are frequently promoted to producers after a brief tenure on a sitcom staff. Many early sitcom writers didn't become producers until long into their careers. Some enjoyed the task. Others greatly preferred writing.

Madelyn Davis Producing is not as much fun. It becomes a little more of a challenge.

Bob Carroll, Jr. It's more work. We still did massive rewrites anyway.

Madelyn Davis You have to okay all the stories and then you have to handle all the props.

Bob Carroll, Jr. On *Alice*, we had probably six or eight staff so we had to work with them every couple of days to get stories.

Madelyn Davis It's a little more fun to just write the thing.

Jack Elinson We were amazed that Sheldon Leonard made us producers on *The Danny Thomas Show*. We figured a producer is a producer and a writer is a writer. I felt a little awkward about it. Now everyone on television is an executive producer. We were some of the firsts to become producer-writers. It was a little rougher because it had to cut into our writing time. It was hard work but it worked out.

David Lloyd I never wanted to be a producer. In a world where everyone's a chief and I'm the only Indian, it makes me valuable.

Jerry Mayer You get to guide something. The money's better. You can write scripts too. It's like arriving—artistically and financially.

Saul Turteltaub I enjoyed producing. It's good to be king. As producer, you make all the decisions. You decide what script to go with, what changes to make, what to cut in the editing room. It's your fault if it's no good but it's your pride if it is. Basically, the producer job in sitcoms at that time was mainly supervising the scripts—writing your own and then bringing in other writers and finalizing the show. Along with hiring the cast and hiring directors. It was fun. It was being in show business, which I always loved.

Lila Garrett I became so busy that I thought it was time to push to produce my own material. Because no matter who you are or what you are, when they have a staff, the staff rewrites you. At that time, I just hated being rewritten, I just couldn't stand it. It didn't make my scripts any better. But I failed to understand that there is such a thing as the sound of the show and every script has to be adjusted really to that sound. It is the staff that really understands the characters, their rhythm, their quirks better than anyone else. I didn't want that to happen to me so I said from now on everything I write, I have to produce. Then there were a lot of changes done by the director once I started to do TV movies and I said from now on everything I write and I produce, I have to direct. And they let me do that. For a while, I was really having the most wonderful time writing, directing and producing my own material.

Irma Kalish It was much different than today when you graduate college and you're an executive producer. We paid our dues, I would say.

Carl Kleinschmitt Now everybody's a producer but they're basically staff writers. It's a different business.

Bernie Orenstein Producing credits in those days meant you were the head writer. It had nothing to do with money. Instead of giving you more money, they'd make you a producer. It appealed to our vanity. You were responsible for casting and what stories were going to be written. We didn't have big teams of writers like they do now. When we bought scripts from outside writers we would rewrite it to fit our concept of the show.

Arnold Margolin I loved producing, especially *Love, American Style*. Mostly because there was no star. I didn't have to put up with any ego, other than my own. It went a lot smoother that way and it spoiled me for the rest of my career when I did have to deal with stars.

Jack Elinson We had to be at casting sessions and other things. I didn't enjoy any of it more than I did the writing. Later, I didn't want to write that much any more so I kind of just stuck with the producing part, which was odd because early in the beginning, I didn't want to be doing the producing part.

Rick Mittleman   I enjoyed producing very much. In those days you didn't have all that much interference. You would get notes from CBS saying you can't say Frigidaire, you've got to say refrigerator. You've gotta say tissue, you can't say Kleenex. That was the kind of notes you got then. You were left pretty much alone as long as the show was rating pretty well. I would supervise the casting and then I would supervise the set construction and the wardrobe and everything that needed approval. I didn't go down to the set very much because I was sure the cast would seek me out, complaining about something. But after the show was on film, then I would go into the editing room. After the director made his first cut, I would go in and make some changes if I thought they were necessary. I really enjoyed it.

Sam Bobrick   I produced a number of shows. It was okay but I didn't like it so much because you had to do so many other things. Some writers would come in and it would just read terrific and the script was really good and some writers would give you a script that didn't work at all. They weren't always the same writers. Sometimes you hit it, sometimes you don't. I didn't like producing because I didn't like going to all the meetings. I was more of a hired gun. I never sold anything that I wanted to sell. Every time I'd sell something that I wanted to write, I'd go in and pitch it to a network and I'd come out with some different show that was theirs. I never felt the love for some of the shows that I worked on that I do for my plays. I got to know Phil Rosenthal, who produced *Everybody Loves Raymond*. He loved his show. He really loved what he was doing and had a big, big hit. And I envy him. I told him, "I wish I could love some of the shows that I was on as much as you did." Of course, he created it and stayed with it and he had a good group of people with him that he liked to be around. You have to be in love with what you're writing. Otherwise it becomes just a job. Not as much fun.

Carl Kleinschmitt   I don't think I was very good at producing. I tended to like the writing part of it better than picking out the shoes part of it. I didn't particularly enjoy the prop man running up and saying, "Which wallet do you think will work here?" I didn't know. It was sort of the beginning of writers becoming producers but staying more writers than producers. There were plenty of people around who knew how to make pictures. My job was to get the material right.

Bob Schiller We did the same thing we did as producers as when we were writers. Everything was rewritten on Norman Lear's shows. It was almost a disease.

It's been said that sitcom scripts aren't written so much as they are rewritten. Although it occurred with less frequency in early sitcoms, rewriting has always been the bane of sitcom writers' existence. Rewriting became even more pervasive as writing staffs grew larger. No matter how much they enjoyed their careers, classic sitcom writers can still get riled up about rewrites that took place decades ago. It's understandably difficult to see your name on a script that doesn't reflect your original intent or input.

Sam Bobrick Then your name is on something you didn't write and for the most part, it's not as good. That's another thing I like about writing plays. Your name is on the play and what they see is what you wrote. That was very important to me that when my name was on something that I wrote it.

David Lloyd I never wrote with a partner but in the larger sense you do because the room pitches the story and the room then takes your script apart and makes it better. Or not always, in the writer's opinion. Sometimes they make changes that you don't care for.

Jerry Mayer In committee, in the writers' room, it just becomes survival. You just want the script to get laughs. You don't even care if the other guy gave you the biggest laugh in the whole thing. Not that you're going to take credit for it but your name is on it and you want it to be successful.

Bob Schiller I hate being rewritten. It was as if Norman Lear had invented the word "rewrite." We used to argue with him all the time. And he would argue back with us. And he would say, "Well, we made it better, didn't we?" And we would say, "No, not better, just different. We'll never know whether it was better because we're doing it your way and you own the store."

Austin Kalish There was more rewriting on his shows.

Irma Kalish Definitely. A lot of it unnecessary.

Paul Wayne There was an amazing amount of rewriting on *All in the Family*. There were three guys that did nothing but rewrite. A lot of my vision was still there though.

2. Careening Into a Wall

Jerry Mayer I wrote spec scripts and met with Norman Lear. We had lunch together at MGM. He said, "Come up with some story ideas." And I came up with one where Sally Struthers' character gets pregnant and has a miscarriage. The other one was about the Jeffersons living next door. He rewrote them a lot.

Lila Garrett My desire to produce and direct my own shows came from the amount of rewriting done on every show. They rewrote you completely on *All in the Family*. I wrote two of them and I practically didn't recognize my stuff. But the people who did the rewriting were wonderful. But I was wonderful, too. And I thought what I handed in was great. But there was epic rewriting on that show. I have to say it was on all of the shows with the exception of *Bewitched*. Most of the *Bewitched* shows went on pretty much as we wrote them.

Jack Elinson It's expected. It's part of the game. Sometimes it was insane. I don't think there's ever been a script that hasn't been touched a little place here, a little place there. I don't think we rewrote that much more on Norman Lear's shows. I never liked having more than two people writing a script. Some shows, every day it's a mob of people. I can't work unless I'm alone or with one other person, maybe two if the second one is good.

Fred Freeman I used to roll out a piece of paper from the typewriter and crumple it up and throw it in the wastebasket. And people would ask me what I was doing and I would say, "I'm eliminating the middle man. Because it's going to be rejected any way."

David Lloyd It's necessary. But Bob Ellison, who was on *The Mary Tyler Moore Show* staff, said it and I agreed with him completely. We changed jokes just because we'd heard them. You'd do a joke at the table reading on Monday — big laugh. Do it at the run through Tuesday — big laugh. Do it at the run through Wednesday — the laugh's a little smaller. We'd heard the joke twice before. And then somebody would say, "We better fix that. We better change that." I thought, we're throwing out jokes that we know work just because we're tired of them and there's no guarantee we're going to find something better.

Sam Bobrick The theater doesn't work that way. They stay with it down the line and wait until the audience is there to tell you. That's another thing that I like about the theater. Good producers will be aware of that. You don't have to make the cameraman laugh three times at the same joke. That's one of the problems I found with a lot of television shows. I replaced a lot of great jokes but that's what you had to do when you worked for some stars.

Arnold Margolin   The first time that somebody did a big rewrite and I saw it on TV, I realized the horror that there was nothing left of mine in the script. But you learn to get over that or you get out of the business because that's the way it goes. But I never really seriously had that problem. We would rewrite ourselves as much as anybody. It's not like we thought our words were precious. Nothing's sacred.

Bernie Orenstein   The first script we sold was to Garry Marshall for *Hey, Landlord*. We wrote the script and turned it in and Garry said, "This is fabulous. This is great. This is terrific." Then we saw it on the air and I didn't recognize one word that we had written. I found out that's how it goes. You turn it in, they like it and they start rewriting. So I got used to that situation.

Elroy Schwartz   I've been rewritten from page one. So much so that I didn't recognize the script. It bothered me. That's not ego, that's professionalism. I was a professional freelance writer. Rewrite me, fine. But take my name off of it. I created a pseudonym for when I got a rewrite that I really hated. I used it on a couple of scripts that I didn't want to be associated with that script.

Bob Schiller   We were working with a producer on *The Carol Burnett Show* who couldn't stand for other people to get their stuff on the show, so he would either rewrite or put our sketches in a drawer. So a friend of mine, Herbie Baker, was going to head write *The Flip Wilson Show* and I sent over some of the sketches we had written for Carol Burnett and he hired us on those sketches. We rewrote them for Flip Wilson and won an Emmy.

Bernie Orenstein   It's difficult to remember what we wrote and what we rewrote. That was the style in those days. A writer would submit a script and you'd okay it and change it to fit the style of the show that you were doing that you knew better than that outside writer. That doesn't take away from the outside writer's ability or contribution.

Fred Freeman   I don't recall huge rewrites from the producers. My attitude, whether we were doing movies or TV, was that if the guy in craft services had a good joke, take it. If you have a neurotic ego, you're going to make everyone crazy. Constantly arguing that you're right, even if you are. Most writers have a healthy attitude. If someone had a good idea and we liked it, we would take it. You should be pretty open.

2. Careening Into a Wall

Bob Carroll, Jr.   On *I Love Lucy*, we didn't have much time for even rewrites. We would fix a few things during the week. But if they threw out a script, we were all in trouble.

Madelyn Davis   We'd be off the air. They never threw out a whole script. In a way, it was a kind of a blessing because nowadays they rewrite and carry on and work all weekend and put whole new scenes in. We couldn't have done that and turned out that many scripts. If they were picking it apart and throwing things out we were through.

Bob Carroll, Jr.   We worked on one show, which shall remain nameless, and they said, "We're going to do the rehearsal on Friday so we have all weekend to rewrite. We said, "Oh, no, you don't. If you don't like it by Friday, you can get somebody else."

David Lloyd   We used to tape *The Mary Tyler Moore Show* on Friday. Now most shows tape on Tuesday so they can rewrite over the weekend.

Sam Bobrick   Toward the end of my TV career, if you wrote a script and at the end you saw 5 percent of what you wrote there you were lucky. They just rewrite, rewrite, rewrite. Doesn't make it better, doesn't make it worse, just makes it different. Some of the shows were rewritten so much that I couldn't bear to watch it. One show called *One Big Family*, a syndicated show — Danny Thomas was in it — we wrote one show and other people took that show and would rewrite it and it would become a different show. Then the director would take that show and make it into something else and it would be a different show. Then when they pieced it together, it would be a different show. You would look at a show and say, "Oh, my God." That's kind of what I knew was the beginning of the end. It bothered me so much to have my name on something I didn't write. I think when I was young and starting out, I was just impressed to be on shows. In the early days, I would say 90 percent of what you wrote — on *The Smothers Brothers* 95 percent of what we wrote — was what they shot. It wasn't until toward the end when they kept getting the big staffs and stars started taking over shows that they changed a lot.

Bill Persky   At a certain point you're making it different, not better. So many writers don't like to go home. They like sitting around joking with each other and ordering thousands of dollars worth of meals from the best restaurants and it becomes like a tradition. It's not fair to the actors. People are changing lines at the last minute. It's a real waste of time but it's become part of the culture.

Austin Kalish   There were some writers in the business who had the affinity for rewriting every script.

Madelyn Davis   We really feel like if you have a script that has to be fixed and rewritten, you'd better get other writers. And we told them. By then we were not kids anymore and we weren't working all weekend. When we started on *Alice*, we had one script ahead and they were having a lot of problems. You work on weekends like that but you're not going to plan your life when you're 50 years old on writing all weekend. You have no life if you do that.

Bob Schiller   You're working over garbage, trying to make it into a flower. And it's tough. And you're never, ever satisfied. The original writer thinks his stuff is good stuff. We always thought our stuff should go on the air as written.

Bill Persky   On *Kate & Allie*, we never had a group rewrite. Bob Randall was a genius. He was the head writer. I would rewrite as I directed. Everybody was home by 7 o'clock.

Paul Wayne   There was a considerable amount of rewriting. But after you got the hang of it, after you got the rhythm of the show, it wasn't so much.

Although some rewriting seemed to take place for the sake of rewriting, it was sometimes necessary to keep the voice of the series consistent.

Paul Wayne   There's a certain pattern that you fall into that people can't possibly know if they're writing for the first time. You got into their characters only through having known their characters. There was a lot of stuff going into that soup.

Rick Mittleman   You're always rewritten for several reasons. The director has comments, the producer has comments and the cast, when they read it, has a hard time with it or say they wouldn't say that. So there are always adjustments. You can't be a supreme egotist when you're writing a sitcom or dramatic show because it is, bottom line, a collaborative effort. Like it or not.

Fred Freeman   You've got to get your ego out of the way. The ego is a killer if you're not open to someone else having a funnier joke.

Ed Scharlach   If you hire good writers and work with them at every stage, there's very little to do in getting it ready for the stage. You have to do some adjusting because you know the show better than they do. With three-camera shows, you have a chance to rehearse them during the week

2. Careening Into a Wall

and see where changes need to be made. You have to be careful not to take out things that are not working because you've heard them many times during the week and they don't seem as funny any more. You have to realize the audience is going to hear them for the first time and they still work. Other things still need to be changed.

Fred Freeman Every show I did helped me learn my craft. With *The Andy Griffith Show*, I liked the emphasis on character development and not having a character suffer by doing the joke that didn't work. You want to do something that's in character. Even on *Bewitched*, you had to pay attention. To me, on *Gilligan's Island* anyone could have done some of the stuff. Yes, they were definite characters. But I said, "If I have to write little buddy one more time." Every show has those things. We all do what we do best. Sherwood Schwartz did what he did best.

Sam Denoff It's more satisfying to do your own show. There was a euphoria that came from writing in our own voices.

Carl Kleinschmitt My experience was that depending on who was running the show, there may have been some better work done after the freelancer turned in the script than the freelancer himself did.

Arnold Margolin For better or worse, the producer has a vision of what the show is and who the characters are and how they talk to one another. You're always trying to make sure that there's that consistency in all the scripts. But you can rewrite to the point of diminishing returns. I've seen that happen.

Lila Garrett When I ran my own show, *Baby, I'm Back*, I recognized that the sound of the show had to be consistent. And no matter how many writers wrote it, it had to sound like it came from the same writer. And a lot people felt about me the way I had felt about all the other producers that I had worked with. So I became much more understanding when I had my own show.

Bill Persky I considered directing to be rewriting and really expanding on what the script is. I direct, not in opposition to the script, but I see things and I'll fix them. I'm not competing. But that's how I direct. That was not always an easy conversation. It got the actors really involved and it was exciting to do.

Austin Kalish When we were producing and working as story editors, we would find people who would come in with no ideas, sometimes we would present them with an idea, lay out the whole story, and they would fall on their asses with it. We would have to rewrite.

Carl Kleinschmitt Sometimes polishing other people's is more fun than actually writing yourself is to make something else hopefully better.

Elroy Schwartz I wrote for what they wanted. I was a freelance writer. If they wanted something, I wrote it.

Although they have many similarities, sitcoms are broken into two distinct styles. One-camera series (The Andy Griffith Show, Bewitched, M*A*S*H) *were filmed out of sequence without an audience and resemble a mini movie. While three-camera comedies* (I Love Lucy, The Dick Van Dyke Show, All in the Family) *were more like a short play shot before an audience. Almost all classic sitcom writers had to adapt to both styles.*

Jerry Mayer On the audience shows like *The Bob Newhart Show*, you would always be there. Even writers that weren't on staff would come. Obviously, it's your baby.

Carl Kleinschmitt I never thought of it as being too different other than on the three-camera shows there was an audience to please. You knew immediately if something worked or not. With a one-camera show you never knew. If the characters are there and you've got a story to tell, it's the same thing.

Arnold Margolin It wasn't hard for me because I had come out of theater. Not that I had been a writer in the theater. But I was used to actors on a stage on a confined set and going from beginning to end in a sequential fashion. I much preferred it.

Bill Persky I think it depends on the show. The three-camera technique was often used where it shouldn't have been because it was cheaper than one-camera. It didn't require travel or as big of a crew. It started because Lucy knew how to work an audience. Because of the financial side of it, a lot of shows started to do it with people who were not theatrical performers. I had no preference other than the material and the actor dictated what you should do.

Paul Wayne People want to know the difference with shooting in front of an audience. I had written a line in an *All in the Family* called "Archie Eats and Runs." Archie eats some mushrooms and at first he thought nothing was wrong with the mushrooms but then he was persuaded that there was something in this can of mushrooms that was poisonous. And so they rush him to the hospital and it turns out there was nothing in the mushrooms, of course. But when it enters his mind that it could have been a can of contaminated mushrooms, he goes crazy. And everybody else goes crazy, too. At the end of the first act where everybody suddenly gets the idea that there might be something in the mushrooms, it builds and builds towards such hysteria that the audience just went crazy. It starts out with Gloria having a minor cold and she can't do anything without sneezing first. Then as Archie builds up in his head that he's sick and he's going to die and they had this running thing where they would get stuck in the door, the line I had was as they're all on their way to the hospital and Rob Reiner turns to Gloria as she tries to go with them, he says, "You can't go to the hospital. You're sick." We wanted that line. But the audience couldn't hear it because they were hysterical. And it didn't matter how many times we did it, you couldn't hear the line. What we did was cut the laugh and did it on a pick up and sweetened it.

Ed Scharlach   We just wrote for whatever show we were hired for. I loved the three-camera because it's like a play in front of a live audience. You get to see your work done in front of a live audience and hear the live laughs and see the performers respond. That's really exciting. But with the one-camera, it's done like a movie and you feel like you're on a movie set.

Bernie Orenstein   We were both more comfortable with three-camera audience shows.

Lila Garrett   I do feel that it's different to write a one-camera film show. It's entirely different. In a way, you have much more freedom. That was one of the fun things about *Bewitched*. The magic gave you a lot of freedom. Three-camera is like writing a stage show. It's all happening right in front of you. But I enjoyed some of the restrictions, but not all, of its being contained like a stage play. They were like little one-act plays except that they were short three-act plays with a beginning, a middle and an end.

Fred Freeman   I preferred one-camera. I think there's a little more control. There's an argument to be made for three cameras in front of an audience. You know where the laughs are. But a feature film can be funny and you don't need a laugh track for it. I didn't like laugh tracks, although I sat in on sessions and said, "Give it a little laugh there." It was a necessary evil.

Rick Mittleman   What was great about doing *The Dick Van Dyke Show* and *The Odd Couple* and shows like that was that they were three-camera shows. And you would go sit there with the audience and you would be introduced during the warm-up and it was like being on Broadway. You would see the show unfold scene by scene. I loved that three-camera technique, not so much visually because it's kind of a flat approach — the cameras are always looking in one direction, usually — but in terms of the writer being part of the audience and listening to them laugh at your own words is a wonderful feeling. In the process of writing, all you're thinking about is the story and character, act endings, things like that. When you did three-camera, you would get confirmation of things being funny, that it was a pretty good script. When you do one-camera, you just have to suit yourself in terms of what you think other people will think is clever. I think after you've been writing three-camera shows, there's a certain rhythm and you can't go too long without something funny but it really is not a problem because it just seems to come automatically. When you're writing a sitcom, whether it's one-camera or three-camera, you're a tailor. You cut to fit. I felt confident I could go on any show, listen to the characters, see how the show plays and sit down and write for it.

Sam Denoff It was tremendously important for us to be there and see a great show being put on because we were learning on the job.

Most television comedy writers also showed their versatility by occasionally working on variety series until that genre waned in the late 1970s.

Paul Wayne Variety shows were different. I'm glad I did that. Once I started getting tired of writing either sitcoms or variety shows, it was a pleasant change to go to the other. Sometimes I was doing both at the same time.

Sam Bobrick Sketches were shorter. And the sketches had to be funny almost from the beginning to the end. Bang, bang, bang. Usually you're writing sketches for funny people. It was just fun. There had to be a reality to some of the half-hour shows that we were writing but with sketches they didn't have to be reality. They could be crazy situations and you'd go from there. I've written several plays with just sketches in there. It's fun to do sketches.

Bob Schiller Variety shows were relatively easy. Danny Thomas was a nightclub comedian, so we used a lot of his material. He was pissed off that we did because once you use it, it's hard to use it in a nightclub. He thought television was killing his living. Then his sitcom came along. He was a funny comic, a great nightclub comedian.

Bill Persky The very word says it — variety. You could do whatever the hell you wanted. You weren't limited. You could just say, "You know what would be fun to watch?" And you would just do it.

2. Careening Into a Wall

Rick Mittleman   I liked variety a lot. I loved doing sketches.

Ed Scharlach   It wasn't like you had a story that you worked on for weeks. You had these sketches that are five minutes long and you just get a concept and milk everything that's funny about it.

Bernie Orenstein   I loved *The Hollywood Palace* because of the people who were on it. I was writing for Crosby and Ethel Merman and Fred Astaire and Judy Garland. Going to their homes to talk to them about what we were going to do on the show. It was a dream for a young kid from Toronto.

Saul Turteltaub   I think I enjoyed the variety shows the most. *The Carol Burnett Show* was great to do because you were writing quick little sketches that were funny. We had a great comedy writing staff. The performers were sensational. It was fun and there was music and singing and dancing, which is show business to me. That's what I like about the business. I want to be Mickey Rooney. My father has a barn; we'll do a show.

3

We Had to Cut the Laugh: Classic Series

Sometimes everything just clicks and a great writer lands on the right show. David Lloyd on The Mary Tyler Moore Show. *Jack Elinson (with Charles Stewart) on* The Andy Griffith Show. *Bob Schiller (with Bob Weiskopf) on* All in the Family. *Bob Carroll, Jr., and Madelyn Davis on* I Love Lucy. *Sam Denoff and Bill Persky on* The Dick Van Dyke Show. *Their sensibilities were just right for these hits. Their scripts for those classics were among the best of their careers.*

Madelyn Davis Lucy had done a "story" show on radio so it was a given that we were going to do married humor. CBS really wanted to do the radio show.

Bob Carroll, Jr. And Lucy, bless her heart, said, "No, I want Desi." Thank goodness she insisted. He was used to working with a crowd from fronting his band. Desi was marvelous. He'd stick his neck out and do things no one had ever done.

Bob Schiller We plotted that one unlike any other sitcom. We tried to think of a funny last scene first. We would try to work toward the funny scene and make it logical. How do you get Lucy with a bunch of eggs dripping and make it logical? And we did the script backwards. Your really funny scene is written first and if you get any funny scenes on the way, it's extra.

Bob Carroll, Jr. We always tried to get one pretty good physical scene in the first half and a real big one for the close of the show.

Madelyn Davis We did something very consciously. Jess Oppenheimer said you have to take the audience along with you. You've seen routines where you say, "Oh, come on. Nobody would do that." Well, nobody would do what Lucy did. But we usually said it early. We'd have Vivian say, "You can't get away with that." And then she'd say, "Well, you got a better idea?"

3. We Had to Cut the Laugh

Bob Carroll, Jr.   Vivian would say, "No." So she'd say, "Good. Then we're going to do it." We kind of cleared that up with people.

Madelyn Davis   Because she was always sort of in a spot and pushed into doing something. You never wanted her to act like, okay, now I'm going to be funny. The audience would see she was in a spot and so what she did was worth a try. Even if it was a dumb idea, she had to try it. We thought the audience would relate to it if we made them like ordinary people. We did it because we thought the audience would relate to it and think it was funny and say, "Oh, yeah. I sold my washing machine to my brother-in-law and it broke." When they came to Hollywood, they just acted like real tourists. All the things they wanted to see. And everybody wants to see movie stars. You can see sometimes where they take the cast to another location because they think they need a change. It doesn't always work. But we were real lucky it did. Going to Hollywood, we thought we were going to get five shows out of it. We just kept getting ideas. Lucy wanted to get into the movies. One thing came after another.

Bob Carroll, Jr.   Changing the setting was real important in giving us stories.

Madelyn Davis   They wanted to get the souvenir from Grauman's and that turned into two shows because there was so much and we got John Wayne. Her trying to get into the act gave us a lot of stories because of her trying to get into the act was a big part of it. She was a frustrated performer. And we said she wasn't very good. Lucille Ball really didn't sing very well.

Bob Carroll, Jr.   But she was really good at not being very good.

Madelyn Davis   She could make being bad hysterical. And that's a trick. You have to know how to do it pretty well to make it look bad. She could do anything if you gave her three or four days.

Bob Schiller   I loved *I Love Lucy*. The results are something — the adulation. Where else do you get to sign autographs? You don't do that for *Maude*. I was on flight to France and they were showing one of the *I Love Lucy* episodes that I wrote. And I was sitting in the front row. And as the credits crawl came along I pointed to my name and then back to me. People say, "I saw *I Love Lucy* last night." I say, "Give me a dime." We got no residuals other than four runs. Four residuals at 125 bucks apiece.

Madelyn Davis   The married humor really worked. It was the combination of Lucy and Ricky.

Almost every television sitcom has been 30 minutes (with commercials) in length. In 1957, Lucille Ball and Desi Arnaz turned I Love Lucy *into a series of hour-long specials. Although not entirely unsuccessful, this experiment reinforced the 30-minute standard, as the half-hour episodes tended to work better.*

Bob Carroll, Jr. When we went to the hour specials, they were kind of tricky. We were so used to the half-hour version. To stretch a story, it's kind of hard.

Madelyn Davis We'd never written an hour comedy. They're kind of strange. We put in musical numbers and guest stars and that's when the first one ran an hour and fifteen minutes. Desi talked CBS into letting him have fifteen more minutes. That's how little we knew. When it was filmed it was way too long. It's tricky because you need more than one plot. You'd have to have a subplot. We got to use some different locations so that opened things up and that gave us new ideas. I recently saw the one with Ann Sothern. I liked that one. Where Lucy and Ricky are playing drums to each other. It was very, very sweet.

Bob Schiller They were harder to plot because you've got to have three or four breaks during the hour. Ideally, you close with a big scene. Getting three or four big scenes instead of one big scene is very different. Guest stars added a little flavor to it.

The 1960s yielded a large group of eclectic hits that ranged from the realistic comedy of The Dick Van Dyke Show *to fantasies like* Bewitched.

Bill Persky It was such a hot show that everybody wanted to write *The Dick Van Dyke Show*. To this day, when people hear what I did, that's the most important credit I have. In many ways *That Girl*, because of the impact that it had on the culture and on young women, is a very meaningful thing. People are more impressed that I created *That Girl* but they are in awe that I did *The Dick Van Dyke Show*.

Fred Freeman I enjoyed *Dick Van Dyke* a lot.

Bill Persky That was like a magic door had opened. To be on *The Dick Van Dyke Show* was the greatest credential you could ever have because it was the most highly respected show.

Sam Denoff He was a husband and a father. It was really a love story like all the great shows are. Something that was important was always at stake. Plus, you put a man and a woman in a room together and you've got comedy.

3. We Had to Cut the Laugh

Bill Persky   Dick and Mary were the first peer couple in a sitcom. He was as afraid of her being upset with him as she was about him being upset with her. Up to that point, except for Lucy, every wife on television was afraid not to please the man. I think it was based on Carl and Estelle Reiner. He had enormous respect for his wife. They really were equal partners. He couldn't allow himself to do something where the woman was less than a peer.

Sam Denoff   The audience would laugh so long, sometimes we had to cut the laugh.

Carl Kleinschmitt   *The Joey Bishop Show* was done on a very small lot called Desilu Cahuenga. And on that same lot, you could find *The Dick Van Dyke Show* being filmed. So in our spare time, which we had little of, Dale and I wrote a sample script for *Dick Van Dyke*. It got to Carl Reiner, who didn't like the script but thought it was good enough to bring us in to pitch ideas. We went in and pitched ideas and ended up writing nine episodes of *The Dick Van Dyke Show*—eight of them in the last season of the show.

Rick Mittleman   It was a very friendly, warm experience. We would all sit in the room. You would come in with five or six ideas. Usually with a beginning, middle and end. But sometimes you wouldn't have the end. With Carl Reiner and Sheldon Leonard, it was great. Desilu Cahuenga Studio was like a college campus. We all went to the café every day for lunch. It was just a friendly, warm college atmosphere. I would be coming out of *The Dick Van Dyke Show* and I'd run into Sheldon Leonard who was also the executive producer of *I Spy*. And he'd say, "Do you ever want to think about doing a one-hour show?" And I always wanted to try. And I would get an assignment. So while I was waiting for notes on *Dick Van Dyke*, I'd be off writing *I Spy*. And then I'd see Aaron Ruben, the producer of *Gomer Pyle*. And he'd ask me to write for that show. It was a people machine. I was working on all three of those at once.

Carl Kleinschmitt   It was fun. But it also posed a challenge to write jokes. Morey and Rose Marie had to be funny. If there were out-and-out jokes, it would usually come from them. We were writing about a comedy writer type about which I had no familiarity. Certainly Carl Reiner did because he worked on *Your Show of Shows* with writers and *Caesar's Hour*. He had experience with an actual roomful of writers. Situation comedy in those days was not a roomful of writers. We didn't sit around the office and say funny things to each other.

Sam Denoff Those characters were comedy writers. They were funny for a credible reason. Carl said, "How many funny insurance salesmen do you know?"

Jerry Mayer On *The Dick Van Dyke Show*, Morey Amsterdam was a joke writer so he could come up with all that stuff. Because with character stuff, it can be funny as hell but the character is not telling a joke. *M*A*S*H* was a good show to have jokes because both of the guys were joke tellers. Alan Alda's character was glib. So it wasn't phony. If you did that in *All in the Family*, it would seem weird. Don't try too hard because then you can hear the typewriter keys of the writer. You hear the writer. It takes you out of the thing. It's like tiptoeing through a minefield.

Lila Garrett One of the first ones we wrote was *The Dick Van Dyke Show*. We wrote a script for them but I don't think it was ever aired. We got tremendous instructions from Carl Reiner. I learned most from our early experience with *The Dick Van Dyke Show*. I thought that was the best written show on television at that time. Carl Reiner was a wonderful guy. We never did write the script of his dreams. Although the final script that we handed in, he liked very much but I don't think they ever shot it. But Bill Persky, Carl Reiner and Sam Denoff were a tremendous team. We learned a lot about working together and also about how important story was. Just the gags were not enough. There had to be some meat on the bones, for sure, but they really had to be the bones. We learned that from them.

Carl Kleinschmitt Before it got to the table, you did a rewrite with Carl Reiner or Sam Denoff and Bill Persky. You made sure you had it on paper before anybody played with it. There were relatively few changes from the script that hit the table on Monday to the filming a few days later.

Sam Denoff It's just the best because it's still contemporary. It could have run longer.

Lila Garrett Almost anything could happen on *Bewitched*. The magic was very liberating for a writer. It was a gentle show. The insults weren't as devastating as they were on other shows. All comedy is based on human flaws, not on human strengths. Humor is a defense. In terms of *Bewitched*, she used humor to hide the fact that she was a witch. It gave us the opportunity to really let our imaginations fly because she could turn the most bigoted neighbor into a saint if she chose to. And she sometimes chose to.

Paul Wayne One of the basic rules was that she could only use her

3. We Had to Cut the Laugh

witchcraft in dire circumstances. They were supposed to be a normal couple living a normal life. And that's exactly the way it should have been. That was the biggest rule. I think it was a good one. Life had to be treated quite normally. And there was always their secret at stake. I understand that toward the end, this is what Bernie Slade would complain about, when they were sort of going crazy looking for ideas, they would get out of the situation through witchcraft. Which they couldn't before. And I thought that was breaking the rule. And actually breaking a writing rule in that you don't sort of have an automatic out, an automatic exit. Otherwise the audience guesses what you're going to do before you do it. And it's not as much fun for the audience. But that's what they did because they were running out of ideas. After a while, shows just kind of quit by themselves. There are only just so many ideas out there.

Sam Bobrick I only did one but I liked writing with Bill Asher. He was the producer there. Very nice man. And we worked at his house. He had a beautiful house. He was married to Elizabeth Montgomery. God, she was gorgeous.

Fred Freeman With *Bewitched*, I just liked Elizabeth so much. And Bill Asher. They were very, very nice people. It was always nice working for them. It's a pleasure when you work with people that are decent and aren't destructive. *Bewitched* was a fun show to write.

Jerry Mayer I used to be there once in a while when they were shooting it. It was fun to watch it. That wasn't an audience show.

Lila Garrett *Bewitched* was a very enjoyable show for us. First of all, it had Elizabeth Montgomery in it and she became a friend and she was a wonderful, lovely woman and very, very talented. We used to go to parties at her house and it became like a family. So that was really fun. And *Bewitched* was whimsical and that was very appealing. It was an easy show for us to write.

Rick Mittleman That was fun. You could always come up with some kind of crazy story idea because you had the advantage of being able to do magical things, which made it easier. I enjoyed that.

Lila Garrett There were underlying messages when we wrote them. And I think that they thought of it that way. They thought of her being a witch as being a member of a minority. And when she was in a tight spot, she could turn herself or her antagonist into anything she chose. So there was wish fulfillment that satisfied the audience. But there was also an opportunity to point out that she was a member of a minority and there was bigotry against her. She was in a mixed marriage. There was bigotry against her on the part of her husband. He loved her but he was ashamed of what she was.

Sam Bobrick   I found it very difficult to write. Here's a girl who could do anything. She can change the plot by twitching her nose. And it was a very difficult show for me to write because I just couldn't think in those veins. I'd say, "Why doesn't she do this so she doesn't have to do that?" Some people had the knack for that show. I didn't. Bill wanted us to write more but I didn't want to write any more, so we didn't.

Jerry Mayer   I wasn't that wild about *Bewitched*. I thought it was okay. I wanted to write *Get Smart*, which was much edgier. When we had story meetings at Bill Asher's house, Elizabeth was around and it was very glamorous and sophisticated. On the third show we wrote together, Bill Asher said, "I think you went the wrong way at the end of the first act. Come up with something else." And my partner, Paul Friedman — we're still best friends — he said, "Bill, I disagree with you. I think that's a great end of the first act." He not only disagreed, he made a stand. He didn't want to change it. I said, "We'll change it, Bill." So Bill caused us to split. I wasn't pissed at him but Bill didn't want him any more. I thought he was crazy to argue with the boss. So we laugh about that now.

Allan Burns   I loved doing *Get Smart* but it was not my bag. That smart, fast Don Adams kind of stuff was not my specialty. Chris Hayward was better at it than I was. When *He & She* was cancelled, they hired us. Buck Henry was leaving. Mel Brooks never was really on the show. He created it and got all the publicity because he was Mel Brooks. But Buck was the guy who was doing it. We came on as he was leaving. But we helped for that next year to keep that show going, with Arne Sultan and Leonard Stern. Those were fun stories. They were tricky. Taking the spy genre and kidding it was not exactly what I had in mind. I loved *He & She*. That was what I wanted to do. It seems like everything I've done since then has to do with that kind of genre, everything successful I've done.

Lila Garrett   *Get Smart* was great. We wrote two. One was about the justice system and about how pompous justice is. Maxwell Smart sasses the judge and they throw him in jail. "Bronzefinger" was about greed. I absolutely loved it because the sound of the show was very clear and in order to write well for someone else's series, you have to really absorb the sound of the show. You have to be able to talk like their characters talk. You have to be able to think like their characters think if you're going to do something that's worthy for an award and I was nominated for a Writers Guild Award for that show. We did well with those shows. That was a very, very funny show.

Rick Mittleman I enjoyed writing *Get Smart* because it was very jokey and it was kind of fun to take normal actions and make them funny because he was such a klutz. I had a lot of fun with that.

Allan Burns I had no relationship whatsoever with Don Adams, who was very difficult and kind of nasty. I liked everybody else. Barbara Feldon was an elegant woman who really knew where the funny was. Dry, sophisticated, really wonderful. How she ever got along with Don, I'll never know. But there was Ed Platt and all these other wonderful actors. A good show. We teamed up with Leonard and Arne and we did about a dozen scripts that year.

Jack Elinson At the beginning, a lot of people were negative about *The Andy Griffith Show* … that people weren't going to watch a country show, shit kicking. They just thought it was another country show. You could have done the same script and done it somewhere in the Northeast and almost get by. It was a nice family. We didn't country it up so much; it was just nice people doing nice things. It was a hell of a show. It turned out to be a beaut. We just couldn't believe it. The ratings were great and it stayed that way the whole time. The actors were so great. It was funny and it was clean and it was great casting. Best kid ever acted on television was Ronnie Howard.

Sam Bobrick *The Andy Griffith Show* I loved. Andy and Don were so great together, they made it so much better and you were writing comedy routines. And I loved the comedy. I always found I wrote best when I was loving the people who were around. It was easy to write. When you have good actors and you know what they can do, it's easy to write for them once they've established their characters. They were just so great. With new shows, it takes a while to find their characters. Nowadays, and this is an unfortunate thing, if you don't make it in three or four shows, you're gone.

Arnold Margolin In those days, the shows didn't have staffs. There weren't staff writers. Most of the scripts were written by freelance writers. There would be a producer who was a writer or a producer who had a story editor and that was the staff. Writers would come in and pitch. On *The Andy Griffith Show*, we went in with a group of four or five other writers or teams and we would sit with Bob Ross, who was the producer then, and we'd all pitch stories. Then Sheldon Leonard would drop in from time to time and we'd tell him what we were doing and he had such an encyclopedic knowledge of sitcoms that he was very helpful. He'd say, "Oh, I remember that story from *The Ann Sothern Show*. And this is why it worked and this is the problem." It was a great shortcut for the problems you'd run into. You'd do that for a week. At the end of the week, everybody would leave with at least one assignment. It may have been a story you came in with and it may have been someone else's story. You never knew what you were going to walk out with but you knew you were going to walk out with something.

Fred Freeman The show that to me was the hardest to write but was most gratifying to write was when Larry Cohen and I wrote several episodes for *The Andy Griffith Show*. They were sticklers, strong on character. Which was good, I thought. In that sense, that was a good experience. They paid more attention to characters than to jokes. *Andy Griffith* was a challenge to really dig into it and get those characters right. There were terrific characters, like Floyd the Barber. Otis was a fun character. It was a good mix of characters. It was a family of characters that the audience couldn't wait to see.

Arnold Margolin Floyd was great. By the time we got to writing for the show, the actor had a stroke. You could only write short scenes with him and short speeches. They had to prop him up when he was standing up. They had to have some sort of device to hold him up. These were things we didn't know when we sold them ideas for the show. Everybody had their things. Aunt Bee had things she could definitely do and other things that were verboten.

Sam Bobrick We had no idea that it would turn out as good as it did. Because the writers on those shows, we weren't down on the set. We were off writing. So the first time we got to look at it usually was when it was on the air. Most of the time, I would say 99 percent of the time, I was laughing at the stuff because they did it so well. And Don was a good friend of mine until the day he died. Andy is a nice guy. They were so appreciative of writers. That's what I liked about that whole Sheldon Leonard and Danny Thomas organization. I was very lucky to get into that. They were very appreciative of writers. It was so much fun to be around. I did a lot of *Andy Griffith*s.

Arnold Margolin That was an interesting experience because we spent the previous year or two learning how to write jokes, learning how to be comedy writers. We wrote our first *Andy Griffith* and we turned it

3. We Had to Cut the Laugh

in and they gave it back to us for the rewrite and they had taken all the jokes out. We wrote the next script and turned it in and they gave it back and took all the jokes out. We came to realize that *Andy Griffith* was not a show that did jokes. All the humor was out of character. It was a very different way of writing, which as it turned out, was a way we preferred to write. Up to that point, we never thought you could write successful sitcoms and not write jokes. We loved it. Those were great characters. By the time we came on the show they were very well established. We'd been watching them for years. We caught on to that pretty fast. And once we realized they didn't want us to write jokes that made it a lot easier.

Jack Elinson When I meet people for the first time and they ask me what did I do and I tell them I was a comedy writer. I tell them a few of the shows, the one that they all love 100 percent is *The Andy Griffith Show*. It's gotten bigger and bigger.

Sam Bobrick Whoever thought *Andy Griffith* would be shown to this day? A friend of my wife's lost her husband and she likes to go to sleep at night watching *The Andy Griffith Show* because she knows that if everything is okay in Mayberry, everything is okay in the world. That's nice. Isn't it nice that show made her feel good?

Jack Elinson Every year they have a big Andy Griffith week down in North Carolina. They called me one time to come with my wife. It was funny, I was like a king. They touched me; I did *The Andy Griffith Show*. They were so nice.

Unfortunately, it's very difficult to maintain high standards during a long run. Although The Andy Griffith Show *remained hugely popular, ending its eight-year run at the top of the ratings, there is a noticeable difference between the series' black-and-white and color episodes. The beginning of the series' color run coincided with the departures of co-star Don Knotts and producer Aaron Ruben.*

Jack Elinson Naturally it wasn't going to be as good without Don Knotts.

Sam Bobrick It was very hard. I didn't like writing it as much because there was nobody to do the comedy that Andy and Don did. I think Andy felt it. He tried other people but it didn't really work. Not for me. Strangely enough, the ratings stayed up there. When Andy retired from it and it was just called *Mayberry R.F.D.*, the ratings were still high. They were watching the town.

Fred Freeman   One show Larry and I wrote was about Aunt Bee going on TV. And we found it to be so dull. We wrote that show and we were embarrassed to hand it in. No rewrite. Perfect. Most of the time we were rewriting like crazy. But that happens so often. If you think it's awful or you think it's great, they're not going to necessarily agree. There's nothing wrong with that. We all have our own sensibilities.

With quality production companies like MTM Enterprises leading the way, the 1970s and 1980s brought new opportunities for veteran sitcom writers. The best adapted well to a new era that offered greater freedom in dialogue and stories. Many stock plots were retired and replaced with stories based on modern relationships and issues, bringing new life to long careers.

Allan Burns   If I were Grant Tinker, I would have hired Carl Reiner for *The Mary Tyler Moore Show*. Failing that, Bill Persky and Sam Denoff, who were his main guys. Or Garry Marshall and Jerry Belson, who were writers for *The Dick Van Dyke Show*. All better known writers than Jim Brooks and me. Why us? He said it was because what we were doing on *Room 222* felt current and today. He thought it was contemporary and topical and the humor wasn't forced. That's what he wanted it to become. We came up with this idea of Mary being divorced. Every comedy writer I know has a show in files about divorce. Because most people are divorced in the comedy world. Mary loved the idea. Grant loved the idea. We went and pitched it to a couple of vice presidents here on the coast. And the blood ran from their faces. They said, "Divorced? Come on. Please. Of all the things you could do, why that?" We said, "Because it's real. She's 30." This is how unevolved we were at that point. We figured if a girl is 30 and unmarried, we have to explain why. We wouldn't do that today. They thought people would think she had divorced Dick Van Dyke. We said, "No, they won't. First of all, we'll see the ex-husband. And it isn't Dick Van Dyke." We tried to explain that everybody is touched by divorce. Everybody knows somebody who is divorced. There's no blame game to being divorced any more. They agreed we were right and they said they'd support us when we went to New York to pitch this to Mike Dann, the head of programming, and Bob Wood, the new president of CBS. They didn't like it but they said they'd support us. Well, that was the last time we ever heard the word support. So we went to New York. We're at Black Rock at CBS. Mike Dann says, "I hear you want to divorce Mary." We gave him the same rationale and there's silence. And Mike Dann has this

3. We Had to Cut the Laugh

other guy talk. He was from research. He said, "There are four things that American television audiences don't want to see — people from New York, Jews, people with moustaches and divorce." At least divorce wasn't first. They weren't laughing. They said to take this as advice. And the meeting was over. We were still going to be on the air because they had a deal for 13 episodes. But we knew we hadn't done well at this meeting. As we're leaving, they told Mary's manager, Arthur Price, to get rid of us. We were out at the elevators while they were talking to him and we knew what it was about. Arthur came out with this look on his face and we said, "They hate us." And he said, "Pretty much. They don't trust you. They think you're leading them down the wrong path." It didn't make any difference that Grant and Mary liked the idea. So Jim and I get on a very long flight back to L.A.; just hugely depressed. We considered our options whether to quit before we got fired. Or we could think some more. And the upshot of it was that Grant and Mary had treated us so well, with such respect, that if we quit it would look like somehow we had a problem with them. We thought we wouldn't want to do that. We thought there might be a way to finesse it if we gave it some more time. In couple of weeks, if we don't come up with something as good or better, then we could decide what to do and let them in on it. In that two weeks, we started thinking about it again. We needed something like divorce that would make it feel real. At that time, we had no newsroom. Jim said, "Having worked in a local newsroom, I know there's something there that we could have fun with and write as interesting. And I know that world really well." So we began to work that way. We wrote about a 12-page treatment. Immodestly, I will say it became sort of a famous treatment. People used to ask us for it all the time. It was half prose and half dialogue; it just went back and forth, doing bits and pieces. It had stuff that was in the pilot. We gave it to Grant and Mary and Grant called and said, "I think you guys hit it out of the park with this one. I really like this." So we wrote the script and it didn't take us very long. In the pilot, we had Mary coming to Minneapolis from another place, which we said was Rochester where the Mayo Clinic is. She had a relationship with a guy and put him through medical school and once he got out of medical school she wants to get married and he wants to wait, which is why she decided to leave. A lot of the back story is in the pilot. So the implication was that they were living together. We always thought it was funny that they wouldn't accept divorce but in those days, with people being as puritanical as they were, we thought they would hate that, too. But they didn't. At least they were off the divorce hook.

David Lloyd Allan Burns and Jim Brooks wrote a wonderful pilot for *The Mary Tyler Moore Show*. I think you could use that as a textbook for how to write a pilot. How in 24 minutes, they managed to introduce some wonderful characters. Get them all in there and get a plot going and back story. It's a marvel of concise pilot writing. You saw where the conflicts were going to come.

Allan Burns Bob Wood turned out to be a great guy. But Mike Dann was a real dark nemesis for us. He wasn't going to forget what happened in that room that day. We were the wrong guys and they weren't going to support us. They gave us the worst time slot they possibly could — putting us between *To Rome with Love* with John Forsythe, who I like, but it was a dumb show, a kid's show, a guy with kids in Rome and added to the mix to make it even more palatable to the American public, they put Walter Brennan in as his father-in-law. What was that? That was our lead in. And on the other side was *Hee Haw*. If you can name a worse lead in and lead out than those two shows for what we were trying to do, I challenge you to come up with two shows that could have been worse. They had just decided that we were gone. We were opposite *The Mod Squad* and a new Don Knotts variety hour. And Don Knotts was hot. Ethel Winant was the head of casting. She was our only ally at CBS at that point. She loved our scripts. Ethel told the story of one Friday afternoon when Freddie Silverman had come out from New York. He was new on the job. The villains all gathered in the screening rooms. Not Mike Dann. He was gone by then. Bob Wood had decided that the shows that were on were not going to work any more, even though they were getting good numbers. They were not what he had in mind for CBS. The demographics were bad. They were all skewing to 60 and above. They did not appeal to advertisers and he was going to do something about it. Bob picked Freddie as a successor to Mike Dann. This unknown, unheralded guy. Freddie says, "I guess we're going to have to watch that Mary Tyler Moore thing." The lights go down, the show goes on and for 26 minutes or whatever there is very little positive response from anybody. The lights go back on. Fred says to somebody, "Get me Bob Wood in New York." And Ethel's holding her breath. He gets Bob at home. He says, "Bob, I just saw the *Mary Tyler Moore* pilot. We have to change the schedule." Ethel was thinking he meant they had to get it off the schedule. He said, "We can't afford for this show not to succeed. It's exactly what we've been looking for." Ethel was the one who was right in the room and everybody else hated it except Freddie. They shook up the schedule and took us out of Tuesday night and put us on Saturday at 9:30 and put us behind a new show with Herschel Bernardi called *Arnie*, which was a pretty good show that lasted a couple of years. It was a decent lead in for us. Very gutsy move on Freddie's part.

David Lloyd Mary was very WASPy, white bread. I have been told by all the Jewish writers that I'm WASPy and white bread. I think I've gotten less so after 43 years in the television business, but I was. I don't know, maybe there's a little Murray in me. I got quickly into a bantering relationship with Betty White that was akin with Sue Ann's with Murray on the show. I felt very comfortable with that show, much more so than I have with many of the others. *Frasier* was very WASPy. Maybe I've come full circle.

Jerry Mayer My agent was out of town and his partner calls and says, "Jerry, guess what happened? I got an offer for you to be story editor on *The Mary Tyler Moore Show*." I said, "That's fabulous. That's great." He said, "I turned them down." I said, "What do you mean you turned them down?" He said, "They weren't offering enough money." I said, "Who cares? That's the best show on television. How the hell could you turn them down without talking to me?" He said, "Jerry, I'm not an errand boy." I said, "You call them back and tell them I'll take it gladly." They had already hired someone else. I did get to write a couple of them. It was a lot of fun. In one of them she had to fire someone for the first time. The nicest woman in the world and she had to fire someone. So that's an idea where you say, "Oh, boy. This will be funny." It's usually the idea. I also came up with the idea that Ted would wear Conquistador boots. It was that simple of an idea. I thought it would be funny to have him walking in and feeling very manly. That was just an extra added laugh that had nothing to do with the story idea. But when you come up with an extra idea like that it adds laughs that didn't have to be there. You just get lucky sometimes.

Arnold Margolin They were looking to do a spinoff. We were good friends with Allan Burns and Jim Brooks. We knew Jim Brooks because the first show he had written was *My Mother the Car*. I don't think you'll find that on his resume any more. He could take that credit off. Before the show went on the air, they would send us memos from CBS that we would all laugh about or tear our hair out about. And their producer, Dave Davis, had been the associate producer on *My Mother the Car*. It was a small community. It was tough to write because we had to do an episode of *The Mary Tyler Moore Show* and use all of those characters and at the same time introduce these three characters that were going to be regulars on this new series but weren't regulars on *Mary Tyler Moore*. It wasn't like doing a spinoff when they were already characters on the show. These were totally outside characters that we had to introduce and demonstrate who they were and what their relationship was. At the same time it had to be a story about Mary and all those characters. It was a bitch. It was tough to do. I don't think it was very successful and it certainly didn't sell as a spinoff. I think a lot of the problem was that it was too many characters to service and too much story to tell in 24 minutes.

Allan Burns When it ended, I think it was ready. It felt like, to us, that we were beginning to repeat ourselves. There were certain things that would come up that we kind of felt like we had seen before. We didn't know if we could get through another season. We decided we didn't think we could. Everybody was making noises about moving on. Gavin was getting overtures. Valerie had already gone. Ed felt like it was his time for the spotlight. We talked him into staying for *Lou Grant*. I don't think we could have squeezed another year out of it. Maybe I'm wrong. *M*A*S*H* stayed on for 11 years. *Seinfeld* for nine. Maybe we could have done an eighth year. I was wrung out. I didn't feel like I had much left in me. Better to leave on your own rather than get cancelled. Why do that?

Jerry Mayer I had done a spec *Bob Newhart* and the producers liked it. It was great. I admired Bob as a writer. He never gave us a hard time. He was great. It was terrific writing for him. He had a lot of talent. He very seldom rewrote anything but he might say, "What if I did this?" We'd say, "Absolutely. Go ahead." Because it was always right. It was great at MTM. Jim Brooks and Allan Burns were very friendly. It was a great place to work. Grant Tinker was a great guy. Everyone was nice. It was a lot of talent and a lot of classy people.

The issue-oriented episodes of Norman Lear's early sitcoms provided a thrilling change for audiences, performers and writers. Subjects that would have been unimaginable just a few years before were now fair game. Although revisionist history sometimes unfairly lumps these series in with less worthy imitators, Lear's shows were blessed with the quality of actors and writers to handle "very special episodes"—making them funny, and often dramatic as well, without being heavy handed.

3. We Had to Cut the Laugh

Bob Schiller   We wrote *All in the Family* and *Maude*, which were quite different from *I Love Lucy*. We wrote intelligent jokes for *Maude*. More cerebral. We prided ourselves on that. And not many people could do that. What they call "gag writers"—when I hear that term, I gag. We're comedy writers. We write comedy with some insight. It's not just plain Bob Hope monologue jokes, which are just scattered one-liners. We were able to transcend that and write intelligent humor. It was very, very satisfying. It was satisfying on *I Love Lucy*, but in a different way. I loved *Maude*. Norman Lear called us and asked us if we wanted to work on that show. It was a challenge. We did everything. We did abortion, alcoholism, menopause. We did everything on the air but sexual intercourse. Weiskopf came in one day, he says, "*The Mary Tyler Moore Show* got wind of the fact that we're doing a two-parter on abortion. They're retaliating. They're doing a three-parter on mayonnaise." Weiskopf and I were very upset, jealous of the fact that *The Mary Tyler Moore Show* was getting all the print and all the publicity. It was a good show, but it was certainly not a milestone nor breaking any barriers. It was just a well-done sitcom. I always said we were like the Wright brothers but no one noticed we were flying. I speak to Bea Arthur [circa 2001] and it's on at 4:30 in the morning. She says, "I get up and watch." She says, "Goddamn good shows. Jesus, we were good!" It's the most underrated show of all time. Brilliant conceptually. She had her feet firmly planted in two generations. I just loved that show. Intelligent humor.

Irma Kalish   Before, you weren't really writing relevant shows about politics or relationships between the sexes. They weren't ready for it yet. But Norman Lear had his own clout. The shows lent themselves to it.

Lila Garrett   That was a pleasure, a real pleasure, because there wasn't any hiding any more. If you did a show about bigotry that was what it was about. If you did a show about being competitive and petty, that's what it was about. If it was a show about being greedy, you didn't have to hide it. About being chauvinistic, you didn't have to hide it. Archie was a very chauvinistic guy; he really treated his wife like she was a dummy. She kind of was in a shrewd sort of way. But she had a great understanding of Archie and knew how to handle him. Those were the days in which women didn't confront men and say they were their equal and my opinion matters as much as yours. They handled men. And she was that kind of woman. I thought that the real breakthrough show during my lifetime was *All in the Family*. And it was a show that was created in England but I thought Norman's translation of it was absolutely brilliant, absolutely wonderful.

Bob Schiller We were adaptable, good writers. A comedy writer should be able to write comedy. And we did. We were not the only writers on *All in the Family*, of course. They had some pretty good writers before us — Don Nicholl, Mickey Ross and Bernie West. It was harder to write for after Rob Reiner and Sally Struthers left. We lost two very good elements. Reiner was an excellent writer. Reiner's a good actor and a wonderful director. He was a great foil for Archie. He understood the writing part of the program.

Irma Kalish There was always something serious in it that you dressed up with the comedy to get it to go down better.

Austin Kalish We always tried to mix comedy and drama.

Austin Kalish If you have actors who can do both comedy and drama, that makes it wonderful for a writer. It gives a writer scope. You can write the drama...

Irma Kalish And still have the drama have comedy around it. You had to do that. And vice versa.

Jerry Mayer Now, when I write plays, they all have a serious thing. To me, that makes the comedy worthwhile. Like *Modern Family*, which I like quite a lot. They have some serious stuff. They usually handle it without you tearing up but you say, "Yeah. They're right." When you can do that, it makes the show much richer. Of course *M*A*S*H* did that and so did *All in the Family*. I did one where Gloria is pregnant and everyone's happy and then she has a miscarriage. You get a chance to be serious. When it works, it makes the thing you're doing more important. The laughs will be there because you have the characters. It was Archie, the guy who's always full of shit, but now his daughter lost his grandson so you have a chance for him to be very serious. And you're not going to get laughs in that scene and you don't want them but it makes it an important episode.

Lila Garrett I did one where Archie's job is threatened. I was very proud of that show. That's what happens when it comes to money. Money is the great character destroyer. It takes precedence over everything else. He was afraid he was going to lose his job to his best friend. And he tries to destroy his best friend. The friend has seen a psychiatrist. I was very, very proud of that show. Norman Lear welcomed that idea that for money people will become monsters. Most people, even of principle, have a breaking point.

3. We Had to Cut the Laugh

Irma Kalish   I was on a plane once and there was a guy sitting across from me. After he discovered I had been a writer for *All in the Family* he said, "Oh, that Archie. He's so right. You had him just exactly the way I believe." I realized there were people out there who did agree with him, who believed as he believed.

Saul Turteltaub   Norman Lear was a friend. We got that job on *Sanford and Son* because the previous producer, Aaron Ruben, left. Norman and Bud Yorkin hired us, I think, not so much because we were wonderful writers but because we got along with people. And Redd was somebody that you had to get along with. We were happy to get the job because it was a good show and successful. We did it for three years.

Bernie Orenstein   The Beverly Hills branch of the NAACP questioned whether two Jewish guys could write for a black family. There are a lot of ways to defend that. I could write about things that happened a thousand years ago without having lived there. The main defense came from Redd himself. He came to our defense very quickly. He said that he was very pleased with the writing and that we were the perfect guys to produce it. That finally quieted any objection.

Rick Mittleman   I found that easy to write. Nothing's easy but I didn't have any problems with it. The sarcastic humor of Redd Foxx, for me, I found that insult humor to be very funny and easy to write.

Because they were so talented and reliable, it was not usual for the best sitcom writers to be hired by top producers time and again, sometimes on more than one classic at a time.

David Lloyd   *Cheers* was fun. It was great fun. When you could give Shelley a line based on Diane being smart at Sam's expense, they could be a lot of fun. The introduction of Frasier was wonderful. Bringing him in there gave a whole new thing, because the other guys at the bar pick on him. He's really an easy mark for them. And yet, he loves going there and being one of the boys and being the voice of psychiatry and the voice of wisdom there. He was such a wonderful foil for them. And then we brought in Lilith and that gave us another interesting character and a foil for them. The ratings were terrible the whole first season but NBC didn't have much to replace it with. But then it picked up in reruns and won some Emmys. By the time we went off, we'd done 11 years and NBC offered two more. Ted had agreed to it on a Friday and over the weekend his then girlfriend, Whoopi Goldberg, persuaded him not to. That he should be a movie star.

Jack Elinson *Andy Griffith* and *Danny Thomas* were the big ones. The others were great but those were the two big ones. I was with Sheldon [Leonard] and Danny [Thomas] for 12 years and with Norman [Lear] for 12 years. Lucky me. I felt very comfortable with *The Danny Thomas Show*. One of the things I felt on that show was that it's really like me. I'm a New York guy and I talk this way and I felt comfortable there. I wasn't doing a hillbilly show; I was doing me in a way. So I got a good start in comedy because I knew what I was doing and what I was saying. I should say that's my favorite show. The whole first year he was a widower, so that gave us a lot of stuff. We milked a lot of the things about being out with women. It was really good. There was poignancy in *The Danny Thomas Show*. He didn't mind being serious for four minutes, maybe five. It's powerful stuff if people like the show. Some shows are just folly — jokes, jokes, jokes.

David Lloyd When they got *Frasier* they had an established character. The audience knew him. *God*, he knew where the laughs were. Kelsey was a wonderful actor. He was a given. John Mahoney, a wonderful actor, maybe new to television but he'd done dozens of movies and lot of stage in Chicago. And then this serendipity of David Hyde-Pierce. That's a notch up from the cast on *Wings* and that's all the difference in the world. Plus, they got some better writers maybe. To me that was more fun to write because you could write smarter dialogue. And you could write smart and undercut them with Martin. You could write farce. The late David Angell, who was killed in one of the planes that hit the Twin Towers, came onto the set one day when I'd written on *Frasier* and he counted one, two, three, four, five, six entrances. "David Lloyd wrote this, right?" Because that's farce. Who needs six entrances in a scene? There's such an element of luck there. There's also the element of a good casting person. Jeff Greenberg is the casting director who is very, very good and helped them cast *Cheers* and *Frasier*. The difference between a smash hit and one that goes off after a few episodes is so much luck. The casting, the spot they put you on, the night they put you on. It's such a crapshoot.

When Rick Mittleman got assignments to work on The Odd Couple, *he had the unusual advantage of having seen the show's origins up close.*

Rick Mittleman Danny Simon's brother is Neil Simon. Danny called me and wanted to work together on a script for *Petticoat Junction*.

3. We Had to Cut the Laugh

He had the assignment and for whatever reason at the time seemed a little insecure about writing the show himself. He certainly could. He was certainly a big comedy writer. So he wanted to do it at his house. I went over there and down the stairs comes Roy Gerber, this famous agent. They shared the house. They were both bachelors at the time. And it turns out that is what Neil Simon based *The Odd Couple* on. And Danny got a percentage of the show. He was basically the inspiration for Oscar. And Roy was Felix Unger. The show was fun. That was with Garry Marshall and Jerry Belson. I felt very comfortable with that. I had seen the real *The Odd Couple*. I was there at the beginning. That was a pleasant experience. Tony Randall happened to like me and the writing I did. Jack Klugman, in my experience, was more difficult with the scripts he was handed and had more problems. Tony Randall was very relaxed, very cordial, very friendly. He didn't have too many problems with the script. I thought their performances were fine. I thought Garry and Jerry did a great job producing the show and casting it. That was fun to go on the set and kid with them. That was the three-camera technique with an audience. Felix was a grump. Writing grumpy is easy. I loved *The Odd Couple*. I think it was because of the people involved. It was comfortable and friendly and people were appreciative of your work. Writing is a lonely business when you work by yourself. To see something work or get a pat on the back, I think is crucial to your state of mind.

Ed Scharlach Of course, it was one of the greatest plays of all time. Garry and Jerry were trying to cast it and they went through every pairing. Of course, they wound out with the two best Felix and Oscar possible for a television series. Amazing chemistry between Jack Klugman and Tony Randall. It was so much fun to write for them. They were theater pros. They were great comedy actors.

Carl Kleinschmitt I was on *The Odd Couple* for the first 13 episodes. The first season we did it with one camera. My old friends Garry Marshall and Jerry Belson were running it. They had me come on as a rewrite guy. I listened to pitches and made assignments. I left to write a couple of pilots. I don't think they'd found it yet. I think it became something better than when I was there. I hope that was only coincidental. I think it became a much better show toward the end. I think moving to an audience show helped. Tony certainly was a man of the stage. And Klugman was too. I think an audience's energy helps that stuff. You've got to remember that *The Odd Couple* started as a play. The characters are very funny and play very well to an audience. I saw the play many times. In many ways, I thought they were equal to or better than anyone I saw play it.

Ed Scharlach I think it helped. It's a play and these guys are really good performers in front of an audience. I think it came alive. When you have real people laughing, you have to write to that. It's funnier. It was great. You were writing theater really. Wonderful, funny stories. You knew they were going to score because you had this great cast and this great chemistry between Felix and Oscar.

Not everyone agrees on what constitutes a classic series. Perhaps no series has a wider divide in opinion between audiences and critics than Three's Company.

Paul Wayne We were not doing *Death of a Salesman*. We were doing farce. We were doing French farce. The critics were right. We were not doing *Summer and Smoke*. We were not doing *Cat on a Hot Tin Roof*. We were doing French farce. It was *Three's Company*. It was a show about a guy who lived with two girls and he never got laid. It was exactly what it was supposed to be. I think people liked it because it was funny. It was farcically funny. It was pure farce. I had studied a lot of French farce and loved it and brought to it whatever I had learned by studying all those plays by Molière and all those masters. You just never forget these things. It's not the plot that's as important as what you do with the person's personality, with their character. It's how you push and move and get somebody to work in a certain way because of their personality. The more confusing it is, the better. How do you move somebody to do something that's hysterical? You need to structure things that keep on scraping against each other. If things go smoothly, they don't work as a story. Farce is about two or three degrees from reality. If it's not based on reality, it's nothing. It must be based on something real. It has to make you think of something that's actually happened. It can't be based on nothing. And then it's exaggerated to a point but can't be exaggerated too much because there's a place where it's gone too far. That is where I think the talent lies, in knowing when you've exceeded that point — when you've gone too little or spread your wings too far. When I think of farce, I think about the stateroom scene in the Marx Brothers' *Night at the Opera*, where you get that little room and you just fill it with people until you can't get any more people in it. It wouldn't happen in real life. It's just an extension of what would happen if it got crazier and crazier.

3. We Had to Cut the Laugh

While most acclaimed series provided happy memories for its writers, landing a coveted assignment on a hit didn't necessarily guarantee a positive experience.

Paul Wayne   George Burditt and I had a wonderful idea for *Sanford and Son*. He thinks that one of his son's girlfriends is coming on to him. And that was one of the ones that Redd Foxx didn't do. It wasn't the script. He just decided not to do the show for a while. So they had to give the show to the other guy — Whitman Mayo — and it just didn't work for the other guy. Our luck.

Sam Bobrick   I liked writing the shows for *Get Smart* but I didn't like what ended up happening to some of them. They would be rewritten or Don Adams would do it his way. He was successful; it's hard to argue with him. The first show, I won a Writers Guild Award for *Get Smart*. I put in the original script, the one that we wrote that was never filmed. And the award should be on your writing, not what was filmed. I only did a couple of those because I don't think I liked it that much. I liked the show; I just didn't like what they did.

Lila Garrett   *Maude* was a sad thing for me. I wrote a script for that and I let a very good comedy writer look at the script and he thought the jokes should be harder. He rewrote it and he said he knew the people on the show and this is much more what they're going to want. So I actually handed in a lot of his script with the hard jokes. My jokes are hard, too, but these lacked charm in this particular script, despite what a good writer he was. The *Maude* writers took it and they said they were going to rewrite because they were surprised it didn't sound more like *Maude*. They put it back to much more what I had written originally, without ever seeing that version of the script. I learned a tremendous lesson on that script. Go with your gut. It was a mistake.

Rick Mittleman   I did one *Mary Tyler Moore Show*. That was a hard show to write, for some reason. I don't know why. When you sell a story, sometimes you're not as thrilled with it or as excited about it as other stories you sell because you instinctively know there are certain pitfalls. The show came out fine but I don't think it was my best work, to be perfectly honest. If I was to analyze that one show, I may have made it a little too jokey, which didn't play well with the producers. *The Mary Tyler Moore Show* got rewritten quite a bit.

Fred Freeman   Norman Lear showed us the early pilot of *All in the*

Family. I think he asked us if we wanted to produce it and in my great perceptive knowledge of everything, I said, "Norman, how many years can you do spade and Hebe jokes?" I guess you can do eight or nine years of them. Those are the decisions you make that you regret. But you move on.

4

A Spectacular Idea: Classic Episodes

Despite the pressure to churn out an episode every week and then move on to the next script, classic sitcoms are labeled classics for a reason — their most memorable episodes are instantly recognizable to fans.

I Love Lucy, "L.A. at Last"

Bob Carroll, Jr. You pretty much knew it was going to be funny, setting someone's nose on fire. I'm laughing right now.

Madelyn Davis We carefully checked that it could be done. I don't know how she had the nerve to do that stunt. It was just a scream. Her reaction was wonderful. She liked to tell on talk shows that that was an accident. But no. If Lucille Ball's prop nose had caught on fire there would have been 82 people screaming and three fire trucks.

Bob Carroll, Jr. We'd still be wet.

I Love Lucy, "Lucy Does the Tango"

Madelyn Davis That's great when the audience knows what's going to happen and they're just waiting and can't wait. That's great. When Lucy had the eggs in her blouse and did the tango, the audience has seen them rehearse it. They knew how it ended. And so they *knew* what was coming, they knew she didn't want to tell anyone she'd been hiding the eggs and they knew what the dance was. And it happened. It was the longest laugh we ever had because the audience was in on the joke and they couldn't wait.

The Lucille Ball–Desi Arnaz Hour, "Lucy Makes Room for Danny"

Bob Schiller That was inspired. That was the only great one that we had. The only one I would be real proud of. The rest of them, we managed. It wasn't the greatest show. It was a stretch and it had stretch marks on it.

Writers like Schiller were adept at not only coming up with big slapstick gags for Lucy but also writing complicated scripts that mixed comedy and drama. When television comedy went through a transformation in the early '70s, even subjects like alcoholism, abortion, sexual assault and cancer were no longer off limits.

Maude, "Walter's Problem"
Bob Schiller The toughest one we did was on alcoholism. It's hard to make alcoholism funny. Drunkenness is funny, but alcoholism is a disease. We took a big risk, making one of the two star characters an alcoholic. We became heroes with the National Institute of Health. It was good for the show. It got good publicity. I always say the show ended after six years because we ran out of problems.

Maude, "Maude's Dilemma"
Irma Kalish It was a very bold venture on their part.
Austin Kalish We were able to do it on those shows because Norman had clout. No one else was doing it at the time.
Irma Kalish The networks were very leery of offending the viewers. Today they might do it on cable and HBO.
Austin Kalish Because of advertisers, they were very conscious that people might be offended.
Irma Kalish When we first started writing, all married couples had to sleep in twin beds.

All in the Family, "Edith's 50th Birthday"
Bob Schiller
That was tough to make funny. She was brilliant. She was really wonderful. I do think we succeeded and it got a lot of publicity.

All in the Family, "Edith's Christmas Story"
Austin Kalish We suggested a show to *All in the Family* where Edith thought she had breast cancer.
Irma Kalish But they were already doing a show about a medical problem and they didn't want to do two of them.
Austin Kalish The next season they started to assign the shows. They said, "We're doing one with Edith having breast cancer." And we said, "We know that because we brought that one in." They were taking it away from us. Or maybe they were forgetting. We said, "No. We're doing that show."

4. A Spectacular Idea

Irma Kalish   We were able to do it because there was comedy around it. That show became very memorable for me because shortly after it aired a friend of mine from the East came out to see me and I hadn't seen her for many, many years but we kept in touch. While we were having lunch she said to me, "I have to tell you something. I had breast cancer and I had to have an operation for it." I said, "I'm so sorry. I didn't know. How are you?" She said, "I'm fine. But you know what buoyed my spirits during that dreadful time? I happened to see this show on *All in the Family* about Edith and it raised my spirits. And I was able to get through my hard time." She didn't know we had written it. She just happened to see it and remarked about it to me. But that really impressed on us that the words you write on the page go out there to people.

Austin Kalish   People respond to it and you don't know where or when it hits home. It was very revealing to us. It said that all the words you write go out into the world again and again. It affects somebody in some manner that we don't know. Your writing career is not just words, it's not just fluff, it has secondary meaning because people drink it in.

Irma Kalish   It's affecting their lives out there.

Austin Kalish   We got a lot of outside comments about that *All in the Family* script. Not only from the network but from other networks that now wanted us as writers and producers.

Irma Kalish   It had that lovely ending where Archie, who was so unaccustomed to expressing affectionate feelings, did it in the only way he could. That was good.

All in the Family, "Archie in the Lock-Up"

Paul Wayne   I came in there with a whole bunch of ideas and Norman sat there and said, "Those are some pretty good ideas." And I said, "I have one and nowhere to go with it. It was just an image I had of Archie in jail with a bunch of hippies." He said, "That's it." I said, "What do you mean? I have nowhere to go?" He said, "What do you mean you have nowhere to go? You get him in. You get him out." Genius. That's how you write. You get him in, you get him out. So I got him in, I got him out. It was a spectacular idea. You can't lose with that idea. That's why there were people like Lear. Or Danny Arnold. Or Mickey Ross. They knew. Somehow they knew.

Some series were so successful that a large number of their episodes could legitimately be considered classic segments.

The Mary Tyler Moore Show, "Love Is All Around"

Allan Burns   That interview scene is in our original format, almost word for word. I don't know what it was about writing that scene but we just knew we had nailed the writing part of it. Before the first show was shot, CBS wanted a scene that they could show their affiliates. And we shot that scene in a studio down on La Brea without an audience, just the two of them in that scene. And it was like pulling teeth. None of the elements changed but it wasn't very funny and we didn't know why. CBS saw it and said, "Oh, God. Lose Ed Asner, will you? He's a wonderful *dramatic* actor." He had played it more for drama than for the comedy. We were not quite realizing that until it was cut together. Then we did a rehearsal show with some cameras that CBS had asked us to try as an experiment. They were big and clunky and bulky and hard to get around. And the audience could not see the action on the other side. The cameras filled up the set. We also had two other terrible things — the air conditioning had gone out and it was very hot and the audience was uncomfortable and there had been a bomb scare on the lot that day. Everything was mitigating against anything good happening. The guys from CBS were there. The same scene bombed. Again calls about Ed Asner were coming. Recast it. We said, "Get the cameras out of there and get the place air conditioned and no bomb threat and we think it will be all right." That was on Tuesday and on Friday we went back to work and we had a pretty good scene with Valerie and Cloris and Mary that was the first scene. Then this was the second scene and the laughs started coming. And Jim and I said, "Oh, my God. This is what we wanted and it's happening." And it was just euphoric for the rest of the show.

Jerry Mayer   When he says, "You've got spunk. I hate spunk," because he's a terrific actor you can't take your eyes off him. What's he going to say now? And it's a surprise. It isn't going for a joke. It's just funny. It's character and that's good writing.

The Mary Tyler Moore Show, "Chuckles Bites the Dust"

David Lloyd   I wrote that very easily. The main rewrite was that I had Mary get through the funeral with great difficulty and then break down when she went to say something to the minister afterwards and they said, "No, no. She's got to do it during the funeral." That was just fun to write. That was just joke, joke, joke.

Allan Burns   Usually we would take a long time working a story out with writers. I think it was Jim Brooks who had read about some crazy thing about someone who had put his head in a large tomato can and suffocated. He said, "Boy, if only we could do that, somebody who dies in a really bizarre way." We decided to do something really silly with Chuckles the Clown. And David's eyes lit up. He said, "You're going to let me do that? Great!" I think that script was probably on our desk within five days.

Jerry Mayer   Even when you're laughing at death, it was good to have the weight of something important like that.

David Lloyd   Jay Sandrich is a very fine comedy director. Absolutely wonderful and sort of a mentor to Jim Burrows, the current best sitcom director. Jay would find physical stuff that wasn't in the script and would get funny business. He was very skilled. That gives you all kinds of comedy. But he refused to direct that show because he didn't think death was funny.

The Mary Tyler Moore Show, "The Good-Time News"
Allan Burns   We were starting to see jokey newscasters. There were those guys who were out there chuckling and it was just awful stuff. There was a guy named George Putnam who was a serious guy who suddenly decided he wanted to joke around and it was just awful and we thought, "Why don't we do that with Ted?" For the life of him, he cannot go off script because he knows if he does, he's sunk. And he tries and it's so pathetic for him to think he's funny. And then Gordy is just this natural in being able to do a quip and be comfortable with himself. Then there's poor Ted who can't do it, can't handle it.

The Mary Tyler Moore Show, "Two Wrongs Don't Make a Writer"
David Lloyd   It springs out of the character of Ted. You know that he would not have the scruples to not steal Mary's story. It's perfectly in character for him. And that Mary in her innocent indignation wouldn't believe that he could do something like that. It's all character and it gives you a chance for some fun. Six little adorable baby horses. I remember that. I was very pleased with that line.

The Mary Tyler Moore Show, "Support Your Local Mother"
Allan Burns   They forbade us to shoot it. CBS had an executive assigned to the show. I'll let him remain nameless because he made so many terrible mistakes, this being one of them. He also was a thorn in the side of Gene Reynolds when Gene did *M*A*S*H*. He predicted that *M*A*S*H* would fail. He called us on a Thursday or Friday afternoon and

we were going to start in production on the show the next Monday. He was the most dour person you ever saw — the face of death. He said, "You can't shoot that next script. Rhoda won't see her mother? What kind of character is that? Everybody will hate her." We said, "Not by the end of the show. They'll find out why she doesn't want to see her. They'll find out how much she loves her mother and how her mother drives her crazy and how she'll drive Mary crazy. And that's all part of it." He repeated that we could not shoot that show. We went to Grant and said, "CBS said we can't shoot the show. We got orders." He said, "What? That's funny. That's really funny. Yeah, you can. Go ahead." He's still back at Fox but CBS knows where the power is. If Grant says go, we're going. There was a big kerfuffle about it that we were defying them on this. We made some slight modifications in the character and Rhoda's relationship with her. Very slight stuff. It's self serving to say but we won the Emmy for that show. Nancy Walker was one of the great ladies that I ever worked with. Boy, did she know where the funny is. But the whole week long she was sort of reading the script. Never gave it much. And that continued all week. And this is Nancy Walker, the big Broadway comedienne. Jim and I were frankly a little scared of her. She was about this tall but she's a potent force. And finally we got up the nerve to say, "Hey, Nancy, could you find it in your heart to give us a little bit of a performance?" She said, "I'm not used to working fast. I'm finding all this stuff." Then she patted one of us on the arm and said, "Listen, kids. When the asses are in the seats, you'll get funny." She was hysterical. We had her in mind when we wrote it. That's why we were so afraid of her because we knew we needed her to make it work. If she decided she wasn't going to show us a performance, it wasn't going to work. Oh boy, the stuff she came up with. I still watch that show and laugh out loud not at my own writing but because of stuff that she and Mary did together. They worked out routines. There was a scene where she's staying with Mary so she wants to pay Mary and she's got money and she keeps trying to give it to Mary and they worked out that whole routine together, the two of them with Jay Sandrich. Worked out all the business that made you howl.

The Mary Tyler Moore Show, "The Last Show"

Allan Burns We came to the reading and we didn't know what the ending was going to be. We couldn't for the life of us figure it out. We knew what the set up was — that everybody was going to get fired except

4. A Spectacular Idea

Ted. We just loved that whole notion but we didn't know how to end it. It was Jim Brooks. We were in the rewrite session and still didn't have an end. And Jim came up with that idea of Ted Baxter saying goodbye to everybody with *It's a Long Way to Tipperary*. And we said, "Jim, what are you talking about?" He said, "I think this will work." And we worked on it and somebody said, "What if we replayed the Tipperary thing at the end. It's such a great song. And it's so goofy in this mix. It's such a goofy thing to do that it just may work." I don't remember what the reaction was on the stage because everybody kept saying to us, "What's the ending?" The actors wanted to know where they were going. I don't know how they felt about what we had come up with but nobody protested particularly. We went down and Jay Sandrich staged it and he had come up with the whole thing with the hug — the famous huddle where they walk to get the Kleenex. That was Jay directing, his inspiration. They were nervous about it. That had not been in the script. We fell apart. Jay gives Georgia credit for that. I think Georgia came up with what if they went for the box of Kleenex. That whole idea of not letting go of each other was Jay's. And that led into Tipperary.

The Dick Van Dyke Show, "Coast-to-Coast Big Mouth"

Bill Persky   That final scene is just a classic. It was one of the greatest things Carl did and Mary did. We wrote it because we knew what she could do in a circumstance like that. She got a hold of it and it just flowed. Nobody ever had to say to her what to do. She knew. *TV Guide* picked it as one of the 10 funniest scenes ever on television.

The Dick Van Dyke Show, "Br-room Br-room"

Carl Kleinschmitt   How you got the assignment was you went into a room with Carl Reiner and Sam Denoff and Bill Persky and you pitched stories. Reiner, unlike a lot of sitcom people, wanted stories that came out of personal experiences. When Dale and I went to our first pitch session with Carl Reiner, we came up with things like Laura gets a ticket and fights it in court. It was all the old clichés and Carl said, "No. Tell us what's going on in your life." We couldn't think of anything that was going on in our lives other than just having escaped Joey Bishop. So Dale said something about each of us just having gone out and bought motorcycles with our newfound money. So that became our first episode of *The Dick Van Dyke Show*, which was called "Br-room Br-room." It's a story in which Rob gets a little motorcycle. It won the Writers Guild Award for best episodic comedy script of 1965. When you're 27 years old, you think it's always going to be like that. It was a huge thrill. Maybe it was because no one had done a motorcycle show at that time. And because Van Dyke is so good. It was a great surprise to both of us that it was nominated and that we won the award.

The Dick Van Dyke Show, "100 Terrible Hours"

Bill Persky Another one based on reality. When Sam and I worked at WNEW, there was a strike with the disc jockeys and we were on the air for a week. And we were working around the clock. So we wrote a show where Dick tries to break a record for doing a disc jockey show and staying awake. The physical things that he did in that. He puts a cup of coffee down on a turntable while he's reading a commercial and just the way he reached out and constantly kept missing the coffee cup. If you gave him the slightest thing to do, he would turn it into something magical. He just was a genius at that. He's just brilliant.

The Dick Van Dyke Show, "Farewell to Writing"

Fred Freeman That was fun. It's in the top 10 of audience favorites. He gets a novel that his friend wrote in the mail. Now he gets crazy. He thinks he needs to be a serious writer. He doesn't want any phone calls. He doesn't want to be bothered. He goes in his room, the phone rings, he comes back out and says, "Who is it?" As a writer, it was my own experience of not wanting to be bothered because I had to write this thing and then be, "Is someone at the door?" The procrastination. It was just my own feelings about it. When someone you know has done something good or big like Broadway, you think you're shit, you're worthless. We can all identify to a degree with that when your best friend is now head of a big corporation or something like that. It was fun to have him not writing. I use that show as an example to my writing class. Write from your own insecurities, fantasies and dreams. It'll be identifiable to everyone, not just people in show business and writers. There was a line that Chekhov said about, "When I want to learn about humanity, I look to me." That's true. All we have to do is look into ourselves. Those are the things that ring true. We gave him a paddleball. He's looking for anything to do except write. He sees nudists out. It's just going by your own self. I'll do anything sometimes to avoid writing. I pay the bills. I fix the couch. That's no different from any of us. You hit a common chord that we all share. You don't have to be in show business to understand it.

4. A Spectacular Idea

The Dick Van Dyke Show, "That's My Boy??"

Sam Denoff We wrote a spec script for *The Dick Van Dyke Show* and we thought it was great. Carl Reiner didn't like it but he told us to take another shot. We ended up pitching the idea that Rob thinks Richie was switched at birth. A flashback. He loved that idea and so he spent a day-and-a half working out the story and breaking the scenes with us. That was "That's My Boy??" It's my favorite episode. Carl hired us for that show because nobody had captured the voice before like him.

Bill Persky Everything that was done on *The Dick Van Dyke Show* happened to somebody. When I went to the hospital when my first child was born we actually did get someone else's flowers. There was no DNA then. So I wondered if we got someone else's flowers, how do we know we got the right baby? Everyone says, "Calm down. Calm down." But that was the source for that story.

The Dick Van Dyke Show, "Curse of the Petrie People"

Carl Kleinschmitt My favorite is "Curse of the Petrie People," where Laura receives an obnoxious pin that's basically a map of the United States with diamonds in it that represent the birthplaces of every male in the Petrie family and manages to drop it down the sink and break it in the garbage disposal. I just thought that was fun. I love the title for one thing. We had a lot of laughs writing it and I thought it turned out quite well.

The Dick Van Dyke Show, "Go Tell the Birds and Bees"

Rick Mittleman To me that was one of the easier shows to write because there was so much there.

The Dick Van Dyke Show, "October Eve"

Bill Persky That came about because I had a portrait done of my wife and kids and when I saw it the guy had gotten kind of surrealistic. There was a moment in that one where Dick walked into the gallery looking at the painting. The painting was downstage and he was way upstage and when he turned and actually saw the painting he dropped his head like somebody broke his neck. It was the most hysterical thing. It's like his head came down to the middle of his chest. I don't know how he did it. Nobody said, "Do this." That was his initial reaction. And the bit where he's holding the gratings from the stove and all his tension is in gripping them, that's not in the script. He just did it.

M*A*S*H, "Sometimes You Hear the Bullet"

Carl Kleinschmitt   My agents sent me out on a call to pitch stories to Gene Reynolds and Larry Gelbart. It was the first year of *M*A*S*H*. I'm not even sure it was on the air yet. I remembered the movie so I knew the characters. I came in with an idea that Hawkeye, who was so glib about doing his duties as a surgeon, had never lost a friend of his in the war. I thought it would be a good idea to kill off someone that Hawkeye had an attachment to. That worked. That became an episode called "Sometimes Your Hear the Bullet." It gave them another avenue to go down in that everything didn't have to be fun and games. That was a script that basically seemed to write itself for some reason. If there's one thing that I liked the best that ended up on the screen in television, it's that particular episode. I found that once I started writing it I became emotionally involved in it and that's why, to some extent, it takes that downward turn in emotions after the guy dies. You build him up as this devil-may-care friend of Hawkeye's who's just there on a lark to get material for his book. Once I started to write it, I actually believed in those people while I was writing it. They liked that story from the beginning and when I turned in the first draft, they loved it. That episode was nominated for a Writers Guild Award but lost to the *Maude* alcoholism episode. CBS hated the script. They hated the idea that somebody died. As one executive said, "What is this? A tragedy show? People don't want this crap." In some ways, it helped make the show what it was.

M*A*S*H, "The Ringbanger"

Jerry Mayer   I had read this thing about in the Army they had people they called ringbangers. The idea is that guys who went to West Point when they were in a meeting and making decisions, they would turn their ring around where the big part was and they would bang that so you knew they were from West Point. They were often kind of full of shit because they would use that to make themselves look important. I pitched that story. They liked it a lot. Larry Gelbart was a very nice guy. So I wrote a draft and they said I didn't have to do a second draft. Well, he rewrote the whole thing. But I was so pleased and honored that Leslie Nielsen was in it. That was before he was in the movies where he said, "Don't call me Shirley." There were those little thrills.

M*A*S*H, "Hey, Doc"

Rick Mittleman   I did a *M*A*S*H* and that turned out very well.

I don't think I even did a rewrite on that. There was a classic scene in it that I keep getting clip fees for when they take a clip. I did the show where Major Burns decides he wants to drive a tank. He gets in this Sherman tank and flattens the colonel's jeep. They really flattened a jeep. It was really funny. And that clip gets shown a lot. I would have liked to have done more because it was my kind of show. I found *M*A*S*H* easy to write because the characters were so well drawn. All a good writer has to do is watch the show a couple of times and they get the feeling of all the relationships. Because these are people that see such tragedy with all the helicopter loads of bloody wounded coming in, they have a dark sense of humor. I really enjoyed writing it.

The Andy Griffith Show, "Manhunt"
   Jack Elinson   When we got to the point where we had to do the premiere, we liked show number two, which was "Manhunt." We figured that was the one to open up with. And CBS said we'd rather have "The New Housekeeper," which was so different. The other one was punchier. They were very strong about it. It wasn't like we hated the first show. We got a thing from the Writers Guild for "Manhunt." That was fun. "Manhunt" was my favorite episode. Just a simple story like that.

The Andy Griffith Show, "Goober and the Art of Love"
   Fred Freeman   Don Knotts was very funny in showing his friend Goober how to act with girls. And he's looking through the window at Andy and his girlfriend. The best moment I had was after a show we did, I got a call from Jim Fritzell and Everett Greenbaum and they said, "God, that was a good show." Because they were the guys who really wrote so many. I was so flattered. That was so terrific of them to do that. They were very nice.

The Andy Griffith Show, "Otis, the Deputy"
   Arnold Margolin   At that time it was still permissible and acceptable to do shows about drunks. You can't do that today. Even then we had to be very careful about how we treated that aspect. It was one of the tougher episodes for us to write. I think a lot of it had to do with the fact that Otis was an outside character and we didn't know him as well as we knew the others. I think they only did one or two shows a year where that character had that prominent of a role.

> *With all of its tension, joy and potential for problems, it's hard to beat a wedding for a classic storyline.*

Rhoda, "Rhoda's Wedding"

David Lloyd   Jim Brooks was running that and we broke it up into scenes. He has an infectious enthusiasm. He would get you galvanized and convinced you were being very funny. He has a laugh that's been much parodied, which you can hear on all the tapes of *The Mary Tyler Moore Show*. He would do that with actors. Lines he'd written and heard a dozen times but at showtime he'd get the actors saying, "Wow! I'm killing, I'm making Jim laugh." And I'd say, "It's just amazing how he manipulates that, they fall for that." And then he'd turn and do it to me and I'd fall for it. And I'd say, "My God, he likes my writing!" And so when he got us going on a project like the wedding show, he would infuse us with enthusiasm, which is very hard to resist.

Allan Burns   It was very good. It was hard. We took sections. We divided it up. It was a really funny show.

Cheers, "Woody's Wedding"

David Lloyd   That was the one that was the most fun there. That was just a treat. I had decided I was going to pretty much stop writing for *Cheers*. I was not getting along as well as I should have with the producers. I'd written a bad script for them, which they then rewrote. Probably saved it but it wasn't very good even the way it came out. And I thought I'd gone to the well once too often. And then they decided they wanted a farce for the wedding. And I think the Charles brothers said, "You should get David to write it." And I started on it and started to get enthusiastic about it and said, "We can do this, we can do that." And they said, "Let's turn it into an hour." And I said, "Okay with me." Upstairs door, dumbwaiter, swinging door, door out to the nasty dogs, door to the wine cellar. It was just one good thing after another and I'd say, "Ooh, can I do this? Can I do that?" That was just such fun. I really loved writing that. I guess it would be my favorite. That was just sheer fun to write.

> *Other times it merely takes a particularly inspired story for a hit series to yield a memorable episode.*

Taxi, "Elaine's Strange Triangle"

David Lloyd   Ed. Weinberger was meeting a gay friend in a gay bar in New York and saw a guy coming, looking for a dance partner and Ed.

was saying, "Oh please, God. Oh, please don't ask me." The guy walked by him without looking and he said, "What's the matter with me? What am I, chopped liver?" You'd be surprised how many of our stories were based on things that happened in Ed. Weinberger's life. The dancing with Judd was hilarious. I can't claim credit for that, that's not the writing. I think that's probably why I lost that year, I was nominated for an Emmy, but I didn't get it. Any more than I could have written Mary's performance laughing at the funeral.

Mork & Mindy, "Mork's Mixed Emotions"

Ed Scharlach   We got a Writers Guild nomination for that. It was kind of a complex subject. It was about the various emotional clashes that human beings actually do have. For many years schools would show that as a representation of the things they talk about on a more serious level and we were doing it on a comedy level. It was a very good show. It was Tom Tenowich's concept and we had a very good time writing it together. Apparently, Orkans don't have emotions and he's here on Earth and has basically fallen in love with this beautiful girl that he lives with and she kisses him for the first time and suddenly it frees all the emotions that have been held prisoner. Robin Williams, as this great actor, acted out every single emotion on the entire spectrum. It's all just like Robin doing a one-man show. It still holds up. I was very, very proud to be associated with that. That was the first one we wrote. And it was the first time, I think, the show went to number one in the ratings. That was just coincidental.

Frasier, "Ham Radio"

David Lloyd   My great regret with that is I didn't get an ending for it. I had one but it was really just more of the same. It really wasn't an ending; it was just pushing it a little further. I thought, damn, we never really got a boom ending for it. But up until that time I was having a lot of fun with that because I grew up on radio stuff.

The Odd Couple, "Gloria, Hallelujah"

Rick Mittleman   I particularly had a lot of fun writing one episode that actually got changed a lot. That happens when you're a freelance writer. I had a producer once who said, "Rick, you've gotta get a folder and you've gotta put it in a drawer next to where you're working and every time something is taken out of your script, you take it and put it in a folder marked little darlings. And those little darlings are yours but they'll never be shot. Don't worry about it. Go on with your life." It's true. There was one script I wrote that got a Writers Guild Nomination but it got rewritten quite a bit. I was having so much success that I was surprised to see it rewritten but that's the business. Tony insists that Klugman sign up with a dating bureau and then helps him fill out the application. Thanks to Tony telling him what to put down, Tony's ex-wife shows up as his blind date. I felt it got changed, not for the better, but still got a Writers Guild nomination. I can't complain.

The Odd Couple, "Speak for Yourself"

Ed Scharlach   We did one where Felix met the woman he wound up marrying and subsequently divorcing. It was a flashback. It was fun to do an origin story to decide how characters that Neil Simon put together originally began.

Bewitched, "Divided He Falls"

Paul Wayne   I had written something for *Bewitched* called "Divided He Falls." I was in a grocery store one day and I looked at a *TV Guide* and it said "The 100 Best." I said, "Gee that's interesting. I wonder if I'm in there." Oddly enough, there I was with "Divided He Falls." And curiously, it said they thought it was so good that they repeated it with the second Darrin. I said, "What?" That was something I never knew.

Bewitched, "The Magic Cabin"

Paul Wayne   There was also a thing that I had done called "The Magic Cabin." We had hired Buster Keaton. And it was so good and he was so funny. What had happened was that they had gone to Darrin's boss's cabin, not knowing that it was so dilapidated and rain was coming in through the roof and he said, "Okay, you can use your magic to change it because we're so miserable." At the same time, unbeknownst to them, Darrin's boss was trying to sell it. Some people came and they thought it was a magnificent palace. The idea was that the cabin changed back and forth and the idea I had was a painter on a hill, painting the cabin and every time he looked at the cabin, it was a different cabin. And we'd given the scene to Buster Keaton. So, of course, every time Buster Keaton saw the cabin, it was a different cabin. So he threw away one oil and started another. And by the end of it he decided he was done with painting. You can image what Keaton had done with it. It was just absolutely brilliant. But it was so long it had become unwieldy and they had to cut it.

4. A Spectacular Idea

Sanford and Son, "Steinberg and Son"

Bernie Orenstein We thought that would be a good parody. It had a lot to do with television. It was about selling a show that was plagiarized from Fred Sanford's life. All of us, all writers, have been confronted with shows on television that we've submitted at one time or another that we thought the idea was taken from us. So we wanted to do a show that reflected that. Redd loved that idea. He was perfect when he went into the office of a big shot. We saw him confronting studio executives as being a great vehicle for him.

Saul Turteltaub That show was fun to do. It was a spoof of our own show. We brought in John Larroquette, who played the son. I think it was his first television job. The man who played the father was wonderful — great actor of the Yiddish theater — Lou Jacobi. It was an interesting plot. It was a different idea. You're turning them around very quickly. You're editing one, shooting one and writing one and going quickly through all of them. I enjoyed every one of them.

5

This Is Good: More Hits

Although they don't inspire the passion of top classics, television history is filled with successful series that invoke positive memories for fans and writers alike. Some of these series were the second or even third hit for beloved TV stars. Programs like The Lucy Show, Here's Lucy, The New Dick Van Dyke Show, The Ann Sothern Show *and* Cosby *had to live in the shadow of the star's previous hit.*

Bob Carroll, Jr. It wasn't as easy to do *The Lucy Show*. We had to dig up boyfriends once in a while. You can't beat that old husband-and-wife relationship for comedy.

Madelyn Davis I find myself referring to something and then I think, "Oh, that was that show." Lucy worked with an elephant on that show. She and Viv got stuck in the shower. We did a lot of physical stuff that really worked. Because by now, we knew the formula. We did some good shows. There were some really, really funny shows on *The Lucy Show* and *Here's Lucy*.

Bob Schiller *The Lucy Show* was a success because of Lucy. It was tougher. Much tougher. Husband and wife are natural enemies, at least in sitcom land. You had to manufacture conflict. Having two women. We tried with Gale Gordon. That wasn't as powerful as Desi. Outside of being tied to her purse strings, he had very little power. Also, he was funny, but Desi was the most underrated straight man in America. He was brilliant. Nobody gives him credit. We had had enough of it and we had a great offer—*The Red Skelton Show*. We wanted to do a variety show. It just seemed like it was time to move on.

Lila Garrett I got to do a wonderful episode. But we were really given that story by her staff. Lucy is on skates and she's directing a choir. She kept rolling through the front of the choir and she couldn't help it and they would pull her back. On *The Lucy Show*, the thing you had to think of in every show was what would be the physical bit that Lucy was

5. This Is Good

going to perform. This physical bit was given to us. But I got to know Lucy pretty well. It was thrilling. Lucy was Chaplin. Lucy was a genius. Just amazing.

Elroy Schwartz I had a storyline in mind for *Gilligan's Island* and I sold it to *The Lucy Show*. That was an interesting experience. I was going to give Gilligan superhuman strength. Lucy is in Mr. Mooney's office and there's a Xerox copier being delivered and the copier slips and traps his foot and he's screaming in pain. And Lucy comes over through the small crowd of people and lifts it up and he takes his foot out. They are amazed at her strength because nobody can do that. The doctor says, "You couldn't do that again." So Lucy picks it up and puts it down. The doctor is amazed and he says, "Your adrenal gland that gives you certain strength at a moment of excitement must be stuck." So she gets this super strength. When I wrote that for Lucy, they invited me over and I was sitting there with about ten other people. There's a break and I don't see Lucy. Suddenly, she's sitting next to me. She said, "You must be Elroy because I know everyone else here." I said, "Yes." She said, "Hi." I said, "You don't have to introduce yourself, Lucy." And she laughed and said, "I'm enjoying the script so much, it's so much fun, that I just wanted to thank you for it." That was fun to watch her perform. She was a very inventive comedic actress. You could give her a prop and she could do anything with it.

Bob Carroll, Jr. While we were doing *The Debbie Reynolds Show*, Lucy called and they had met the Burtons at a party somewhere and the Burtons had said, "Can we be on your show?" Lucy said, "Of course." So she called old Bob and Madelyn. Who better to drag in to write that show? So that's how we got reinvolved with Lucy on *Here's Lucy*.

Madelyn Davis It was different. And we had quite a few guest stars. We got some wonderful stories from guest stars.

Saul Turteltaub Dick Van Dyke had moved to Arizona and wasn't going to do any more TV. By coincidence, a company had built a studio in Arizona. It turned out it was only a mile or two from Dick's house. CBS called him and asked him if he wanted to come back and he said that if they could do it in that studio that he'd do it. Immediately, he called Carl Reiner. He created *The New Dick Van Dyke Show* but he wasn't going to go to Arizona every day. So Bernie and I had just finished *That Girl* and we were free and knew Carl, so he asked us to produce it. Carl would read every script and make suggestions and then fly out for the reading and come back for the shooting day. So he stayed involved. I thought it was a good show. I thought it was fun. It wasn't as good as the first one. I thought the first show was funnier. It was the better show. This one I thought was good and it was funny and we enjoyed it. But it didn't get the ratings that the first one did.

Bernie Orenstein Being out in Arizona was a new experience. We had a great group. Hope Lange played his wife. Marty Brill was a terrific comedian. Nancy Dussault. A lot of good people.

Bill Persky It was a fun experience. Saul and Bernie are terrific writers. People compared everything to the original show but those shows were really funny.

Ed Scharlach Carl Reiner had created a new show for Dick Van Dyke and Warren Murray and I wrote some scripts for that series. It was never the magic chemistry the original *Dick Van Dyke Show* had but it was a nice show and fun to write and there were some good comedy actors in the cast.

Bob Schiller We created *The Ann Sothern Show* because she did such a good job on the first hour show with her drunk scene [on *The Lucille Ball–Desi Arnaz Show*]. She had been very popular on *Private Secretary*. She was good friends with Lucy so she asked Desi to come up with a sitcom for her. It was fair. Not a bad show, but not a good show.

Bernie Orenstein *Cosby* was a very good experience. They wanted a couple of older writers on the staff. Bill is an extraordinarily talented comedian. We all know that. But he can drive you crazy when you're trying to write a show. He was not averse to changing everything. And usually for the better. I give him that credit. But it makes it tough for the writers.

Saul Turteltaub Bill Cosby was a person who always added to the show. He was brilliant with comedy. He was brilliant with everything. But *Cosby* was a sad show because that was the year his son was killed. He used to walk down the street or ride in the cab and somebody would wave at him with a big smile. Now they'd have a sad face for him and he knew they were feeling sorry for him and he appreciated it but he didn't want to see it. So we went back to business as usual. He handled that amazingly. He's a great man.

Bernie Orenstein He's a great performer. I thought he was terrific. Everybody liked his character on *The Cosby Show* and this was an old guy who was crotchety. So it was a change. But he performed it beautifully. It wasn't accepted as easily as *The Cosby Show*. People had it in their mind what Cosby was.

5. This Is Good

Although spinoffs have the advantage of using a known commodity from a popular series, they too have to live in the shadow of their mother series. Even when the series becomes a tremendous success—Gomer Pyle, U.S.M.C. outrated The Andy Griffith Show *in its first two seasons—history is often kinder to the original.*

Rick Mittleman It's one of those things as a TV viewer at home on my own time, I never watched *Gomer Pyle*. It wasn't my kind of show. I had a good ear for Jim Nabors. I really did, for some reason. I can't explain why. I could write for Jim Nabors' speech pattern. The way I approached it, I thought of a movie I liked a lot called *Billy Budd*. The story had this young man who was perfect and because he was perfect was treated mercilessly by the first mate. I took that. I took Jim Nabors as Mr. Innocence — pure, decent, kind — and the military sergeant as being like the first mate who was on his ass constantly. I think what made that show successful was the constant conflict between Gomer, who was always trying to do well and would screw up, and Sergeant Carter, who would always be on his case. And it became easy for me to write for a show that I ordinarily would never watch.

Jack Elinson It was really a steal of the plot of *No Time for Sergeants* without actually doing it. Aaron Ruben did that show and asked me write for it. It was country humor, too. Jim Nabors was the heart of the show. The character did everything with a smile. Frank Sutton was a very good actor, too.

Carl Kleinschmitt I did and didn't enjoy writing for that character. I thought the Frank Sutton character of Sergeant Carter was more interesting. My favorite episode of that is called "I'm Always Chasing Gomers." Sergeant Carter has had so much trouble with Pyle that he jumps on a plane to go home to his mother to spend a weekend. And Gomer, for some reason, gets on the plane and is there for the weekend so Carter thinks he's having hallucinations, seeing Pyle everywhere. I thought that was fun. I don't think it's a great show. It was a nice show. All the shows on that lot had that in common. They all ended on a nice note. Danny Thomas believed in what he called a treacle cutter. Just when you didn't think you could take any more sweetness, you'd put in a kind of edgy joke.

Sam Bobrick I didn't like writing that show. I loved Aaron Ruben. When Aaron went over to produce that show, he brought me over and we wrote for him. But I had a hard time with it because I realized that there was nobody smart on that show. The sergeant was dumb. Gomer was dumb. Where Andy Taylor was smart. He was the glue. He was the guy that kept it all together. That show came from a different place. While a lot of people did like it, I found it tough to write. I really did.

Carl Kleinschmitt   It's not something I would want to watch over and over again but it was a nice show. And Jim Nabors was one of the nicest men you'd ever want to meet in your life. The nicest man. I didn't know him well but a few years later I was working in London and across the street I saw Jim Nabors. He looked over and he crossed the street and couldn't have been more gracious in saying hello. A lot of actors aren't that nice. He made Gomer a character and it's absolutely nothing like Jim Nabors. The first time I heard him sing I thought it was a ventriloquist.

Sam Bobrick   This is terrible to say but my kids were surfing the Internet and they happened to hit on an old *Gomer Pyle* show and they said, "Dad, look. It's *Gomer Pyle*." And I looked at it and I listened to it for about 10 minutes and I said, "Oh, my God. He was retarded!" I just didn't like writing that show very much. Jim Nabors himself was one of the nicest guys I've ever met. I love Jim. But the show didn't work for me like some of the other shows I enjoyed writing. I don't even remember how many I wrote. I don't remember that show that well. That's the show that I think made me want to go off and do something else.

Bob Schiller   I thought *Archie Bunker's Place* was dull. It didn't have the elements of *All in the Family*. It's not like a husband and wife or a father, daughter and son-in-law. Not like a family.

Ed Scharlach   Tom Tenowich and I had worked together on *The Dean Martin Show* and he asked me to be his partner again on *Mork & Mindy*. That was an interesting experience. That was one of my dream jobs, to be able to write for Robin Williams. His amazing abilities made you stretch as a writer. It was a lot more fun and free. We had a lot of laughs. The best shows happen when the writing staff and the cast are in harmony. We were all really close and it made the show so much more fun and the quality so much better. We did things that you couldn't do anywhere else but all the stories had to have an emotional point. Eventually, the magic wears off. It's very, very difficult. ABC put us on Sunday night. The ratings immediately sunk. The network panicked. Jane Fonda said she wanted to do an episode and loved the show. ABC said to make it an hour. She was a major star but that's not why people watched the show. A movie came up so she couldn't do it. So they put in Raquel Welch.

5. This Is Good

Totally different from Jane Fonda. It was an interesting week. She was very nervous about doing a show in front of a live audience. She took her nervousness out in ways that were funny to us but not productive to the show. Then they tried bringing in T & A with sexy girls on the show. It's the exact opposite of what a family show like *Mork & Mindy* needed. So that didn't work. But it lasted four years. I'm very proud of the shows we did. It was a great treat to write for Robin Williams, Pam Dawber and Tom Poston.

Allan Burns I look at *Rhoda* today. Not so long ago they sent me some DVDs of it and I thought, "This is good. I don't remember it as being this good." Charlotte Brown, who became the producer, did a hell of a job.

David Lloyd I think Charlotte was very, very good. I would struggle with her when she wanted me to do something and I wanted to do something else. I chafed under that but she was right. She was usually right. She understood the dynamic of this young woman, single — Charlotte was single — much better than I did. So I think she made that show good.

Allan Burns We made what I think was a bad choice in casting with Joe. He was a good actor but he didn't have those comedy rhythms and chops he needed to keep up with Valerie. Valerie is very generous and a very nice lady. She's pretty easy to work with. I think this was probably the first divorce in television history that was because they were comically incompatible. That was the reason for their divorce. We tried keeping him on for the whole process of the divorce instead of just cutting it off. I think it was sad to have her have to admit defeat. That the character wasn't going to work. I don't think Valerie took any joy in David Groh being let go. It hurt David deeply. It hurt her, and it hurt all of us, but she realized that it wasn't working.

David Lloyd In retrospect, I think it was a mistake — I think they all did — to get her married so soon. Joe was a mistake and I think they found that out. Because until they got rid of Joe, the show kind of hit that peak and went straight down. Something other shows have learned to resist. When there's a romance, they've milked it and milked it and milked it. Niles and Daphne milked it for years and years and years before you let it pay off.

Allan Burns I don't think it was necessary for them to get married. I think it worked better when they were dating and kind of feisty with each other. David could play that really well. But once they were married, it became serious. Fred Silverman made one of the only mistakes I think he's ever made relating to us in ordering us to get them married. He was right in one thing. He said, "We'll be number one in the ratings." And we were that night. It was huge. We beat *Monday Night Football* and it was hot. Howard Cosell said something to the effect of the crowd in the stands that night was a little sparse and he guessed it was because everyone was home watching Rhoda's wedding. But it was much too early. We wanted to drag it out to at least the end of the first season.

Fred Freeman   Joey Bishop was a very destructive guy. He was very unhappy in his life. Joey scored when he was a guest on *Jack Paar*. He was a good counterpunch. Quick. But that doesn't mean someone like that deserves a lead on a show. They are supporting actors at best.

Sam Denoff   He didn't have the talent or the temperament of a Dick Van Dyke. He also didn't have a Carl Reiner running his show.

Bill Persky   Garry Marshall and Jerry Belson worked on *The Joey Bishop Show* and they would come over to *The Dick Van Dyke Show* and say, "We had to get away from the cemetery and come to life." Joey was the most depressive guy in the world. We only did a couple of shows with Joey and it was arduous.

Carl Kleinschmitt   Dale and I began writing for Joey Bishop 12 to 16 hours a day, writing scripts and then rewriting scripts that other writers had submitted. Garry Marshall had left and in Garry's own fashion he said, "Here are the boys who will replace me." It was great training but a thoroughly frightening experience working for this man. He was very difficult. But we learned how to write under pressure. We learned how to write fast, even if it wasn't very good. And according to Joey, it never was. It was good training. We'd be sitting at a table at the reading and we'd hit page five or six and Joey would take the script, throw it in the air, curse and say in his inevitable way, "I will not do this shit! I'm a comedic genius. Go back and do it again." So we would go back and do it again. Joey would always call us "fellas." He would never call us by our names. He would call my house at 3 o'clock in the morning. It was an interesting experience. As another comedy writer, Harry Crane, told us, "It's like being in the Marine Corps. It's boot camp. If you can get through it, you can survive anything." It was good training but not an entirely pleasant experience.

Fred Freeman   The last show we did was *Empty Nest*. They made us an offer we couldn't refuse. It wasn't really our kind of show that we liked that much. But it was a well-done show. We ran the show so we had to look at everything, including costumes. We only wrote two of them ourselves because we were busy getting the other ones in shape. We were brought in by Paul Junger Witt and Tony Thomas to run the show. The rest of the staff, I think, really resented us because I think they thought one of them would be picked to run the show. It wasn't always pleasant. Sometimes we were there until two, three or four in the morning, writing. It wasn't a show that I would have naturally chosen to write. But we started to get in the rhythms. Richard Mulligan was a very talented guy. He could be difficult but he was smart. It was a good cast. It was a good show for what it was.

Still other hits lived in the shadow of the series that preceded them on the schedule. Although their placement on the schedule provided them with an advantageous head start, series like Too Close for Comfort, Wings *and* Chico and the Man *were generally considered to be slightly watered down versions of* Three's Company, Cheers *and* Sanford and Son, *respectively.*

Austin Kalish   *Too Close for Comfort* was an interesting show because we could do broad comedy. We brought in Jimmy Bullock. When they started, they had two girls in the show and they were not comedic. We had Ted. We had Nancy, who's wonderful. We needed something with the young people because that's who they were trying to attract. We brought Jimmy in. He read for us and he failed. We brought in a lot of other people. Then I asked to bring him back. We brought him to the network and he read the same shitty way that he read the first time. They were about to dump him. I said, "Do me a favor. Give me five minutes with him and I'll bring him back and we'll try it again." I read him the scene and I said, "Do it exactly the way I'm doing it." And he did it for me, repeating the timing. I said, "Do that. Nothing more. If they ask you to do something else, we won't let that happen." We came in and he read exactly like I directed him to do and he got the job. He was on the show for five years.

Irma Kalish   That was a good show. It was a fun situation.

Austin Kalish   We gave him things we thought he could do. He had a certain charm about him. A certain silliness.

Irma Kalish   And he played off Ted really well.

Austin Kalish   He was wonderful on the show. He was a necessary addition to the show. When Lydia Cornell was in a scene, she would do her lines and then she would look around the stage. She was a line sayer.

Irma Kalish   We had something in a script where it said, "She gives him a raspberry." She looked around and said, "Where is the fruit? Where's my raspberry?"

David Lloyd   I got to really think Steven Weber was a wonderful comic. I wanted to write a Brian show on *Wings* and they would say, "No, it's got to be a Brian and Joe show." But Joe wasn't as funny. I think Tim Daly learned comedy as the show went on. It was a good cast. They found Tony Shalhoub. They had to bring him back. David Schramm is a much-neglected actor. He's terrific. Lowell was skewed, a dumb guy. Giving them the back story where Brian had betrayed Joe, there was some real anger and resentment under the surface there. And they had to eventually overcome that to be really close and really fond of each other. But it was never too far from the surface, which is good. That gave them a nice tension when they were working together. The network fought the producers on a lot. I think it was a learning experience. I think they learned from that.

Ed Scharlach   When I was with *Happy Days*, it was low in the ratings. It hadn't caught on yet. And *Chico and the Man* was in the top five shows on television. It was very discussed and popular and in the zeitgeist. It was exciting for me to realize that I was going to be on this very popular show, coming off this show that wasn't at the time. Ironically, *Chico and the Man* only did okay and didn't stay on that long and *Happy Days* became this gigantic juggernaut. But it was fun because Freddie Prinze was such a star and he was a nice guy. And to work with Jack Albertson, one of the great Broadway actors of all time. Ultimately, I was writing by myself and things weren't going the way I liked. I didn't have the warm mentorship that I had on other shows. It's the only time I actually quit a show. It wasn't going the way I had experienced before.

With sitcom writing dominated by urban, white males, writers were often challenged by writing for rural, ethnic, female or teenage characters.

Jack Elinson   I used to wonder about myself. I'm a Jewish boy from the Bronx, what do I know from cowboys and country stuff? On *The Real McCoys*, especially. As I got involved with the first shows, I had seen enough cowboy stuff and I learned a lot just watching. It was no big problem for me. I came up with words that I made up myself, country words. I enjoyed that part, because I certainly was not in my ballpark—*Andy Griffith* and *The Real McCoys*. It was created by Irving Pincus. Can you image Irving

5. This Is Good

Pincus is the top guy on a country show? He came from the Bronx, too. It was a pleasure though. Walter Brennan was sensational. Dick Crenna was a wonderful actor.

Bernie Orenstein   There was a film called *Cooley High*. We tried to write a one hour one-camera television version of *Cooley High*. We were not successful. It was not good. Fred Silverman, to his credit, said, "Forget all this serious drama. Give me a half-hour, three-camera comedy." So we did that. There was really no relationship to the film. It was very successful and very funny and lasted a number of years. We liked doing that show. The kids were new to television. We tried to infuse a moral element in most episodes of that show and we were fairly successful.

Saul Turteltaub   Bud Yorkin was no longer a partner with Norman Lear. He had left the television business but was still an owner on *Sanford and Son*. He wanted us to concentrate on that. But we talked him into joining us. That's how we formed TOY Productions. We did *Sanford and Son* and *What's Happening!!* at the same time. Then Fred Silverman asked us if we'd be interested in doing *In the Heat of the Night* as a TV comedy. I don't think I ever said no to a job offer in my life. We put together *Carter Country* with Kene Holliday and Victor French. We got two years out of that.

Rick Mittleman   I did *What's Happening!!* It was a show with a black cast primarily. I liked working on shows like that. I found writing black or white or Hispanic really no different. Funny is funny. Sometimes as a writer you can put a little dialect in but you don't have to worry about it because the cast will take care of that. Particularly on *What's Happening!!*, because I wasn't that hip. They were kids. And there was a great actress on that, Shirley Hemphill. She was terrific. I had no problem writing funny and letting the actors take care of the dialect and expressions. It's just like what I did on *Gomer Pyle*. I never had any trouble writing for that or *What's Happening!!* or *Sanford and Son* or *Chico and the Man*. It never seemed to be a problem.

Saul Turteltaub   Shirley was a funny lady. She had a funny personality in real life. She was a comedienne. We had heard about her and seen her perform. We auditioned little girls and Danielle Spencer was perfect. She just had the right personality and charm and sharpness and tartness and she was wonderful. She today, by the way, is a veterinarian. Mabel King was just unhappy with her part. She didn't want to do it. We all agreed it was best. But I don't think it was best, frankly. That cast was perfect the way it was. When she left, we lost a lot of strength, family kind of stuff. After she left, it was the last year we did the show. I think it was a mistake to let her go. But if she wanted to go, we were going to let her. We stayed friends. I liked her very much. She was a nice lady.

Bernie Orenstein They were all very good on the show. They were excellent. Fred Berry was not an actor. He played himself. It just took off. Fred Berry was a little difficult to get along with. He saw himself as a superstar. Shirley was excellent. Shirley was a very talented comedienne but also felt her role was more important than anything else on the show. However, they were young and they were new to the business. I chalk that up to youth. Most of the people on the show were very nice.

Jack Elinson *Good Times* was a brand new show and they needed writers. Norman Lear knew about our work and we were honored. It was terrific. We were so happy that they let us do that because up until that you really couldn't do too much of that stuff. We just loved that they allowed us, through Norman pushing, that we could just say it like it is. We were the first ones to really come out with what was happening today. Bad things. Good things. I was very proud of that show.

Irma Kalish But there was always racial tension.

Jack Elinson The cast resented the fact that we were doing it. We had one writer that was a good black writer. But you couldn't find many black writers a bunch of years ago. It wasn't a happy place. John Amos was terrible. Esther Rolle was okay. They were very down on us. The thing that almost broke it off, a black magazine, the cover says, "Bad Times on Good Times." Isn't that clever? And we said, "What the hell is he talking about?" And he wrote a whole article and we were not in it. This was too much so we walked into Lear's office. We said, "What are we going to do?" And he said, "Quit the show." It was right in the middle of the season. He's kind of clever in his way. So we went and quit the whole show. The sorta looks on their faces, they couldn't believe. A day went by and they came to us and said, "We don't need for you to quit the show. We just want to do a little more with our folks." It was bad, it was really bad.

Irma Kalish We came in at a crucial time. They had just lost John Amos. They had a problem with him. He's gotten to be such a wonderful dramatic actor these days. There was a lot of racial tension going on in the show before we came in.

Austin Kalish There was a lot of pressure. They didn't want the show to go off the air. It was a big show.

5. This Is Good

Irma Kalish They didn't want it to be a fatherless family.

Austin Kalish They brought in Moses Gunn, who was very good and a wonderful actor.

Irma Kalish Eventually, we also had to do the show without Florida. We had to find a way. We had Willona be the star. Ja'net DuBois was very good. That was also the year we put Janet Jackson on.

Austin Kalish I said, "Let's get her. It will be great publicity for the show." And it was.

Irma Kalish She played Penny, a little abused girl.

Austin Kalish It was a good show. And I cannot tell you how many people remember that show to this day, that she was the abused child.

Irma Kalish They were very conscious of their customs. We did a show once in which Willona had a boyfriend. He came to see her and he saw the daughter in the family and he hit on her. And she was very upset about it and she threw him out. And we said, "You could slap him." She said, "Oh, I couldn't do that." She couldn't slap a black man. We said, "You can do it." We asked her to do it once when we did the show and then she wouldn't have to do it when we did the second taping. When she did it, a cheer went up from the audience.

Austin Kalish It shocked them.

Irma Kalish We once did a show where Michael found money on the street and wanted to turn it in. One of the cast members came to us and said, "He would never do that, you know. A poor kid would never turn it in." We had to defend the story.

Austin Kalish It was consistent with the character. We always fought for the characterization. That was our strength. Any time we got on a show, we understood the characters. We didn't do anything but what that character would do in certain situations. Unless it was extraordinary situations for a particular reason.

Sam Bobrick Peter Engel came to me and said he had a deal for two shows at NBC. He said they want to do a show about a schoolteacher and they want to do a show about detectives. I knew that very few detective comedies work. You had *Barney Miller* and you had *Get Smart*. They tried a lot of them that didn't work. But a schoolteacher, that always works. This is luck. It was supposed to be about a high school teacher, which I liked. I wanted to write about high school kids because I think they're the most fun. Young kids like to look at older kids. Older kids won't look at younger kids. We went to meet with Brandon Tartikoff and I had a whole bunch of ideas about the high school thing but he wanted to do it about his third grade teacher. It didn't make NBC but somehow it ended up on Disney. I already had another job with Grant Tinker. When they put it on, I couldn't go back to work on there. I really didn't want to do it anyway. It was on, I think, for 13 shows and then something happened. I think it went off the air and then they decided to change it into the high school. They still gave me credit for creating it because they still used the same principal and that's the show I originally wanted to do about a high school. Peter came up with the name *Saved by the Bell* I guess, instead of *Good Morning, Miss Bliss*. So they gave me credit for it but I never did a show for *Saved by the Bell*. I've got to be honest with you, I never watched one. But I got credit for it because I created the first of what it became. It was very nice because the money was very well spent. Success comes where you least expect it sometimes.

Jerry Mayer   I used to say, "I never want to produce a show or write for a show that I wouldn't watch on my own." And that's what *The Facts of Life* was. It was about a girls' school. It could be a good show but it wasn't one I would have watched. It was a good show. A lot of people told me they grew up watching it. We went to a fine girls' school in Beverly Hills just to see what it was like and get the ambience. And during that, one of the young girls that was taking us around as our hostess was Mindy Cohn. Charlotte and I both thought she was funny and cute. And we hired her.

Jack Elinson   I was trying to fight it off. What do I know about a girls' school? I always felt funny. I remember thinking to myself I've mostly done girl shows. I can't write girl shows. It just happened. I left most of the writing with the writers. The first thing I did as a producer was find a girl team because this was a girls' show. I didn't think for a million years I could do what girls could be doing on the script. We found a hell of a team. So it actually didn't turn out to be as tough. The one thing we had to do, they had seven girls. The first thing we did was get rid of some of the girls. Because they all had a line to say. They pouted if they only had one line, it was terrible. So we got rid of all the girls except the best ones. Then it really took off.

Jerry Mayer   NBC thought it had potential but they thought it had too many girls. One of the girls was Molly Ringwald and she was one they wanted to get rid of. I thought she was probably the best one. But they wanted a tough girl in there. We read Nancy McKeon and she was better than anyone else. It didn't change much. It just made it simpler than having all those girls. In this case, the network was right. There were too many.

Irma Kalish *The Facts of Life* was good. We had George Clooney. I've said, "If I knew he was going to grow up to be George Clooney, I'd have paid much more attention to him." I didn't have any problem with the cast other than the normal things that happen. We wanted to do a show where the character of Blair stayed out all night and actually spent the night with a boyfriend. The network was willing to let us do it as long as we made a point of saying they had protection and it wasn't just an overnight boyfriend, it was a boyfriend she had for a while. But the actress wouldn't do it. It was against her beliefs. So we got another actress, the one who played Natalie, to do it, with the same provisos. The actress who played Blair wouldn't even be in the show. She refused to be in the show. They said they could hold her to it by contract but I said it would be all right. Let her go. We'll write her out of that show.

Jack Elinson *The Doris Day Show*, the first year it was on, it wasn't a big hit but they were renewing it for a second season. They had to get somebody new over the show. The guy who had it the first year, they didn't want any more. We aren't all that crazy about it. Everything she had always done in the movies, she was a sharp city-like person. She was not somebody from a farm. That was the major change. It helped. She became sharp, and romantic things could be done. We were surprised that it lasted five years. It was going from country to city that made the whole difference, which is not so brilliant. It's pretty obvious. You had to depend on other people to be funny with her. She got a lot of funny lines but she wasn't funny like a Danny Thomas was funny. But she's a good enough actress to be funny with a funny line. I wouldn't rank that as the best show I ever wrote.

Ed Scharlach She was the number one movie star for many, many years. It was very exciting to write a show for someone who was such a superstar. It was fun to write.

Television comedy in the 1960s was heavy on wacky sitcoms, often with a fantasy element. Although not generally beloved by critics, these series were often fun to write.

Elroy Schwartz Jim Aubrey, "The Cobra" at CBS, I guess he was aptly named, took this meeting with Sherwood where he told him his thought for *Gilligan's Island*. He approved it, never believing the show would go beyond one season. He wasn't sure you could do 13 episodes. Sherwood came to Rocky Kalish and me and gave us three pages of what was to be the pilot script. We sat down and wrote it, for which we got amply screwed. The pilot was shot with two girls who were secretaries and they just didn't work. When they didn't work, they got Tina Louise and Dawn Wells and recast the show and shot it again. No one at CBS believed there was more than one year in *Gilligan's Island* because where are you going to get stories for the people stranded on an island? Well, you did. You got stories. That was a fun show to write. Jim Aubrey was wrong.

Fred Freeman *Gilligan's Island*, I just thought, was silly. My Northwestern snobbish days of writing plays came into play. I used to get a little bit drunk to write it. I would get silly as hell writing *Gilligan's Island*. Larry and I did five shows. The first one we did, they liked it so much that they put it in as part of the opening show on the air.

Elroy Schwartz The cast was fun to write for. The characters were fun. They were zany. They were in sharp contrast to one another. The Howells were above everything. Their attitudes were in sharp contrast to Gilligan and the Skipper. The Professor could recite anything.

Austin Kalish The show was a lot of fun. It was craziness to write. We could write funny things. There are some shows that you have to struggle to write funny.

Fred Freeman What I thought was so funny was Sherwood showed the pilot to Larry and me and probably six other writers and when it was over we all looked at each other. Then Sherwood said that it was going to be a microcosm of society. And all we would need are these seven people. Well, by the second and third episode we were bringing people onto the island. We were going to run out of stories. But it was fun. We got noted for the one where we brought in Wrong Way Feldman. He was our version of Wrong Way Corrigan. Hans Conried played him.

Elroy Schwartz When you have seven people on an island, you've got to have someone come in and then disappear. Somebody got lost and wound up on the island for one episode and then he's gone.

Lila Garrett To give you an example about how sensitive this industry was in those days about a show having a message, let me tell you about a story I didn't sell. I tried to sell a show to Sherwood Schwartz for *Gilligan's Island*. It was very, very early in my career. This island is meant to be a satire, a microcosm of the world. They have a CEO stuck on the island and a nubile movie star and then they had this pure spirit in Gilligan. So

5. This Is Good

this is a chance to do a satirical piece about our society. So let's do greed. We had a story where Thurston Howell is feeling very melancholy because he doesn't have a place on the island. He doesn't have any function on the island and he's used to being the head guy. So they get together and try to create a reason for him to be happy. They decide to create a currency on the island and in order to get fish or a plant or fresh water, we'll each have our own stall and you'll have to pay for it. They decide to use the pebbles in the lagoon for currency. They're all different colors and sizes. The blue will be the cheapest, the green ones next and the brown ones at the bottom to be the highest. They think it's silly but they decide to do it. Now they start collecting these pebbles and now some have more than others and at night they go to the lagoon and they start diving in and they're bumping into each other late at night to get the real valuable ones at the bottom. They end up bringing their pebbles back into the creek because they're becoming just like the people in civilization. Before they weren't competing, they were cooperating. Even Howell is the first to agree. It was a hilarious story, may I say. Sherwood Schwartz said, "Eh. The economy is boring." I said, "Economy? They almost drown each other trying to come up with the right pebbles. It's an obvious satire. We're not talking about the economy. It's a story of greed." And he said, "I don't like it. What else have you got?" [This despite the fact that Schwartz greenlit *three* separate stories about an exact double of one the castaways showing up on the island.] So I said that we didn't have anything else right now but we'd be back. Every scene was hilarious how seriously they take it. How they forget who they are and they're transformed by greed. And in their world trivia becomes major. It was a terrific opportunity. It got back to my agent that I argue. Your reputation can be harmed very easily. A big agent said he wanted to hire me but he didn't want me to argue. He said that everybody thought that. It had gotten around. And the truth is that I argued very little because I learned very quickly that these people in these executive jobs are very set in what their pattern is. I understood that. You had to get a script out every single week and either the writer was willing to do it or they weren't willing to do it. And generally speaking, I never once did a show that I wasn't willing to do. I had just misunderstood that show.

Fred Freeman I don't look down on *Gilligan's Island*. I did look down on it when I did it. It was so silly. Tina Louise thought she was better than the show and of course her career went nowhere. She wouldn't do the movie version. My theory with that and *The Beverly Hillbillies* was that people like to watch people that are stupider than they are. I don't know if that's true or not but that's one perception I had. It was silly. Everyone just took it for what it was. I began to stop denying that I wrote it when I realized it's appealing. It's silly. It's goofy.

Elroy Schwartz Kids like it because it's zany and fun. It was an escape. An escape from reality. It was interesting for me because I lived in New York and went to see *South Pacific*. While I was in the audience watching that, I was in the South Pacific despite the fact that there was a snowstorm on the street. You're lost in what you're viewing. I think that was true of *Gilligan's Island*.

Fred Freeman Everyone thinks it ran for years. It only ran three years.

Elroy Schwartz The show was picked up for the next season. And then the show was cancelled after it was picked up. Bill Paley's wife wanted to know why *Gunsmoke* wasn't in the lineup. It was her favorite show and she wanted it back in the lineup. He looked around for an hour and he cancelled *Gilligan's Island* and put *Gunsmoke* back on the air.

Austin Kalish We had more fun doing certain comedies. We had more fun doing *F Troop*. It was wild comedy.

Irma Kalish We got on *F Troop* because we had an assignment on another show at Warner Brothers that didn't appeal to us at all. It was a comedy about some kid that was auditing a college class. Being at Warner Brothers, we knew *F Troop* and wanted to do *F Troop* so badly.

Austin Kalish So they said they'd try us.

Irma Kalish We were able to transfer our assignment to *F Troop*.

Austin Kalish All of a sudden, we got so many assignments from it.

Irma Kalish Along the way, of course, many people have asked us, "What was your favorite show?" Whenever they asked us, it was the show we were working on.

Austin Kalish In truth.

Irma Kalish Looking back, at least for me, it was *F Troop* and *All in the Family*. Two entirely different kinds of shows.

Austin Kalish It wasn't hard for us to write.

Irma Kalish It was fun. Look at the characters — you had the Indians and the girl and the blustering sergeant and the corporal and the captain.

Austin Kalish If you had the characters, we could work with it.

5. This Is Good

That was a show we loved to write. It had the comedy there to be had, even if it wasn't a simple thing. The situation was that good that you could write sketch things for modern things but put it back in that time. We were even able to put in something political. Instead of "better red than dead," we had an Indian say, "Better red man than dead man."

Elroy Schwartz *McHale's Navy* was fun. Good, zany characters. When you're doing comedy, it's easy to write zanier characters.

Rick Mittleman I always had a problem with Ernest Borgnine because Ernie wanted to be the funny guy. He wanted to be Captain Binghamton or Ensign Parker. He wanted to accidentally put a foot in the bucket and walk along with one foot in the bucket. We kept trying to tell him he was the center of the show, the core, the one sane person on that PT boat. You can't do that or you'll ruin the show. But he always wanted to be funny. And if anybody isn't funny it's Ernie Borgnine. Tim Conway was getting all the laughs. And Joe Flynn. The producer, Si Rose, was a guy who treated writers mercilessly. Nothing was ever quite right. It was a very difficult year for me. There was constant rewriting. You couldn't make the man happy. That was a rough year. Although I was thrilled to have my first staff job.

Bill Persky We had done a *McHale's Navy* because we knew Tim Conway from *The Steve Allen Show*. We became friendly with him and he got us a script assignment. We wrote a script that I thought was terrific. But there was a producer there, Si Rose. The same day that we had handed Carl Reiner a draft of "That's My Boy??" we had a meeting with Si Rose on our *McHale's Navy* script. He started the meeting and he had a note on every page of the script. It was the most painful experience I ever had as a writer. We only got halfway through the script by lunch. We went to this Chinese restaurant and we were so depressed. I said, "We're obviously not suited for this." Then we went back and it was an awful afternoon. He hated everything. We got back to the office and the phone rang and it's Carl. I thought if Si Rose hated us, I could only imagine what Carl Reiner thought. And he loved it! We had the best and worst experience in the same day.

Austin Kalish *My Favorite Martian* was interesting to write because it put your thought process into the future. But we were able to write the jokes as long as we set up the premise. What they figured was sand up on Mars was all diamonds the way we played it. You could write a show using that premise.

On the other side of the coin, the '60s also featured several warm family comedies. Although these series were sometimes soft on comedy, they provided an interesting change of pace for their writers.

Irma Kalish *Family Affair* was very nice.

Austin Kalish We loved it because we not only wrote it, we did the rewrites on it. We wrote 25 shows. It was about one-fifth of the shows. When there was trouble on the show, like one time the little girl broke her leg…. We were on a vacation on a houseboat in Stockton. We got a call. We had to find a way to write the show with her broken leg. We wrote it and rewrote it in a day or two.

Irma Kalish Our kids were all school age and a little older than the kids on *Family Affair*. We would wait for them to come home from school in the afternoon, with pen and paper in hand we would ask them if anything funny happened in school that day. And we would quickly make a story of it.

Austin Kalish They wanted to get paid for it.

Irma Kalish When they realized what we were doing, they asked for more allowance.

Austin Kalish Little Buffy was the producers' third choice. They didn't want her. They couldn't get the people that they wanted.

Irma Kalish She was older than her character. She was two years older.

Austin Kalish But she looked the part.

Irma Kalish She hated that doll, Mrs. Beasley. She hated that doll.

Austin Kalish Dragged it around.

Irma Kalish You'd never know it to see her play with it but she would just drag it across the set.

Austin Kalish It was well cast. She was wonderful in the show. She was absolutely wonderful.

Irma Kalish The kids were great.

Elroy Schwartz I wrote a script for *Family Affair*, which I think is the best script I ever wrote and Ed Hartmann was part of that. The script was called "Christmas Came a Little Early." Jody and Buffy had a little friend who had leukemia and she was dying. The storyline was to have her celebrate Christmas early because she wasn't going to be alive at Christmastime. And that bothered me. I went into Ed and told him that bothered me. I said, "Isn't there a miracle drug or something that I can invent to continue her life?" And he said, "Elroy, our audience is children. They have to learn to live with life and death. They have to believe that there is death. Write the script the way it is. Because she's going to pass away. And they're going to celebrate Christmas early." That's they way I wrote it. It was real. Ed kept me there by having the little girl going to pass away.

Irma Kalish Don Fedderson was a great one for expressing love. You had to write it or rewrite it that when Bill came home it would be "Hi, Uncle Bill. We love you." You had to express it.

Austin Kalish You couldn't imagine love. You had to show it. You had to say it.

Irma Kalish We got used to writing it very loving.

Austin Kalish We did several for *My Three Sons*. They were fun to write because we were writing for Ed Hartmann. And Ed Hartmann believed in us. He saw in us what I saw in Irma and Irma saw in me. We would develop a story with him. It was always right. We had his language for the show. There's an importance to that happening. Someone has language for a show and the characters and you develop that language. And you don't take those characters out of that language.

Irma Kalish The shows were interesting from a production standpoint because they had a big star — whether it was Fred MacMurray, on another show [*The Smith Family*] it was Henry Fonda, on *Family Affair* it was Brian Keith. There was also *To Rome with Love* with John Forsythe. So they didn't shoot in sequence. It was a single camera. They had to do the show so they could do many shows ahead and do all the scenes with the lead character. Then they could let him go for the rest of the season and shoot the rest. John Stephens, the production manager, was very good.

Lila Garrett *Petticoat Junction* was run by Jay Sommers, who was a great guy. He really knew the sound of the show. I admired the character of the leading woman. She was a single mother and I admired her and appreciated her smarts and I appreciated the fact that she was bringing up her daughters and she was the equal of every man in town. I appreciated the fact that the people running the show appreciated that. When she felt equal, she was equal. So I enjoyed that show. I make it sound very solemn. The bottom line in all these shows, for my personal enjoyment, is that they were funny. But I thought that *Petticoat Junction* had some spine and that's what kept it on the air. It wasn't just the fact that it was a hillbilly show.

Austin Kalish It was fun to write *The Flying Nun*.

Irma Kalish   We'd come up with unusual story ideas. On this particular show, it was called "The Conversion of Sister Shapiro." It was about a little Jewish girl who happened to land on the island and likes Sister Bertrille. She decides she wants to become a nun. It was a great story and they loved the story but the network came in and said, "Go ahead with it but you can't say she's Jewish." We couldn't *say* she was Jewish. We could say she was on her way to her brother's bar mitzvah, we could say her name was Shapiro but we couldn't say she was Jewish.

Austin Kalish   That's how powerful network was and it drove us up a wall.

Carl Kleinschmitt   *The Courtship of Eddie's Father* was a very sweet show. It's easier to write if you're not going for jokes all the time. It's much easier than trying to find laughs. There weren't a lot of laughs in *The Courtship of Eddie's Father*. For what it was, I thought it was really well done.

Other hits provided their writers with a mixed bag of good and bad memories.

Arnold Margolin   ABC had announced its first season of doing 90-minute movies of the week. It was Barry Diller's idea. Someone at Paramount sold them an idea for a movie called *Love, American Style*, which would be three half-hour stories about love that weren't connected at all. Just an anthology. They asked us to write one. They loved it. They didn't like the other script that they ordered and they asked us to be executive producers on the movie and supervise the writing. So we rewrote the script that they weren't happy with and asked some friends in New York to write the third episode. We were putting together this 90-minute movie and as we were editing it, someone, I wish I knew who because I would like to give my eternal gratitude, suggested that we also just cut it down to an hour version and submit it to ABC as a pilot. In those days ABC was in huge trouble. Nobody had ever done an hour comedy anthology. They bought the show. Then we had to figure out how the hell to do it. We figured it out and it was very successful. It was a lot of fun.

Bernie Orenstein   It was a nice experience. We liked working at Paramount because it was a big studio lot. We really felt like we were in Hollywood.

Ed Scharlach   We did like 80 segments a year. I wrote my own scripts and worked with writers that came in to work for the show. *Love,*

5. This Is Good

American Style wasn't just TV writers. We had a lot of movie writers and playwrights. We did every kind of comedy there was. We had a lot of stories going at the same time. It was one of my dream jobs. It was an amazing experience.

Arnold Margolin   It was crazy. We were totally different than anybody else. Because it was an anthology and every story was different and people didn't have to write the same characters week in week out, people could come in with all kinds of wacky ideas. We had some stories that were as short as six minutes long. We had a lot of stories. And the blackouts, as we called them. Garry Marshall and Jerry Belson wrote most of them. They used Japanese pseudonyms.

Ed Scharlach   One of my favorite things that I got to write on *Love, American Style* was a satire of movie musicals. I got to write the lyrics for nine songs. Charlie Fox, the famous composer, did the music. He told me to join ASCAP. So I did and I got more money every time they showed the show from ASCAP than I ever did from the residuals for writing that show.

Carl Kleinschmitt   When *Funny Face* folded, I still had one script remaining on my contract for Paramount and I ended up producing what was the pilot for *Happy Days*, which appeared as an episode of *Love, American Style*. There wouldn't have been a series except *American Graffiti* came out and the '50s were hot again. The success was due to casting Henry Winkler as Fonzie. It gave it a dynamic that was never intended in the pilot. Garry's original script was a very soft, sweet script. The father was not Tom Bosley, it was Harold Gould. He had also been Marlo Thomas' father on the *That Girl* pilot.

Ed Scharlach   The first year of *Happy Days* was one-camera. We went for a sweet, nostalgic coming-of-age feel more than laughs. We wanted to dig into what high school kids went through emotionally. And it was a sweet little quiet show. Someone realized these kids could be funny. When they experimented with three cameras, the kids just came alive in front of an audience. It went great. It was night and day. It was a major factor in making the show such a hit. I don't think they expected it to be the hit it was. It influenced Garry to do his other shows three-camera.

Jack Elinson   *One Day at a Time* had a good premise. That was a very important thing. They had a little trouble at the beginning. A man and his wife wrote the pilot script. When it was brought to the table it didn't really work. Norman asked us if we would try to do it. We did it and it was dynamite, just dynamite. It was great, if I say so myself. I remember doing some good shows. That ran nine years, a show I never thought would have.

Bill Persky After we did the pilot of *Kate & Allie*, they put it on for six shows. The show took off and people loved it. Because of that, Brandon Tartikoff put on *The Cosby Show* because he could see that a family sitcom could work again. I loved that show. It was reflective of the society. I raised my oldest daughter by myself from the time she was 12. I knew about being a single parent.

Bernie Orenstein I enjoyed doing the show because both of the women were terrific. I think they were uncomfortable with Billy leaving the show. They depended on him very much.

Saul Turteltaub As we learned when we got to *Kate & Allie*, they were thinking of canceling it. It was ordered for 12 weeks and we were proud that we got picked up for the year. It was not an easy job. Nobody was happy over there about us coming in. Jane Curtin, especially, had gotten used to Billy Persky, who had directed it and produced it. Now he was gone. We came in as the stepfathers. We had no trouble with Susan Saint James. She was wonderful. But Jane seemed to be unhappy with us from day one and we could never break through that so that was never fun. Although it was a good job because the two of them were so good that there were no pickups. We would tape the show at 6:30 and we could plan to make the curtain of a theater show at eight o'clock if we wanted to. We did the show and we were out of there and home. It was terrific.

Bob Carroll, Jr. We were on the lot at Warners and they had had one year of *Alice* and they were having trouble with producers quitting. Alan Shayne called us into his office and said, "While you're here, would you like to think about doing *Alice*?" We said, "Give us a moment. We'll go look at some tapes." And we were on the lot and we said, "Fine."

Madelyn Davis We didn't know if they hired us because we were handy. Also, they'd had a lot of problems and we didn't know that. We might have been a little more reluctant. But it all worked fine. They were a great cast and a good premise. We were on it for eight years. We brought experience. We get along with people pretty well. We don't have a lot of ego and thrash around. You just say, "Come on. It's a TV show. Let's get it on." We sort of calmed everybody down.

Sam Denoff While we were doing the last season of *The Dick Van*

Dyke Show, Danny Thomas comes to us and says, "I want you to do a show for my kid."

Bill Persky I have always been a feminist and the idea of doing something that changed the role of how young women were being done on television was very appealing. Marlo was doing *Barefoot in the Park* in London and she was sensational. She really is an icon. Women in their fifties and their sixties, I'm a real hero to them. In all candor, Sam was not a feminist. Sam and Marlo fought constantly. So I was like the bridge. Sam was a great contributor and he was funny but he did not like Marlo being the boss and she was the boss. It was essential to have Marlo's voice in the show. No male writer could have done that. We could interpret what it was for her. But she was adamant about who the girl had to be. *That Girl* was Marlo. She was going through the same things. God knows, as Marlo Thomas it was easier than an unknown girl. But she went through all those same struggles with her father. When she wanted to move out to her own apartment, Danny couldn't understand that. They had this mansion. To Danny, the only reason a Catholic girl would leave home was to get married or become a nun.

Jack Elinson They asked me if I wanted to produce *That Girl*, not write it. Persky and Denoff were the writers. So it was kind of a new thing for me, kind of easy for me. Something I don't have to write. I never once had to tell them how to do a line. Just stay away from these two guys because they were really good. It was very exciting being back in New York. The pilot was made and it was sold and they asked me if I wanted to produce it. I wasn't comfortable about her, Marlo. I smelled trouble there like she might be a pain in the ass. So I didn't take the job.

Bill Persky ABC wanted to replace Ted Bessell. They were adamant about it. The research didn't support him. But we had done a dumb thing in the pilot. We had made him her boyfriend and her agent — two diametrically opposed characters. The agent wants to send her off and the boyfriend should be supportive. We had created a schizophrenic character and he didn't work as an agent or a boyfriend. They wanted to get rid of Harold Gould as the father. I think that had an ethnic aspect to it. I think Lew Parker, in the long run, was a better choice. Lew was a very endearing guy. Where Harold, in that role, was a stronger but harsher kind of guy. We couldn't lose Ted. And Marlo loved him, too. As it turns out, Ted Bessell was the most popular co-star on television for five years and every young girl only wanted to meet a guy like Donald. I am a great enemy of research.

Bernie Orenstein   That was quite pleasant. It was our first producing job. It was a big step up for us — two young guys who had never produced before. It was a lot of responsibility to work for a big star on a hit show. We were welcomed. We had a terrific star. Marlo was very creative and had very good ideas. She was very helpful. She was extremely talented and knew exactly what she wanted. Ted Bessell was brilliant and the unsung hero of that show.

Ed Scharlach   It was great. It was way ahead of its time to have a young, single girl living alone. Marlo was great. Her sister, Terre, is one of my best friends. It was exciting. The big show at the time was *Batman*. *That Girl* had not gone on the air yet. I would tell my friends I writing for a new show called *That Girl*. And they'd say, "You mean, *Batgirl?*" They thought maybe it was a spinoff of *Batman*. I think one reason they brought us in was because it was about a young woman and her boyfriend and Peggy and I were a male/female writing team. They thought she'd write the girl and I'd write the boy but, of course, it doesn't work that way. You write everybody. We were in the age range. It made us appealing to write for *That Girl*. Denoff and Persky were my mentors, along with Garry Marshall and Jerry Belson. My stepfather, Harry Crane, was also very encouraging. Denoff and Persky were brilliant, very patient and funny.

Arnold Margolin   They were high energy, fun guys to work with.

Rick Mittleman   Working with Sam and Bill was very pleasant. I didn't work with Marlo at all. As I understand it, she was somewhat difficult. As a writer, I would have already turned my script in and be working on something else when they would go to the table and read the script for the first time with the cast. So I was never a party to that. My memories of *That Girl* were pleasant.

Bernie Orenstein   I thought Bill and Sam were terrific writers. I learned about character development from Billy. They were terrific help. They were very strong executive producers in terms of the direction of the show and being encouraging to us as new producers. There was a New York writing community that was in Hollywood and everybody was very friendly and helpful.

Sam Denoff   Marlo was great but she didn't want to do the show with an audience because she was very concerned with her appearance. It probably would have been a different show with an audience.

Bill Persky   I think *That Girl* needed one camera because it was a glamorous show. It was a more personal show with long periods of soft, gentle and dear moments. With multiple cameras, you can't do that. You have to have that audience laugh at least once every page.

Ed Scharlach Marlo and Teddy were wonderful. They had a great chemistry and were very funny. They were inspiring to write stories for. They could be funny and there was a touch of reality in their relationship. Teddy was a funny guy and Marlo was really, really smart and a great actress.

Arnold Margolin We wrote several episodes of *That Girl*. The first episode we wrote turned out to be the premiere show. It wasn't the pilot but they didn't show the pilot first. They wanted to do an episode where Don meets Ann Marie so that was the first one to go on the air. We had seen the pilot. We got it from seeing that. We didn't do a lot of rewriting on that. They liked it and that's what they shot. We had a good feel for that show, I thought. We had a knack for being able to write other people's characters, which I have learned over the years that there are some very good writers who have a hard time writing for other people's characters. Some people have a very distinctive voice and they can't adapt it. Others can. I don't even know if it's a skill. It's a knack. That certainly gave us some visibility. We enjoyed it. I thought that was a character Marlo had down pat. She knew that character. She knew that show. Ted was great. Loved Ted. The supporting cast was great. We just had a ball writing that show. Some shows were easier than others and that was one that came pretty easily for us.

Carl Kleinschmitt There was a lot of rewriting. Danny Arnold could be difficult. On the other hand, if you gave him something he liked, he could be wonderful. I did one script called "Bad Day at Marvin Gardens," about a Monopoly game. I was procrastinating. I got a call from Danny and he said, "How are you doing with the script?" I said, "Great. I've done the first act and I'm halfway through the second act." He said, "Terrific. Because the script I planned to do has fallen through. I can't shoot it. Can you finish it tonight and bring it in tomorrow?" I said, "Sure." And then I sat down and wrote, "Fade in." I had not written the script. I was making this up because I thought I had another week or so before I had to turn it in. I sat down that night and wrote the script. When I handed it in, Danny said it was the only time in his tenure at *That Girl* that he took the script, sent it to mimeo and had it on the table the next day without touching it. That was a highlight for me.

Paul Wayne The script I did for *That Girl* was the best acted that

I ever wrote for. And the least worked over. It almost came back exactly the way I wrote it. There was a thing that didn't have a subplot. It was one idea that grew and grew and grew. That was the kind of thing that I loved to do. It was just one of those things that I felt was performed better than practically any sitcom that I'd ever written. It just was glorious to watch.

Carl Kleinschmitt   Dale and I did an episode called "Anatomy of a Blunder." We enjoyed that a lot because anytime you put a blind man together with a woman who can't drive a stick shift, it's easy. That was fun.

Arnold Margolin   I always loved the idea of some incongruous physical thing happening. We did have fun with that and drove the prop people crazy and the director having to have a bowling ball stuck on her foot. Something stuck on somebody always works well. It worked well on *Love, American Style* a number of times.

Sam Denoff   ABC wanted to give us two more years but Marlo wanted to leave for her movie career. What movie career? That's the way it goes.

Arnold Margolin   We got bored pretty fast with writing the opens where someone would say, "That girl." So we'd always try to come up with some weird way to do it. We'd usually, for the hell of it, put some silly thing in the first draft to drive the producers nuts. Some stupid thing. Usually something too filthy to put on the air but just to keep ourselves amused. Then we'd write something we could use.

Ed Scharlach   We'd spend two days trying to get it right. You had to do it in a surprise way that hadn't been done before. So we would have fun trying to figure that out. It had very little to do with the story.

Jerry Mayer   I did a pilot and I went in to ABC. The people I was pitching to for ABC were Tom Werner and Marcy Carsey. The pilot didn't get picked up. Most of them don't. About two weeks later I get a call from Tom Werner and he says they had just done a movie of the week and they were going to do a weekly comedy show and he'd like me to run it. And I said, "Oh, great. What's the name?" And he says, "*The Love Boat.*" And I had seen the first *Love Boat* movie of the week and I thought, "Jesus, this is corny as hell." And I turned him down! And I always use that when people ask my advice, I say, "Don't ask my advice. I turned down *The Love Boat.*" It ran nine years. They took wonderful cruises. They got paid a fortune. I said I had something else I couldn't get out of. I suggested Ben

5. This Is Good

Joelson and Art Baer, who I had worked with on *The Jonathan Winters Show*, and they got the job. These things happen in careers with writers and actors. You look back and think you should have taken that or you're really glad that you didn't take that. You make some mistakes and you make some right moves.

Carl Kleinschmitt The producer of *1st & Ten* was a big football fan. I couldn't care less about it. He and his partner wanted to do a show so they could be close to football players and be around their idols. So I wrote a pilot that I thought was pretty clever. Then I saw a copy of what had been shot and it bore little to any resemblance to the show I created. So we had a big fight. I never had anything else to do with it. I guess what makes it interesting was I think it was the first comedy show on HBO and it ran for five or six years.

David Lloyd What attracted me to *Amen* was Ed. Weinberger and a lot of money. I left *Cheers*. I worked on *Cheers* for 10 out of the 11 years. Because he came and offered me a huge amount of money including a percentage of the adjusted gross. And that's pie in the sky. I should have known better. I kind of hated it. I really did. I wrote seven episodes, I think, and some of them were fun. I didn't like Sherman Hemsley. He could be funny and some of the others could be funny. He is a good comic if someone can tell him what to do and convince him he ought to do it. So I wrote some episodes that I thought were fun. At first they were going to have some spirituals in it but we didn't have the luxury to have much singing in a 22-minute sitcom. At the end of the first year I said, "Forget that. I'm going back to *Cheers* if they'll have me." Which they did. I also did three more years of *Amen* at the same time because Ed. said, "You'll come in at twelve. You don't have to go to the table read. You don't ever have to see the actors." There was only one actor I didn't want to see. I liked some of the other actors quite well. I've seen them since. "You don't have to do that. Just get in there and rewrite it, run the room so I don't have to stay around. At 6:30 you can go home, no matter what. I'm assuming that you'll do your best to keep it on track." He had a couple of old guys on the show. Artie Julian went back to *Duffy's Tavern* on radio and everything triggered a story in him. So we were trying to get a rewrite done and my job was to keep dragging them back to get the script done. Those were productive years for me financially. It wasn't because I was mad, crazy for the show. It was just because that was too good a deal to pass up.

Allan Burns I hated *The Munsters*. Chris Hayward worked in partnership with Lloyd Turner, a very funny man. Chris was hysterical. But Chris was impatient and underpaid. So he and I teamed up. Lloyd, at that time, didn't seem to have ambition beyond Jay Ward Productions. Chris did. I did. In those days, in animation you were in a world of older, quirky guys. Much older. I'd look at these guys and I did not want to be what they were when I was 50. They were just weird and quirky. So Chris and I put our heads together and pitched ideas to each other. We wrote some scripts together for shows that were on the air, trying to crack in. We did *McHale's Navy* and things like that. We came up with this idea for something called *Meet the Munsters*. We envisioned this family of very weird people. We sort of stole the idea from Charles Addams and his *New Yorker* cartoons about these weird-looking people who lived in this house and were just bizarre. We had no agent. Nor did we have Writers Guild representation because writers for cartoons were not covered by the Writers Guild. So we're looking for an agent and we found a guy named Les Colodny. We went in and pitched some ideas and he'd already read some of the stuff we'd done. He didn't seem to be overly impressed until we told him this idea. So we were encouraged by that. He called us a month or so later and told us he liked the *Meet the Munsters* idea. He was at Universal now, working at comedy development. He said that was an idea he'd like to develop. So that made us happy. We had a number of meetings with him. And we started working out a story and wrote the script. And he'd read it and take the pages. Then there was silence. We'd call his office and he'd be in a meeting. We got another agent. The other agent called us one day and he says, "Hey. Why didn't you tell me that Universal is shooting *The Munsters*?" We said, "That's the first we've heard about it." It turned out that Les Colodny was taking our pages and feeding them as his ideas to two staff writers at Universal — Ed Haas and Norm Liebmann. They were not culpable. They didn't know where this stuff was coming from. They liked it. They revamped it. That's what they shot. Because Universal owned the Frankenstein character and the Dracula character for movie rights, they decided to take their characters instead of the characters we had written, which were just sort of bizarre, weird people. We hated that whole idea. And they'd also stolen it from us. So we went to the Writers Guild of America and why they even agreed to meet with us, it was another one of those serendipitous things. We told them the story and the executive director's eyes sort of glittered and he said, "Maybe we can help you out."

5. This Is Good

And help us he did. The Writers Guild went to Universal and must have made veiled or maybe not-so-veiled threats of lawsuits and they settled and gave us a settlement mostly based on merchandising and a credit of "From a format by." We became sort of friendly with Liebmann and Haas. But we were *persona non grata* at Universal. But it helped my wife and me buy our first house.

6

I'm Going to Acting School: Flops

The right premise. The right cast. The right staff. The right time slot. It takes a lot of talent and luck to make a hit series. Just one wrong element can lead to a flop. That failure can particularly sting when the writer is also the creator of the series.

Bob Schiller It's riskier to create a show. You never know if it's going to be a hit. We created a show called *All's Fair*, with two people we thought couldn't miss — Dick Crenna and Bernadette Peters. It was a wonderful premise, based on my marriage. I married a woman 25 years younger. And added to it, she was a left-winger and he was a right-winger. He was Bill Buckley and she was Jane Fonda. We may have let them down with the writing. But that show should have gone. Should have been a hit. It got pretty good reviews. I don't know. I really don't.

Fred Freeman Once Larry Cohen and I sold a show called *The Good Life*. Great cast — Larry Hagman, Donna Mills, David Wayne, Hermione Baddeley. But we wrote the pilot and we sold it but we struggled so much with the next episode because we did everything in the pilot. We cut ourselves off at the story. It was ridiculous. We didn't know where to go with the damn thing. It was a premise with promise, like a lot of shows. That was embarrassing. It was a good pilot and a bad series. Larry Hagman was a crazy, funny guy.

Bob Carroll, Jr. I liked *The Mothers-in-Law*.

Madelyn Davis Someone gave me a couple of tapes and sometimes you write stuff and you see it later and you say, "Oh my!" but this was still very funny. I was quite pleased with it. It was not a huge hit but it was respectable. Eve Arden and Kaye Ballard — we did a lot of physical stuff and it was funny.

Fred Freeman Larry and I did a show that was on the air for eight

6. I'm Going to Acting School

weeks, called *Empire*. Harvey Shephard at CBS loved it. I think the reason we got on is his wife loved it more. People on the East coast hated it because it was about corporations. It had some funny things in it. But it didn't have a character that you could identify with. You've got to have someone you care about and we should have emphasized that more. It was about a young guy going into the lion's den of a board of directors. Patrick Macnee was in it. And people were coming to watch rehearsals because it was funny. We had a good time. We enjoyed writing *Empire*. We had great character actors. It's always rewarding when the cast really likes the writing and they really like what they're doing. It doesn't mean it's going to be a hit or anything because who knows. None of us knows what's going to be a hit. We didn't pay enough attention to the main character, who was the straight man. He was coming into this den of lions. We had Perry King, who was good. He wasn't funny enough for the network and we said, "He's not supposed to be funny. Everyone around him is funny." So they made us go with Dennis Dugan. He's fine but he had too cynical of a way about him so there was nothing innocent there. But I don't know if that's what killed it or not. The pilot was pretty good, I thought.

Lila Garrett *Baby, I'm Back* had a very strong social point. At that time, black families were thought of as being matriarchal. There was this theory that a lot of black women had been deserted by men who couldn't get jobs. They weren't lazy but there was a lot of prejudice against black males and they were demoralized as a group. The women made the money and brought up the kids. I wanted to do a show that said when they got jobs and they were a part of society they did not abandon their families. They wanted a family like everybody else. That's why it's called *Baby, I'm Back*, because it's about a black father who was a gambler, couldn't get a job and did abandon his family. But when he started to work in the parimutuel window, he came back to get his family. But guess what? His wife was about to get married to an officer in the Pentagon. It was a marvelous series. CBS cancelled it because Norman Lear would only give them a new show he had if they put *Good Times* on for another season. It was a tragedy for me. It was very, very unfortunate because it was a wonderful show. It was hilarious. It was sexy. I had two great kids in it. One of them was Kim Fields. The other one stopped acting but he was wonderful. Denise Nicholas was fantastic. Demond Wilson was great. It really hurt my career. That's the business. The business was not forgiving.

Bill Persky *The Montefuscos* was written to be called *Sunday Dinner*.

It was written to follow *The Wonderful World of Disney* on Sunday night and everything about it was an Italian family meeting at the parents' house on Sunday after church to watch the ballgames. The whole show took place on Sunday night. NBC put it on Thursday. It made absolutely no sense. I think it could have succeeded on Sunday night, I really do. I think that show really worked and it was funny. It was a big, lovable family but when they're coming home from church at 8:00 on Thursday night and sitting and watching football games, it makes no sense. On Sunday night it would have been sweet and dear and wonderful. Ron Carey was one of the sons. Linda Dano was in it. It was a wonderful cast. I feel it never had a chance.

Sam Denoff   We did *Big Eddie* because we wanted to do a show with Sheldon Leonard as an actor. It got off to a great start. They had us on behind *All in the Family* and the ratings were terrific. So CBS said, "We love it. It's great. We like it so much we want to move it against *Sanford and Son*." We begged them not to do it but they did and we were gone a few weeks later. In a case like that, it has nothing to do with your work.

Bill Persky   I was never really a big fan of *Big Eddie*. It was logical to have Sheldon do something like that. But when we sold it and *The Montefuscos* at once it was all the talk in L.A. that two independent producers with no studio involved sold two shows. I said, "We can't do two shows." Everybody is going to be split and neither one of the shows is going to benefit from that. *Big Eddie* was a reach, in my opinion. It was a disastrous period for us.

David Lloyd   On *Mr. Sunshine*, we had this professor that was already cynical and acerbic. His nickname is given to him ironically by his college students. He's divorced and lost his sight in an accident. He's got to start everything again blind. They got a good cast. I thought it was a lot of fun doing it. But it didn't last very long. But I thought we did some good episodes. Jeffrey Tambor is wonderful.

Carl Kleinschmitt   Paramount owned the title *Funny Face* and they wanted to use it. It was a Fred Astaire movie that had nothing to do with what our show was about. Sandy Duncan had made quite a hit in a bank commercial and had a role in a Disney movie, *The Million Dollar Duck*. Tom Miller from Paramount and I pitched this very crude idea that she was this girl who comes out to Los Angeles from some place in Illinois and is going to school to be a teacher but she pays for her rent and tuition by being a commercial model. She was dumb enough to say yes and we

6. I'm Going to Acting School

were dumb enough to do it. In all honesty, the pilot was not bad. It was a softer show but we had characters in it. As soon as CBS bought it, they had us take the characters out. We lost Nita Talbot who was very good and very funny. Frank Aletter played her ex-husband. They played the heads of the agency that handled her career. The first note we got from CBS was to lose them. Fred Silverman was running CBS and he really didn't want anyone around Sandy Duncan. That's a very difficult show to do. Over the course of the 13 episodes we did before she got her eye tumor, we had a landlord and his wife, we tried several best friends. It just never worked. Part of it was we weren't allowed to do the show we wanted to do originally. And maybe part of it was our own shortcomings. I took it a little personally at times. I bore a great deal of dislike for the man who was the West Coast guy. He turned out to be the same guy who thought the "Sometimes You Hear the Bullet" script for *M*A*S*H* was wrong. It just didn't work. It came back for another 13 weeks as a three-camera show run by a funny guy, Arne Sultan. And that failed, too. I thought Sandy Duncan was a fresh, original talent at the time but someone that may not have been cut out to do a three-camera comedy show.

Fred Freeman We thought we were going to have three shows on the air and then nothing. I'm sure every writer has that same roller coaster. We did a pilot called *Sedgwick Hawk-Styles*, which was Paul Lynde as Sherlock Holmes. It fit him perfectly with the flamboyance of the outfits. We had three shows that were supposed to be on the air at once—*Sedgwick Hawk-Styles*, *The Pruitts of Southampton* and *Occasional Wife*. They were all on the schedules and an executive at ABC said he didn't want Paul Lynde as a star on his network and threw Paul Lynde off. *The Pruitts of Southampton* was supposed to be with Beatrice Lillie and they ended up with Phyllis Diller. We wrote it for a much more sophisticated comedienne. We were not consulted. They paid us and we went on our way. They were going to take *Occasional Wife* off because the ratings weren't good. The ratings got better but they still took it off. It was a regular sitcom with nothing extraordinary about it.

If nothing else, some flops give a writer the opportunity to introduce an extraordinary talent to the audience.

Allan Burns Grant Tinker hated *The Duck Factory* and cancelled it. He thought it was unfunny. He thought it was awkward and it didn't work. He was pretty brutal about it. It was my first shot at doing a one-camera show and that could have been a mistake. I just felt that it fit better. There was something about the style of the show that felt like it needed to be one-camera. Partly because I intended to use a lot of animation in it. As it turned out, we didn't because animation takes too long. So we could only use little bits and pieces. I meant it to be more integral and that wouldn't have worked for a three-camera show, obviously. I took it completely from my experience with Jay Ward. I thought Jim Carrey was playing pretty much who I had been. A young, kind of innocent kid among all these weird older people for the most part. Teresa Ganzel was very funny. Jack Gilford was funny. Jay Tarses was funny. I thought he did a really good job. Jim Carrey was really good. It was the first thing he ever did right out of nightclubs. His standup was a little different then. He relied more on impressions. The impressions he does are just uncanny. They were both hilarious and serious. He could do Leonid Brezhnev and make you laugh and segue into Katharine Hepburn and Henry Fonda in *On Golden Pond* and do both parts absolutely accurately. And be not just funny, but touching. And I saw him do that at The Comedy Store in West Hollywood and I knew he could act. It wasn't just funny; it was really acting going on there. Amazing. Part of the failure of that show I lay at my feet. The characters that Jim played after that were so off the wall and wonderful. The character that he played in *The Duck Factory* was pretty straight. When we cast him, I should have realized there was more there than what I was allowing him to do. I should have written to that and made it a funnier show. I really take a lot of responsibility for the fact that show didn't work out. Jim was like a sponge. He just admired Jack Gilford so much and he really played off of him and there was this father/son thing that happened with the two of them, I thought. As much off-camera as on. Jack's character was based on a guy I worked with at Jay Ward. He was kind of a lost soul. A kind of sweet man. Jack just nailed it. He and Jim would go off together and Jack would spin stories about show business. Talk about a life in show business. He and Zero Mostel got blacklisted at the same time. He used to tell stories about having to resort to working at kids' camps in order to make money. Jewish kids' camps in the Catskills. He was a wonderful guy. One of the sweetest men. Never bitter about it. Sad about it. But I never saw any bitterness. Jack was a wonderful spirit.

Fred Freeman Oh, God. *First Impressions* was not very good. We were supposed to supervise two writers and half way through the process they realized they weren't experienced enough to do it. We needed an office

6. I'm Going to Acting School

at the time and they gave us an office at Orion. So we said we'd write it. We didn't think it would ever get on. But they put the stupid thing on the air. Brad Garrett was a sweet guy. It was one of those shows where we couldn't believe they were putting it on the air. What are we going to do? We tried it. It wasn't our format.

Arnold Margolin *A Family for Joe* was a great experience. It was the most fun I'd had in a long time. It started as a TV movie. At first I was thinking of it as just a series. Robert Mitchum agreed to star. It took a lot of time to set up the premise so NBC wanted to do it as a two-hour movie and we had Bob Mitchum who was a big enough star to carry a movie. The movie was fun. It had a lot of heart. It was very successful. It tested through the roof, especially Mitchum. Brandon Tartikoff didn't like it. He didn't want to do the series. He kept testing it but it kept scoring bigger and bigger. He didn't want to do that kind of a show but he couldn't let it go because he knew we'd take it to CBS. And it would be embarrassing to have it be a success there. We decided to do it as a comedy. The movie was kind of a comedy and a drama. Then he buried it. Put it in a time slot where it was never going to work. Nobody really saw it and it never really had a chance. Those things happen. Robert Mitchum was great. He was a wonderful comic actor. He could do comedy. He was very conscientious and he never complained. I was used to actors always complaining about their parts. After we'd been shooting the movie for about a week, I got nervous. I went to him and asked him if he wanted any changes or if there was anything he didn't like. He said, "You write the words. I say them." He was an old-fashioned Hollywood movie actor. That was his job, like a plumber. He came to work every day at nine o'clock, he did his lines and he went home. That was a dream situation for both the movie and the series. He was great to work with and he had a million great stories. One day on the set of the movie he was a little loaded so we had to loop some stuff but when he looped it he was perfect. One take and he got it. That was the only time I ever had any kind of problem with him. Juliette Lewis was impossible. He wanted to kill her. We read her with the network in a whole room of people and she gave this incredible reading that was unbelievable. Funny. Great. And that was the last we ever saw of that performance. We never could get it back. She was just a contrarian. She didn't want to do anything we wanted her to do. She was certainly a pain in the ass.

Saul Turteltaub When we created *One of the Boys*, in the back of our minds, we thought Mickey Rooney would be terrific for it. We wrote that as a spec script. We had this idea about a man who's put in an old-age home and his grandson can't stand it so he brings him out and brings him to live with him in his college apartment and his roommate can't stand it. That sounded like a typical great sitcom. We had Dana Carvey, Nathan Lane and Meg Ryan. We had heard that Dana Carvey was a bright young comic up in San Francisco. We flew up to see him in a nightclub and we came back really high on him. There were a whole bunch of kids sent in and out by casting people but we figured he would be right because he had a great talent for impressions and could be funny at that. We found him right away but we couldn't find the other guy so easily. It was last minute. It was between Nathan Lane and another guy and we just picked Nathan. It turned out that he was sensational. Mickey Rooney loved him. He thought he was the most talented. He was right. He saw a great talent in Nathan. It was just amazing. The people on that show were just fantastic. But the show was a mistake on our part. We sold it as him being in the apartment with these guys, ruining their lives every time any girl would come up. Getting in the way and being a pain in the neck. Then when we sold the pilot and it was terrific, when we got the go ahead, we added some people and tried to say something and make it a little more socially conscious. It was stupid and it ruined the show.

Bernie Orenstein I loved that show. We had a terrific cast. I don't think Nathan Lane had done anything before. Now he's the biggest star on Broadway. It was a cute show. Very funny. We had a disagreement with the network, which I believe helped it being cancelled. They wanted changes made to a particular episode on the day we were shooting. We refused. I'm not sure that was so smart.

Allan Burns I thought *Eisenhower & Lutz* was overlooked. When CBS cancelled *Eisenhower & Lutz*, I was so upset because I thought it was a really great cast. I decided I was going to make another show with the same cast. Scott Bakula got offered *Quantum Leap* because he thought he might do better in a drama. Although I thought he had done a good job. So we cast Bob Hays. Bob is really one of the most underrated comic actors, I think. I never understood why he didn't have a huge career. He's very funny and a good actor and serious about his craft. He should have had a good television career. I was trying to shove it down CBS' throat that they had made a mistake and that's why I wanted to do another show with that same group. Both Scott and Bob were the nicest people you'll

6. I'm Going to Acting School

ever meet. I've been very lucky to work with the nice people that I've worked with. Talented and nice. I thought *FM* worked better as a show, for me. Good people. Pat Richardson is a very funny lady. There was some good romantic tension. We made a pilot and I thought it really worked. We didn't get on the schedule. I called Brandon Tartikoff and said, "Hey, Brandon, what are you doing? This show really has the possibility of having some legs." So he said he'd pick us up for five more shows and air it in the summer. It was the kiss of death. It was just his way of letting me down easy. We ran behind *Night Court* and didn't do very well. We ran behind *Cheers* and did very well. But there was another show lurking and it was *Seinfeld*. They got the same assignment. They did a little better than we did. I think I could have chose *Seinfeld* myself. They also had *Wings*. Even though there were some guys associated with that show that were very talented, I hated it. I thought it was unfunny. It just felt jerry-rigged to me. It didn't work, as far I was concerned. I didn't like all the characters. It had some very talented writers, the guys who later did *Frasier*. After he cancelled *FM*, Brandon said we weren't playing on a level field. At the point we were on, he didn't need MTM any more. He needed Paramount because they were giving him *Cheers*. That's why he picked up *Wings*. He said, "It's not as good a show as yours. But I had to pick it up." I think if *FM* had been picked up, it would have been on the air for five years. It was cooking. The relationship between Bob and Pat Richardson was wonderful. We had Lynne Thigpen and Lynne was wonderful. DeLane Matthews was in this, too. Grant Tinker called me up and said, "I can't figure out why they didn't pick your show up. I love that show." He was gone from NBC at the time. I was pleased to get that phone call and frustrated that it couldn't make any difference.

Saul Turteltaub *E/R* was, I think, a great show. It had a great cast. It was Elliot Gould and Mary McDonnell, Conchata Ferrell. The hospital administrator was Jason Alexander. A kid came in to read for a part. He was terrific and we hired him. It was George Clooney. By the end of the second rehearsal, Bernie and I looked at each other and decided to make him a regular on the show. This kid is sensational. We signed him to do a whole bunch of them. He was so good. Not just with the comedy. The second show he did, he played Conchata Ferrell's nephew, she found out she had breast cancer and he was so moved and so saddened by it. It was a great dramatic performance. He was marvelous. He was likable and great to work with. I think the trouble with that was the mixture of comedy and tragedy, because we had people who died on the show. I just think the public didn't like that mixture. It was different on *M*A*S*H* but for some reason this setup didn't appeal to them. The scripts were good and the actors were great. I can't tell you what the problem was. With other shows, I can tell you what the problem was. This one should have stayed. When it was taken off, Harvey Shephard, who was the head of CBS, called us into his office and said, "I hate to do this but the show is not getting the numbers and I can't justify keeping it on. I like it. I think it's great. But I'm going to have to take it off."

Bernie Orenstein   It was fairly well received but it was cancelled after a year. It was a very interesting show. George Clooney had a small part. We saw Jason Alexander in a Broadway show and brought him out to be on it. Those were little casting coups. I think we had a pretty good eye for talent. It was different than most shows. We liked doing that a lot. I thought it was one of our better shows.

It's certainly understandable that networks, producers and stars would be tempted to spin off supporting characters into their own series. However, not every supporting character can carry his or her own series.

Saul Turteltaub   Bernie and I wrote the pilot for *Grady* and we did that wrong. It was our mistake that that show wasn't successful. The cast was wonderful — Joe Morton, Carol Cole, Haywood Nelson and Rosanne Katon. In the pilot, he buys them a painting on velvet, which they wanted to hide because it was so terrible. Then when he realizes what a dummy he was, the whole show he's so depressed. It was awful. It was dumb of us to do that. Because he was always good when he was loud and jumping around and all that. It was a big mistake on our part. They were all wonderful performers.

Bernie Orenstein   That didn't work. It didn't have Redd. Whitman Mayo was very talented. But Redd was Redd.

Jack Elinson   *The Bill Dana Show* didn't get the ratings and that's all it takes. The studio audience always loved him. He got big laughs. It was just too bad. Don Adams was in that show, too, before he became a big star.

Bill Persky   I loved Bill Dana. He was very popular and he was doing a lot of stuff at the same time. Maybe the character didn't work in large doses. It was great in nightclubs but to have that character for a half-hour, there was a lot of the same things over and over.

6. I'm Going to Acting School

Bob Schiller *Pete and Gladys* was nice. But Gladys was a Lucy wannabe. I once told her she was doing something wrong or not doing the way we had it in mind. She was a pain in the ass, Cara Williams. She says, "Who are you to tell me that?" I said, "Well, I'll tell you. I used to write for a girl who used to imitate the way you act. And I think I'm an authority on that." She laughed.

Saul Turteltaub Next door to Fred Sanford there was supposedly a building that they turned into a hotel. It was called *Sanford Arms*. It was about as unsuccessful as you can get. It was a bad idea from the start.

Jerry Mayer I was hired to produce a show called *Tabitha*. It was fun. When we cast we picked Robert Urich and Lisa Hartman. They were very nice and good and easy to work with. When we read Tabithas, Pam Dawber read and I wanted her. She turned it down for some reason. When we were casting for Aunt Minerva we needed someone funny. I go out in the room and I pass through where all the actresses are waiting. And there's Patricia Morison, who was in *Kiss Me, Kate* and was a big Broadway star. At this point she's in her sixties. And I think a big star like that but she's not funny. We read her and she wasn't funny. She was kind of trying too hard. She wasn't a natural clown and Karen Morrow was. So we hired her. She went out and bought a beaver coat as a celebration.

David Lloyd Cloris Leachman is a marvel and they got good people around her on *Phyllis*. Henry Jones. I loved Henry Jones. And they got Jane Rose, whom we'd used on something else. She was wonderful. Judith Lowry was terrific. They got a good woman who of course was murdered, Barbara Colby, whom we'd used on the *Mary* show when Mary went to jail for protecting a source and they put her in jail with a couple of hookers. One of them was Barbara Colby. And everybody was very impressed with her and said we've got to use her for something. Losing her was a blow. As far as having an emotional center that made them go on loving Mary and made them care about Mary and Murray and Lou; Phyllis is hard to care about. You want to watch her. She's funny as hell. But they had Ed. and Stan running it and then they hired the Charles brothers who went on to create *Cheers*. So they had good people there. When I would go in to pitch stories, that was fun. There was some strong supporting cast. It is hard to feel warmly toward Phyllis because she is so off-putting. Very funny but you're not going to cry over her. There was a joke on that show that if I had to pick one or two jokes that I wish I'd written but I didn't, that would be it. It was the show where Phyllis' daughter is dating a boy of normal height whose parents are both midgets. And Phyllis is very concerned about the possibilities down the road. Dick Schaal played the dumb guy in the office. She tells him, "My daughter wants to marry a normal-sized man whose parents are midgets." He thinks and he thinks and he says, "Has she found one yet?" My kingdom for that joke.

A popular star is also no guarantee of success. Audiences may love a performer in one series but remain lukewarm toward him or her in a less ideal premise.

David Lloyd   I think there's a lot more vulnerability in Betty White than in Cloris. Now Jim Brooks, who is a *huge* Cloris fan, I'm sure wouldn't agree. But I think Betty, even as Sue Ann, there were moments of vulnerability. She wanted Lou's affection. And I never saw vulnerability in Phyllis. I wrote a terrible pilot for *The Betty White Show*. Ed. Weinberger and Stan Daniels were off, the handwriting was on the wall, they were leaving MTM, they were going to Paramount. They hadn't figured out *Taxi* yet but that was what they were going to do. Jim Brooks was going to go. They'd gone off to do something, then they'd gone off to Las Vegas to help write something for somebody and I was left writing *The Betty White Show* and I was resentful and irritated and so on and what I wrote just sucked. And we went to the table with it and got almost no laughs. Stan and I pitched a whole new script, I think each of us contributing about half of it. And it worked out great and it found all the jokes in the relationship. Just from page one we redid it. The jokes were coming. Nobody was bothering us. And thereafter, Ed. and Stan were gone. Bob Ellison and I had to do that show and a guy named Dale McRaven and it was fun. We were really enjoying the hell out of that one.

Bill Persky   That was a lovely show. Those guys were terrific writers. There was a lot of rewriting and a lot of fixing and Betty White was superb through the whole thing as both an actress and a person. As was John Hillerman.

David Lloyd   Betty is so great. She's so terrific. Maybe the supporting cast, outside of John Hillerman, wasn't as strong as *The Mary Tyler Moore Show* but there were some good possibilities there. John Hillerman was wonderful playing comedy. He was a perfect foil for her. Just perfect. And we had great fun doing that. Everybody likes the chance to put somebody in drag. Klinger had been doing it for years and years on *M*A*S*H*. And when we came along we thought ours was kind of legitimate. After

6. I'm Going to Acting School

all, it's a police show, she needs a stuntman. So they got a guy built like an ape. He was a tough guy. They put him in whatever outfit Betty was wearing and I'd start to laugh right away. What killed us and what really killed Betty was that subsequently in public statements the network said, "We may have been hasty canceling that one," once it was too late. We couldn't believe it because by a lot of standards we had a very decent rating. We had no notion it was coming. I was in the middle of writing I think my seventh script for that and Bob Ellison called me and said, "There's no way to break bad news, we've been cancelled." And it was like, "What?!"

Saul Turteltaub *You Again?* was a show that we were hired to save, so to speak. That show was on and they picked it up for part of the year and we got it picked up for the rest of the year. We got a year out of it. The problem was between *The Odd Couple* and *You Again?*, Jack Klugman did *Quincy*, which was not a comedy. It was a dramatic show where he saved the world every week. He made a statement and he was dramatic and he wanted to do that on this show. This didn't call for preaching every week. This was a guy who had a son come back into his life, and the comedy would have to come from interfering with his life. He just didn't want to play any comedy. He wanted to make a speech. We got a call from NBC and they picked us up but said if we were going to come back after that we had to do comedy and forget the preaching. Jack still wanted to do that and that was the end of the series.

Bernie Orenstein They were in trouble and wanted us to come in. We had known Klugman. John Stamos did a very good job. Klugman was very tough to work with. Away from the show, he was about the nicest guy you ever wanted to meet — friendly, enthusiastic, funny. But when he came to the show, he felt he should rewrite every word that was ever on a script. And he made it very difficult for us and any other writers on the show. However, we got through it. Jack is very good. He knew what he was doing although I'm not sure his writing talents were up to his acting talents. John Stamos came out as the hit of that show.

Ed Scharlach Gabe Kaplan had a huge success with *Welcome Back, Kotter*. But a lot of that success was due to the kids — one of them being John Travolta. Now NBC had Gabe Kaplan coming off a huge success and thought whatever else they put him in would be a huge success. They paired him up with a country guy, Guich Koock. A fish out of water, a New York guy in Texas. We had a nice cast. At first it looked like it could be a hit but they put us on opposite *Magnum, P.I.* so nobody watched us.

The ratings were low and everybody's spirits sank. Right before it went on, we didn't have a title yet. Someone at NBC decided to call it *Lewis & Clark*. That was a really dumb idea. Not only was it tough to find the show but it sounded like it was a show about explorers, not a comedy.

Bernie Orenstein   *A Touch of Grace* was one of our greatest experiences. Shirley Booth was a superstar actress who had the greatest respect for everybody who worked on the set. She was revered by everyone because of her background and her great talent and her reputation and her niceness. She couldn't have been nicer. I loved Shirley. She was brilliant. She was able to portray a woman with great, great dignity and tremendous humor. She knew her way around a joke, I'll tell you that. That show was not accepted as well as we had hoped. It's kind of interesting that the shows we liked doing most lasted the shortest time, with the exception of *Sanford and Son*.

Arnold Margolin   *One Big Family* [starring Danny Thomas] wasn't a great experience. It wasn't fun. It wasn't clear from the beginning what the premise was. I never had a clear idea of who the characters were. It was very hard to get a grip on what it was. It didn't work. Nobody understood what it was about and where the fun came from.

Sam Bobrick   We didn't stay with *The Paul Lynde Show*. We were at that point where we wanted to write plays. We did the pilot and we didn't want to stick with the show. We did get to know Paul Lynde, who was a very funny man. We'd go to a restaurant with him, and he was on a daytime show — *Hollywood Squares* — and when we'd leave, people would follow him like he was the Pied Piper. They just loved him so much. He was really a sweet, funny man. I liked him. But we didn't want to do the show. That kind of hurt us. People would not want us to do pilots because we wouldn't stay with the show. But at that point we didn't want to. I don't think we realized all the money that was to be made if you stayed with a show. We didn't want to kill ourselves. We both had families. We didn't want to be gone all the time. It was a good choice.

Allan Burns   Our new agent called and said there was something we might be interested in with the Smothers Brothers. They were hot but they hadn't done any television. We loved them. We thought they were great. Four Star Television wanted to do a series with them. Aaron Spelling was going to do it. It was a great television company. Dick Powell ran Four Star like it was a movie studio. It had all the trappings of that. It was never down and dirty. It was classy as hell. Aaron had come up with some-

6. I'm Going to Acting School

thing and he's no comedy writer, God knows. He had come up with something where Tommy was an angel and it was very badly written. We came up with fixes for it. We said, "Let's not do it seriously. Let's kid it." At that time there were all these shows that were like *My Favorite Martian* and *Bewitched* that took this fantasy stuff and went with it. Our thought was to turn it on its head and make it a satire of those shows. Which is what we intended it to be and we wrote about six scripts. And the brothers at that point loved what we were doing. We made a pilot. Four Star in this case went into partnership with Alberto-Culver, who made hair products. There was no network attached to it. The pilot was very funny. The brothers were great. Mean, but great, as it turns out. They took it out and sold it within, I think, the first two days of the pilot being out there. CBS bought it. We're on our way with it. The people at Alberto-Culver were so happy with it that they had a mass screening of it for the people at the plant. These are not the people you want to do satire with. That was not our target audience. Our target audience was young people who were hip and would get what we were doing. So they did the screening and they hated it. The people on the line didn't get it. Alberto-Culver panicked. Aaron, who was being very proud of it up to this point, panicked. They fired us off of it and brought in a couple of hacks. Aaron was executive producer and brought in another guy who was a real comedy hack to "funny up" what we had done and make it less satirical. It was the second show in a row where we were embarrassed by what happened to it. It sounds like ego on my part, but it was really funny. We got some early reviews of the show as we had done it that verify that it was a funny show. The guys who wrote those things wondered what happened to it. It was criminal what they did to it. The show lasted a year. Bombed. It was a good show and they turned it into garbage. And the brothers weren't happy and they couldn't wait to get out.

Arnold Margolin   I don't think they were good enough actors. Once they had a variety show that was their environment. They owned that. They knew how to be themselves; they just weren't very effective as actors.

Bill Persky   Along with *The Boys* [a 1974 unsold pilot], *Working It Out* is one of the two greatest disappointments in my career. We had an on-air commitment because of *Kate & Allie*. I wanted to do this show about a relationship from the beginning and each week it would progress. Papers around the country loved it. They loved Jane Curtin. They put it on Saturday night at 8:30 when all of the people who are looking for relationships are out looking for them and the only people at home are babysitters. It couldn't have been on at a worse time. I loved that show.

Irma Kalish Brian Keith was married to a Polynesian woman and he wanted her to be on *The Brian Keith Show* as his girlfriend and the network wouldn't have it. So he said, "Okay, then I don't want any love interest on the show at all." So we didn't have one.

Austin Kalish There was no relationship between the characters. It was a tough show to do at that point because you couldn't set up relationships.

Sam Bobrick I was working for Grant Tinker. He was a nice guy. He made a deal with CBS to have Dick Van Dyke and Mary Tyler Moore back-to-back. There was really no interest at that time for either of them. They had a producer and the whole show was about Dick coming to this small town where his son runs a theatre. The shows just weren't working so I was assigned to that show. I tried to sell a show with Louie Anderson that didn't sell so they asked me if I'd take over *The Van Dyke Show* and I got Ron Clark to come in. We had to burn off a bunch of scripts that were not working. Finally, we were starting to write nice scripts for Dick. In fact, he came in and said, "The scripts are really getting better now." But they cancelled us. They put us on too soon. It wasn't the show I would have done for Dick Van Dyke. We were producing it and working the late hours. It just wasn't working. We finally had Lois Nettleton come in. She was going to play Dick's wife and Ron and I spent the whole weekend writing a script for the two of them and it was really great and that's when they cancelled it. We didn't even shoot that script. I think if we had gone in that direction, maybe it would have worked. But the whole other thing, the playhouse, was forced. We just couldn't make it work. Dick was nice. He was a sweet man. We were behind the eight ball when we took over that show. It was just so many things to work out. But that's where I met my wife, Julie. We became friends and have been married for 12 years. So some good came from it.

Austin Kalish *Oh Madeline* was crazy.

Irma Kalish It was a very difficult show to do. She [Madeline Kahn] was a brilliant comedienne but she didn't want the guy to be her husband.

Austin Kalish She didn't want that actor. She wouldn't let the guy kiss her.

Irma Kalish And it was taken from a British show where the guy had two wives and had to carefully tiptoe between both situations. But

6. I'm Going to Acting School

when they brought it here, they said we couldn't have a woman doing that with two men. She was very upset that it wasn't the same kind of show. But she was brilliant.

Likewise, very successful producers and writers can't always duplicate their success, and consequently have a fair share of flops on their resumes.

David Lloyd For *Doc,* Ed. Weinberger said that everyone loves the notion of the little old family doctor who makes house calls in the middle of the night to deliver a baby. Barney Hughes was wonderful. Barney Hughes was playing little old men from the time he was 35. But then you had Liz Wilson who's a good actress but not a real comic strength. It wasn't really a comedy cast. We were going softer. We were going for emotion. It did often and I was very pleased with that. It came back for a second year and they brought in some new people to run the show and everybody left, including Mary Wickes. She stayed for one episode and then left. And they suddenly started going very heavy for the bedpan humor and that sort of thing. And it went down and off very fast.

Paul Wayne That didn't go very well. Barnard Hughes was a lovely man to work with. We did the best we could with that show. It was a mellow show. I think that was the problem. I don't know if they were afraid to step out into real farce comedy. It was one of those things. Sometimes you either go too far or you go not far enough. They just didn't know where the line was. It was a soft show. I had Steve Martin in a show. I had an idea about him wanting to be a comedian. He had a terrific desire to be a comedian. But his father, the doctor, wanted him to become a priest. The executive producer was Ed. Weinberger and he got it in his head that the end of the show should be what the Barnard Hughes' character, Doc, wanted it to be. I thought, "Why?" It's his life. Steve Martin's character's life. He should be what he has the urge to be. Everybody goes through this. I can't tell you after all these years that I was right and he was wrong. It's just that instinctually I felt that it would just pull the show down. I kept running into that week after week after week. There was nothing I could do about it.

Allan Burns *Paul Sand* was a show that just didn't work. Good idea, fairly well executed but it didn't work. We were overburdened. We had too many shows going at once. It was the stepchild. And we didn't have time to give it the time it needed and it was kind of our fault. Paul Sand wasn't a leading man. That was the main problem. Paul, coming out of improv, was used to working that way — improv in the scene. Well, you can't do that in a three-camera television show. He would throw the other actors for a loop. Where's the line? It just got awkward. He also had a very hard time remembering lines. Not his fault. It was just one of those things. He just wasn't a leading man. We had convinced ourselves. Freddie Silverman thought he was a leading man and wanted to do a show with him. He did an episode of *Mary* where he played a tax auditor, where he was very funny. Mary thought he was wonderful. But he never quite got comfortable in that role. The relationships he had with the women in the show never quite seemed real. Penny Marshall was in the show. Steve Landesberg. Jack Gilford. Mike Pataki played Paul's brother. Also a really good actor. Very good cast. Penny was a friend of Jim's and he was reluctant to cast her because he didn't think she was quite up to it yet and I talked him into casting her. She was sure ready when it was time to do *Laverne & Shirley*.

David Lloyd That's never a good situation when they're working on three shows at once. It wasn't ideal.

Fred Freeman *Apple Pie* was a very upsetting experience. It was a 1930s depression comedy. We thought Norman Lear would bring more humanity to it in some ways. We were rewritten. It was on the air for two weeks. I can't say who was right but I didn't like the rewrite they did. Even though I like the guy that did it. I didn't like what they did. When you don't have control, you're going to be rewritten if someone else doesn't see it your way. That's just the nature of any business. It's about who has clout.

Carl Kleinschmitt Sheldon Leonard was a major player in television and he had done most of his shows for CBS. NBC wanted to be in business with him. He loved to travel and he thought it would be wonderful to spend some time in England. He loved London so he wanted to do a show there. Some moronic executive at NBC thought it would be a wonderful idea. So that was *From a Bird's Eye View*. I had never been out of the country and I thought it would be a wonderful experience. It was very different. What I treasure about it was that I got to spend time with Sheldon Leonard and his wife, Frankie. They were just wonderful people. Just regular people. The best part about it was him. He was a wonderful man. Just a decent human being. It was a hard show to do in that it wasn't fully developed. We never had a grasp of what it was about other than one girl was British and one American. I had no idea who Millicent Martin was and she was huge in England. The other girl, Patte Finley, was an unknown from Amer-

6. I'm Going to Acting School

ica. I don't think we did well by them. When it finally showed here in the United States, Cleveland Amory wrote in *TV Guide* what I think was the best review I've ever read. The first line was, "This show was filmed in England. Unfortunately, it was also filmed in English." That pretty well summed it up. It was a failure on many levels.

David Lloyd   Ed. Weinberger and Stan Daniels and Jim Brooks were doing *Taxi* but they had an idea for a lawyer show called *The Associates*. And they had used their clout, because *Taxi* was good and their credits were good, to get the spot right after *Mork & Mindy*, which was the top comedy of the week, just a huge hit. And that was one of those real mixed blessings because the ratings for *The Associates* dropped off very sharply and that's all the network looked at. And *The Associates* was short lived. And I think that had great potential. It was a very interesting show. Not something we had seen up until now. And heavily researched. And a fantastic set. You came out whistling the set. It was just amazing — a two-story law library. But it was an ill match for the timeslot. Not that the show was too smart for the audience; that would be much too arrogant. None of us was too smart for the audience. But maybe the setting was a little too rarified — associates waiting to move into very high-paying jobs. Maybe people didn't find them that sympathetic as characters, I don't know. My God, we had Martin Short, we had Joe Regalbuto who went on for a long run on *Murphy Brown*. We had Alley Mills. Wilfrid Hyde-White was very funny but also absolutely maddening. I wrote a show that I liked a lot on *The Associates* in which Wilfrid Hyde-White's old nemesis, who was also Joe Regalbuto's law professor, comes in. And it was John Houseman playing the character that he played on *The Paper Chase*, which we could do because *The Paper Chase* was written by the same man who wrote the book *The Associates*, on which the series was based. So it was all in the family. And so Houseman came in and he's pleading the case for the other side and Wilfrid Hyde-White's going to do it for their side. And the two of them, I gave them a scene together, in which we're going to see these two codgers go at each other. These two old codgers could not remember a line between them. I have never a seen a scene take so long to shoot.

Carl Kleinschmitt   *M*A*S*H* had just won the Emmy and the next day or so later, Gene Reynolds and Larry Gelbart had a meeting with ABC. Gene had worked with Karen Valentine on *Room 222* and Gene saw her as a public interest person. *Karen* was based on that idea. I have to credit Gene Reynolds. He wanted to do something about politics and the way the country worked. This was right after Nixon had resigned. Gene is a very serious guy about some issues. He went on to do what I thought was a wonderful show, *Lou Grant*. Because they had just won the Emmy and they were hot, ABC gave them a deal for 13 weeks. I don't know if Larry and I got it that much. If we had our wits about us, I think we would have gone deeper rather than going for obvious jokes. It didn't work on a comedy level and it didn't expand anybody's knowledge of how Washington worked so it was just a failure on many levels. This was a show that probably needed another 13 weeks or a year to find its legs. We fiddled with characters. We changed casting. We never got a clear idea of how funny or serious it should be. Poor Karen, who's very good at what she does, was never sure what she would be doing next week. It went from one extreme to the other and I don't think we ever got a handle on it. As it turned out, nobody watched it anyway.

Ed Scharlach Buck Henry was one of my idols and we got to write a show that he was writing and producing. A brilliant, brilliant comedy mind. I had admired his work as a writer and performer. We walked into his office to have the meeting on our story and he had two typewriters set up with paper in them. He said he was working on two screenplays in between producing this very funny series, *Captain Nice*. He said, "The typewriter on the left is a movie version of *Catch-22* that Mike Nichols is going to be directing. On the right, I'm writing another movie for Mike Nichols based on a book called *The Graduate*." He had an amazing mind. The show was very imaginative and we could be pretty loose. He had created *Get Smart* with Mel Brooks and it had a lot of the same loopy humor except it was a takeoff of super heroes. I think it would go real well now. It was a ball to write for him and the show. Some of the greatest shows aren't discovered by the public. Some shows that I never thought would have gone anywhere somehow captured the audience's imagination.

In spite of the success of M*A*S*H, The Odd Couple *and* Alice, *it is extremely difficult to recapture the lightning in a bottle that occurs with a hit movie comedy.*

Arnold Margolin I got a call from Ken Hecht, who I had helped start off as a sitcom writer, and he was working with Bob Brunner and they were running *Private Benjamin*. Ken said, "I want to offer you the worst job in show business." He was right. The previous year they had all kinds of problems with Eileen Brennan and with Lorna Patterson. If they

6. I'm Going to Acting School

didn't like a scene, they would just walk off the set and they'd have to shut down production. My job was to stay on the set all the time and do rewrites on the spot if one of the stars had something they didn't like or didn't think they could do. Whatever the problem was, I was the set psychiatrist and writer. That was my job. It wasn't a pleasant experience for anybody.

Madelyn Davis *Private Benjamin* just didn't work.

Bob Carroll, Jr. It was one-camera, which we weren't used to, really.

Madelyn Davis They seemed to want something else. Sometimes things don't work. Then everybody tries to fix it and it all just disintegrates in front of your eyes.

Bob Carroll, Jr. We were used to having sustained comedy right in front of an audience. Just doing this scene, that scene, that scene wasn't our type of thing. We couldn't do our type of stories that we liked.

Ed Scharlach When *The Ghost & Mrs. Muir* started, it was much more based on the movie. Very adult, wistful, romantic. In the movie, these two people love each other but it's never consummated because one's dead. It's this beautiful, touching story. They kept that quality at first but then they discovered if they made it more about a ghost it would appeal more to kids. I think the quality went way, way down as a result.

Some series fall out of favor with their networks due to controversy — as serious as religious concerns over mixed marriages and as frivolous as a plot about a toilet.

Jerry Mayer I liked *Bridget Loves Bernie*. I was curious why it wasn't picked up. I enjoyed it. We thought it was light stuff but there are always groups out there that have their feelings getting hurt.

Rick Mittleman That was an unusual show for its time. Bernie Slade created it. I was happy to see it, being Jewish myself. It was a warm, human, feel-good show and it cut through some stereotypes.

Sam Denoff *Lotsa Luck!* was based on a British show, *On the Buses*. The studio audience loved it. They loved Dom DeLuise, who was so funny. They loved Kathleen Freeman, who was great, and the way she said, "Stanley." The first show got big laughs. They were going to buy a toilet. Well, a bunch of affiliates in the South got offended and dropped us.

Bill Persky I loved *Lotsa Luck!* We did *Lotsa Luck!* designed to follow *Sanford and Son* on Friday nights. Knowing that *Sanford and Son* was kind of outrageous and a little lascivious — it took some chances — we constructed *Lotsa Luck!* to follow that. The pilot was about them buying a new toilet. NBC thought the show was so good that they would start off Monday night with it. I said, "It's not *that* good." I knew on its own there would be resentment for certain things on Monday night at eight o'clock. But following *Sanford and Son*, it would be a logical progression. It didn't do well. Dom DeLuise on that show was brilliant — and Kathleen Freeman. It was a really lovely show and funny. But it was too hard and too harsh for the time slot they put it in.

Although an offbeat premise can face an uphill fight to capture an audience, it often provides an interesting experience for the series' writers.

Jack Elinson   I liked *Wait Till Your Father Gets Home*. That was the first animation thing that was about real people. That had never been done before. We really had a lot of fun with that one. The voices were great. We enjoyed it. Without it being animated, it could have been real people. Just the fact that it was animated was an usual idea. Now, there are a lot of animated shows. That was a good show.

David Lloyd   It was a long shot to make a Western comedy. It was called *Best of the West*. I don't know if it had been done before, a straight out-and-out Western with bad guys and a sheriff. I thought it was a very nifty idea. Carlene Watkins was terrific. Leonard Frey was a very funny man and a wonderful actor who was a very skewed bad guy in the show.

Flopping with a truly outrageous premise is one of the surest ways to draw a critic's ire. Some of the most notorious flops in television history provided sizable targets for their critics.

Allan Burns   Oh, God. You had to bring *My Mother the Car* up. We have to talk about that? Again, it was another one where we wanted to kid the whole idea. The guy who produced was Rod Amateau. And he was a good producer. And a good director. It had some funny people in it. Jerry Van Dyke was funny. Avery Schreiber playing the villainous guy, Captain Manzini, that was Rod's idea. Having this moustache-twirling villain. It seemed like it was going to be funny but except for Avery and Jerry, it wasn't. And Jerry was not funny in the way he got funny later on. He was playing a little too straight. He was trying to be his brother. Trying to be a leading man, and he wasn't. It wasn't very good. We had fun writing the scripts and then the fun went out of them when we saw them because of the other actors. The woman playing opposite him wasn't funny at all.

6. I'm Going to Acting School

But it sold. Grant Tinker bought it when he was at NBC. We went through this crucible of *The Munsters*, *The Smothers Brothers* and *My Mother the Car* before we came out the other side. And we went through a pretty hellish time. We made okay money but that wasn't the point. We wanted to do something we were proud of.

Arnold Margolin It wasn't difficult to write because we weren't writing well. We didn't learn until about a year or so later that writing could be difficult if you did it well. They were happy with what we were doing so we just kept doing it. The thing we discovered about *My Mother the Car*, unfortunately too late, is that nothing is more boring than looking at the screen and listening to a guy talking to an inanimate object. Cars don't make good characters. They had a very good actress with Ann Sothern but you don't see her face. There's no human element to it. It's hard to be like *The Odd Couple* when one of the people is not a real person.

Elroy Schwartz It [*It's About Time*] got in trouble in the ratings. Sherwood came to me. He would always come to me when he was in trouble with a script or a show. He wanted to bring the cave people back to the present rather than the astronauts being in the past. He came to me with that on a Thursday and needed a script on Monday. I gave him a script on Monday. They shot it on Thursday or Friday.

Arnold Margolin Everything was what they called high concept — a car that talks, the world's richest man and a pair of brothers where one is an angel. That's probably why the series didn't work. It's difficult for a high concept show to maintain that premise. The successful high concept shows that I've worked on were ones where after the series got on the air people forgot about the high concept and just tried to do what works, usually just character chemistry. You couldn't make *O.K. Crackerby* sympathetic. That was the problem. The best episode they did, and it wasn't ours, was where one of his sons wanted a unicorn, I think, for his birthday. So the one thing that he couldn't buy was a unicorn. But anything else… Who cared? That didn't work.

Carl Kleinschmitt I thought *The Brady Bunch Hour* was the dumbest idea I ever heard in my life. Which it was. The nicest thing about it was it allowed me to buy a house in Santa Barbara.

While it can be relatively easy to make an adjustment in the supporting cast, if the audience doesn't warm up to the lead performer, the series is likely dead in the water.

Saul Turteltaub *Chicken Soup* was a joke. It was terrible. Jackie Mason had done a Broadway show and ABC loved the idea of doing a television show with Jackie because Carsey-Werner had great success with doing *The Cosby Show* and *Roseanne*, using comedians as stars of TV shows. They thought they could do that with Jackie. They saw Jackie married to a Gentile. Being an Orthodox Jew, I couldn't do a show with Jackie Mason married to a Gentile. I said I'd do it if he was in love with her because love is an involuntary act but marriage is a voluntary act. They said it was okay to do it that way. When we cast it, we used Lynn Redgrave. That was a big mistake because it was hard for the audience to believe that beautiful girl would be in love with little Jackie Mason. The casting didn't work at all. It wouldn't have worked anyway because he couldn't act. The show was wrong to begin with. We realized halfway through the first show that the show should have been him in a delicatessen giving advice to everybody and solving or not solving problems. He couldn't act at all. He could kid better than anybody but couldn't play a character. You'd show him a million times where to stand and he'd never stand there. He just never got it.

Bernie Orenstein I think we made a couple of basic errors that caused it to be rejected. Mostly that the romantic part of it was not acceptable. Nobody could believe he was attractive to a beautiful woman. I think that was a fair criticism. Jackie cooperated and worked very hard. I thought he was pretty funny. It just didn't work.

Arnold Margolin *The McLean Stevenson Show* was a strange experience. They had already shot like nine episodes but the guys that had been producing and writing it left. I came in and brought in a new staff, including a couple of new people that turned out to be really good—Carol Gary and a kid at UCLA, Sheldon Bull. He'd written a spec script and I loved it. He had a very successful career. It was definitely in trouble. The problem with that show, and I don't mean to speak ill of the dead, but McLean was a very funny actor but he couldn't handle being the star of a series. It's very important, especially in a three-camera show, that the star of the series set the tone on the set. He couldn't do it. He was so insecure that he just couldn't be the star. I remember one show, he stopped the show in the middle of shooting and turned to the audience and said, "You'll all have to leave." The audience had to leave. He was just too neurotic to handle that responsibility. Because it is a lot of responsibility to star in a show. That was one of the problems. It was too little too late. I

6. I'm Going to Acting School

brought in one new person but they wouldn't let me recast. I felt it needed a different point of view from the casting to be successful.

Ed Scharlach   McLean Stevenson's management, I guess, convinced him that if he was a major star on *M*A*S*H*, that if he left *M*A*S*H* he could be a bigger star on his own. He got a deal with NBC and, of course, the biggest mistake he made was to leave *M*A*S*H* because he was wonderful in that and nothing else he did ever worked for him. It was an uphill battle. McLean was a really good comedy actor but he wasn't a star. He didn't have the charisma to carry his own show, I think.

Rick Mittleman   David Swift created *Arnie* and he wasn't able to stay with the show. I was hired by him to produce *Arnie*. It was very exciting for me. It was the first show I got sole producing credit on. My only problem with that show was the star, Herschel Bernardi. I liked Herschel but like so many actors, he was insecure. Very insecure. He was hired because on Broadway people considered him a comedian. Herschel was not a comedian. He could sing and act but he wasn't a comedian. For some reason, the people at Fox thought he'd be perfect. If I wrote a scene for Dick Van Dyke where he's having an argument with Mary Tyler Moore, it would be very funny the way Dick and Mary played it. If I wrote that scene for *Arnie*, when Herschel did it, it would look like he wanted to kill his wife. He couldn't find the humor in a lot of scenes. He was a good dramatic actor. He was a product of the famous Yiddish theater. Off camera, Herschel was lovely, although he had his problems. He was a very difficult guy on that show. I did a show called "One Strike and You're Out." On the show, the guys on the loading dock go on strike. The question was, since Arnie had worked on the loading dock and was now on the board of directors, will he cross the picket line. And I had him crossing the picket line in the show. I got a call from Grant Tinker, who was at that time head of television production at 20th Century–Fox, and he asked me to come in. I come in and Herschel is sitting there with his lawyer and he said, "I'm not going to do that show. Because I wouldn't cross that picket line." We weren't doing the Herschel Bernardi Show, we were doing the Arnie Nuvo Show. I said, "This has nothing to do with you." He said, "I won't do it." That was Herschel. I finally made a few changes where he still crosses the picket line but I changed some dialogue. It made him feel better that he had some impact on the script. We did the show and he did cross the picket line. Otherwise, we would have had to throw the show out. Frequently, he wouldn't like the ending of a scene.

Even after he read it and said everything's fine, after we'd start to shoot it he'd say, "I don't like the ending." So I'd get a call to come down to the stage and ask him what he wanted to do. I'd say, "Okay. We'll do it your way and we'll do it the way it's written and we'll see how it looks in the screening room." I'd tell the cameraman, "Don't bother putting any film in the camera." So we did it my way and that was the last I heard of it. The ratings were fairly good. After one year, I was on a cruise and I got a ship-to-shore message saying that CBS picked up the show but they didn't want to pick up me as producer because I didn't make *Arnie* funny enough. Well, the show went to a second year and that was the end of it. The ratings were not as good as when I was producing it. Maybe having nothing to do with me, but that's the way it worked out.

Sam Denoff I was a big fan of the book that *Turnabout* was based on. Steven Bochco wrote the original pilot script and it was great but it wasn't funny. He's not a comedy writer. So I rewrote it with Michael Rhodes. Sharon Gless was perfect but John Schuck was wrong for the part. He's very talented but we should have had someone who was more macho because then it would have been funnier when he converted into being a woman. But the network wanted him.

Jack Elinson *Run, Buddy, Run* was a good show that I loved. Jack Sheldon was a funny stand-up comic, great saxophone player. He wasn't an actor. We were trying to make him an actor. He was just himself. With a better time slot it could have been a hit, who knows. I met him after we got cancelled. I asked him what he was doing and he says, "I'm going to acting school."

Bob Schiller Desi wanted us to write *Guestward, Ho!* It came from a book. It was written by the guy who wrote *Auntie Mame*. It was about a dude ranch being run by an Easterner. A fish out of water thing. And we said, "Why Vivian Vance? They're not going to buy Vivian. She's too associated as Lucy's sidekick." Desi said, "Ah, don't worry about it." And that's exactly what happened. Then we rewrote it for Joanne Dru.

Irma Kalish We had a show called *Out of the Blue* with 13 writers on staff.

Austin Kalish We were running it. They put an actor in, Jimmy Brogan, who did stand-up comedy. They gave him a show. He wasn't a Robin Williams. He did warm-ups for shows.

Irma Kalish They gave us a huge staff.

6. I'm Going to Acting School

Austin Kalish Irma stood on one side of the table and I stood at the other.

Irma Kalish They decided it would be a good learning experience.

Austin Kalish The network thought we were great teachers and they would learn the craft. So they brought in all these writers.

Irma Kalish And the star said we didn't know the rules of comedy.

Austin Kalish On the first hello with this guy, he says we didn't know the rules of comedy. There are no rules of comedy! He was that brazen.

Irma Kalish That was not one of our favorite shows.

Sam Denoff *Good Morning, World* was based on our experiences at WNEW. William B. Williams used to say, "Good morning, world," at the top of his show. That's where the title came from.

Bill Persky We had gotten a 26-week commitment from Procter & Gamble from us having worked on *The Dick Van Dyke Show*. The first pilot was with Ron Rifkin. He was adorable in the part. The network and the sponsors decided he was too Jewish so we had to redo it. You just couldn't fight them. We also cast the wrong girl for his wife. In the process of redoing it, we were looking for someone to play the wife and this young girl came in to read the scene and in the scene she was having tea with her friend. And this young girl came in with a teapot. She wasn't the image of what we were looking for. We were looking for the next Mary Tyler Moore. And there just wasn't one. But this girl was adorable. We knew she was spectacular. We told her she wasn't right for the wife but she was going to be the best friend. She said, "I read the script. She doesn't have a best friend." I said, "That's until you came in." And that was Goldie Hawn.

Sam Denoff We had used Joby Baker on *The Dick Van Dyke Show* but we'd forgotten how much trouble he had remembering his lines in front of the audience. He'd just get flop sweat. And they never responded to him. That was the show that we thought would go. More so than *That Girl*. But we did discover Goldie Hawn through that experience. She wanted me to be her agent.

Bill Persky We cast Joby Baker, who was an adorable guy. Carl Reiner particularly loved him. We'd seen him do some theater and he was terrific but he could not remember lines. That just killed the timing of everything. Several years later they were having a sale because they had closed the studio and sold it to someone else. They were selling props so

Sam and I went back. We were walking through and there was this lamp and on it was a piece of masking tape with a line of dialogue on it that Joby Baker had pasted there. That explains why he was so resistant to changing the staging.

Ed Scharlach   It was a great premise. Really, really good cast. The least-known person at the time was Goldie Hawn. Any product that Persky and Denoff did was very well thought out with stories based on real things. Intelligent, reality-based comedy stories.

Rick Mittleman   Joby Baker was not a comedian. It was hard to find where the laughs were with Joby. Ronnie Schell was a stand-up comedian and he was terrific. Denoff and Perky brought the same sense of humor to that show that they brought to *The Dick Van Dyke Show*. I just don't think the audience was all that enthralled with Joby Baker, who's a fine enough actor. He did some Disney movies and things but he just wasn't a comedian. There is an art to it.

Carl Kleinschmitt   I thought it was not a bad idea but miscast.

Sam Bobrick   Getting the right guy is the thing. And sometimes you can't blame the show because the networks won't do it with some actors and they'll want another one. I remember doing a show and we wanted Fran Drescher and they said no. She would have been great. The next season she's on the air with *The Nanny*. On the same show, we had Claire Danes. They said, "You've got to get rid of her." She became a huge star. A lot of network interference. I've always found that to be a problem. We had fun. But it didn't work. They had Goldie Hawn on the show. Persky and Denoff were great guys. Because they were trained by Sheldon Leonard and Danny Thomas. They had great respect for writers.

While it's easy—in hindsight—to spot the flaws in most flops, some hold up remarkably well. The failure of two late '60s series, He & She *and* My World and Welcome to It, *defies simple explanation. A husband and wife series reminiscent of* The Dick Van Dyke Show, He & She *foreshadows the sophisticated adult comedies of the '70s.* My World and Welcome to It *is perhaps even more ahead of its time. Loosely based on the stories of James Thurber, the series used fantasy sequences, flashbacks, animation, narration and the main character addressing the camera long before these techniques became cliché.*

Allan Burns   Leonard Stern hired us to work on a show called *He & She*. He hired us to do the show with him and Arne Sultan, also a leg-

6. I'm Going to Acting School

endary comedy writer. One of the most neurotic people I've ever met in my life. He had been a stand-up and like most stand-ups, he was really neurotic. But funny as hell. And he had a huge heart. As did Leonard.

Arnold Margolin It was only a show that lasted for a year but it was a very prestigious success in the business and everybody associated went on to have a lot of success in their careers. We had a great season but the show didn't get picked up. I remember CBS said, "It's the best show we've ever cancelled." We had a lot of fun on that show. We learned a lot.

Allan Burns There was really something going with Dick [Benjamin] and Paula [Prentiss]. And then there were these subordinate characters that were all fleshed out. Interesting characters. Kenny Mars, who played the fireman who lived next door. The firehouse was right next door to where they lived. And Hamilton Camp, who was just a pixie. One of the funniest little gnomes you've ever known. And Jack Cassidy.

Arnold Margolin We learned to really understand the characters and let the humor flow from who the people were and not try to write jokes. It made it so much easier because they were really good characters and well-defined characters that Leonard and Arne created. So it made it easier for us. Jet Man was a dream to write for. He was such an outrageous but clear-cut character. Jack Cassidy was great in that role. But all of them had very distinct personalities—Dick and Paula, Kenny Mars and Hamilton Camp. They were all great. They were terrific. Aside from *Love, American Style*, it was the most fun we ever had and we would call it the best work we ever did in television. In large part, it was because of those characters. It was a good experience.

Allan Burns We had more fun on that show and we learned so much about laying out a story. It was the first time we had ever really worked in a room with a bunch of writers. It was mostly six of us—Leonard and Arne, Chris and myself and Jim Parker and Arnold Margolin. I was scared to death. I was very shy. Being in that room with those guys, a lot of whom were heavyweights, especially Arne and Leonard, I was almost intimidated by the wit and jokes that were flying around that room. I've never been a joke writer. I just don't write jokes. I can write funny, but I don't write jokes. That was a great experience for us. Leonard and Arne in the pilot they wrote created wonderful characters. And it was marvelous. The pilot was fabulous and just full of heart. It was touching and funny as hell and sweet. We probably wrote eight or ten of them, very often working in the room with Arne and Leonard. We would work on the story with them. We'd have our ideas but mostly they came from Arne and Leonard. They had wonderful ideas and they knew where they wanted the show to go. We just started writing better. I hadn't learned to write yet. That year I did. There were two writing nominations for the show that year for the Emmys. One of them was their pilot and the other one was a show that Chris and I wrote that had been their idea. We just figured they're going to win because what they did was so good and they created the series and they deserved to win. So we go to the Emmys that night and our names get called. And I am mortified. How was anybody dumb enough not to realize they had created this thing and they deserved it and we, going from an idea they had given us, win the Emmy? We were so unprepared and we didn't know what to say and we got up and stammered. We weren't as gracious as we should have been. We were humble. I've always wanted to make it up to them ever since. About six or seven years ago, the Caucus of Television Writers and Producers, they gave me an award. I had a speech prepared because Leonard was one of the people in the caucus and I gave this heartfelt thank you to Leonard, who wasn't there that night. He was sick or something. He never got to hear what I said about him. He was my mentor.

Arnold Margolin   I loved the pilot. And the one where they get married for the second time was my favorite one we wrote. The best man is a fireman and he gets called away during the ceremony and he takes the ring with him and they have to end up using the Jet Man ring to take the oath. It was silly but it was smart. Paula brought heart. She had great empathy and warmth. You just fell in love with her. Unfortunately, the audience didn't fall in love with Dick. But he was very funny. Dick was very knowledgeable. He really understood the show and had a keen eye for what was working and what wasn't working. He was like the field general on the set. There was never any actor ego there at all. It was pretty unique.

Ed Scharlach   That was really a kick. Paula Prentiss was a major movie star. Leonard Stern was one of the great comedy legends. He was working with Arne Sultan, a great comedy writer. Our friends Arnold Margolin and Jim Parker were on that show. We were going to the meeting to get our story for *He & She*. Leonard, Arne, Arnold and Jim all had beards. I never wore one. Peggy and I were going to the meeting so we went to a novelty store and both Peggy and I walked into the meeting with fake beards. It was fun to write. Leonard was very charismatic and a character. He'd had all this phenomenal experience.

6. I'm Going to Acting School

Allan Burns I think it was badly placed on the schedule. The shows around it were not compatible with it. CBS' strength in those days was shows like *The Beverly Hillbillies, Petticoat Junction, Green Acres*, those kind of rural shows. And here's this sophisticated show with lovely Paula Prentiss, who was one of the most original comediennes. Nobody was like Paula. The strangest readings but funny as hell. And Dick playing opposite. This deadpan guy. It was like a more sophisticated Burns and Allen. He would just react to Paula and he was dry and wonderful. She was so wonderful. And Jack Cassidy. That was really fun.

Arnold Margolin I think it was just too hip, too sophisticated for the time. I think the network was uncomfortable with Dick Benjamin. He wasn't warm and cuddly but he was very funny. He was a great foil for Paula. It was too sharp, too sophisticated for CBS. They got uncomfortable with it. Their other shows were *The Beverly Hillbillies* and those kind of shows. They were more of a conservative, rural network. It just didn't work.

Allan Burns *He & She* meant everything to what I was able to do with *The Mary Tyler Moore Show*.

Arnold Margolin I just showed a friend of mine an episode on YouTube a couple of weeks ago and it was amazing how it held up.

Paul Wayne *My World and Welcome to It* was wonderful. That's a show that should have gone on. I think the trouble with it was its positioning at 7:30. I think the network thought, because of the animation, it was geared toward kids. Of course it wasn't. It was an adult show. That was a show that I just loved to do. It was a sweet show. It was just absolutely amazing.

Carl Kleinschmitt That was interesting. I was working in London when that show came about so I did long distance calls on it. When I came back, I saw the work Danny Arnold put into it and all that was involved in the animation and everything else and I thought it was really a good show. It won an Emmy and it was cancelled. It was really innovative. It may have been too early for the time, it may have never worked, I don't know. It was very close to Danny Arnold's heart. Then he went on to have a hit in *Barney Miller*. It was not easy to write because Danny had a very strict idea of what it should be like.

Lila Garrett I loved that show. I was nominated for a Writers Guild Award for that show. I wrote two of them. I think one of the shows was about bullying. And it was an anti-bullying show. And the other show was about ego. He was supposed to write cartoons for his daughter's newspaper and his daughter was a child and he was very proud to do it. And they rejected his cartoon. It was hilarious. It was way ahead of its time. Everything was a social point on that show. Marriage and violence and bullying, freedom of speech — it was all in there. It wasn't as obvious maybe to other people as it was to us. But we got a message across when the rule is don't send a message. And that was the rule in those days. Don't send a message. It's tricky.

Rick Mittleman I got a Writers Guild nomination after the show was cancelled, which was rather interesting. It was very innovative because it wove animation into live action before it became more commonplace. I loved Thurber. I'm a New Yorker and Thurber was part of New York. At the Algonquin Hotel, where Thurber lived, there were all kinds of Thurber sketches on the wall. I stuck very close to the Thurber story. I think one of the successes of the show is that it was true to Thurber and he was unique. The character was cynical but still he was gentle. It was like he was spitting into the wind sometimes.

Every flop did beat the odds in one respect— it got on the air. Every year, dozens of potential series don't even get that far.

Fred Freeman The crazy pilots we did that never went. They were fun to write. Larry and I did a lot of pilots. The executives loved to hire us, they'd laugh at our stuff and then they wouldn't put it on the air. They hired us to do Henry VIII as a half-hour comedy. It was very funny. There was a court jester and he made his pastry maker a pope. We also did a whole thing on the Underground Railroad. We got paid for it but it never went to production at all. It was crazy stuff. We did a weird one with Andy Kaufman. Andy was very sweet. He would always say, "Mr. Freeman." That was not very good. They had something in Andy but they didn't know what to do with him. We tried things and we made him a robot. It wasn't one of my best half-hours.

David Lloyd We did a pilot [*Don't Call Us*] that I wrote with Ed. and Stan backing me, with Jack Gilford, whom I adored. And the notion, and I thought was a good one, was two brothers who are agents — one of them, the Gilford one, was a Broadway Danny Rose but before *Broadway Danny Rose* because this was years and years before *Broadway Danny Rose*. An agent who loves all his bad, hard-to-book acts — his old ventriloquist and his old magician. And his brother, who's a hotshot sharpie, who wants

6. I'm Going to Acting School

hip things to get them on television, who's got his eye on the dollar. And I wanted Jack Weston, whom I thought would have been wonderful as the less sympathetic brother. And they made us, the network, made us cast somebody about 20 years younger than that because they said, "You've got two old guys? You think anyone's gonna watch a show about two old guys?" And so we cast this other very good actor, not very funny actor, very good dramatic actor as the brother. And any last shot it had in my mind, the show I had pictured writing, that I thought I was writing, went out the window at that point because he just wasn't funny. Those two old guys, one who was venal and one who was idealistic, seemed to me to be a good show.

Sam Denoff   We did a pilot called *The Boys* with Tim Conway. I think it was some of the best work he ever did. We based it on Billy and I, our personalities. We got the title from the way they always called comedy writers "the boys," even when there was only one or they were women. Everybody called us the boys. It looked like the pilot was going on and then it tested really badly so it didn't go. Then a few years later when I'm in New York to work on *On Our Own*, I found out that someone at the network hated it and he skewed the research to make sure it wouldn't get sold.

Bill Persky   It was so funny that Jim Brooks and Grant Tinker and Allan Burns who had done the pilot for *Paul Sand* in that development season had seen *The Boys* and thought they had no chance to try to sell a comedy against *The Boys*. It was so brilliant. It was Tim Conway's favorite. When I talk to him today and ask him when was the last time he watched *The Boys*, he'll say, "Last week." It was so special.

Bernie Orenstein   We did a show called *This Week in Nemtin*. We wrote that with Sam Bobrick and Ron Clark. It was a news comedy show. CBS assured us it would be on the schedule. They were just waiting for Fred Silverman to come back from his honeymoon. They kept assuring us it was 90/10 that we were going to be on the air. Then one day they told us to stop worrying because it was still 80/20. I said, "Ooh. What happened to 90/10?" Sure enough, when Fred came back he decided he didn't want to do it, he wanted to do *Me and the Chimp*, which lasted about a week and a half. Then Fred called us many years later and thought we could sell that show.

Fred Freeman   The one we really liked that they wouldn't put on was called *The Continuing Story of the Shameful Secrets of Hastings Corners*.

It was a satire of soap operas. We had Hal Linden playing twins. One twin was the mayor of the town. The other twin was in Argentina playing cards with Hitler. It was a crazy satire. The trouble with satire sometimes is that there is no character that you're identifying with. It's a play of ideas rather than characters. Like George S. Kaufman said, "Satire is what closes on Saturday night."

Bob Schiller We did one that was very good, with Eddie Albert and Georgann Johnson. She was Tony Randall's girlfriend on *Mister Peepers*. And it was called *Living in Paradise*. Paradise was the name of the trailer park. And it was a lovely thing. It was when Alan Horn first came in when Norman Lear was getting out. NBC said, "We like the pilot. We'll give you an order for six." And Horn tried to show his muscle and said, "You can't break up Weiskopf and Schiller for six shows. You've got to give us 13 or none." So they gave us none. That was a good show.

Irma Kalish We did a lot of pilots. We never got one on the air, unfortunately. We had one make the schedule but get pulled before it went on. We did one pilot where we actually did our story about a husband and wife writing team.

Austin Kalish It didn't make the schedule. There were other pilots along the way that you think you have a chance at it but it didn't happen. We think we deserved it. But certain things didn't happen. We're not bitter. It's okay.

Arnold Margolin *Harry and Maggie* was an interesting experience. It was a very funny script. We had a great cast—Don Knotts, Eve Arden, Tom Poston. We shot it. Jay Sandrich directed it. We took it in to test it. I was never a big fan of testing but I did learn some things from watching people turn the dials. The interesting thing about that show was there were a lot of big jokes and the dials would go up on every joke and as soon as the joke was over the dials would go back down. The audience just didn't fall in love with the characters. The characters weren't sympathetic or empathetic enough. The jokes worked great but the characters didn't. And you can't blame it on Eve and Don because, God knows, they were successful in other series they did. It was just the roles we wrote for them. We must have gone to their strength as joke tellers and not bothered to create any vulnerabilities for them. That was a good lesson to learn. Unfortunately, it cost us a series. If we had a scene that was full of warmth and heart, I think it would have made all the difference in the world. I didn't make that mistake again.

6. I'm Going to Acting School

David Lloyd I did a pilot [*Not Until Today*] for Darren McGavin, who was a piece of work. He was a very difficult man to work for. The network liked it and came to Grant Tinker and said, "We'll order 13 episodes." And I said "I'm gone. I'm going to Paramount. I'm not going to work with that man again."

Bill Persky I wrote *Bobby Parker and Company* for Ted Bessell. I didn't have a deal anywhere. I wrote it because I wanted to write it. It was about me. It was about a guy and the things we all go through. It was very specific and very personal. We screened it at NBC and at the end of the screening every guy in the room could identify with it. But they couldn't yet put a thing about a guy in therapy on the air. They said it was too soon for that show.

Fred Freeman They put us together with Albert Brooks. I always thought he was one of the funniest guys. He made me laugh a lot. That was an embarrassment because we developed a format with Albert and we had a network meeting. Everyone came because of Albert. There was a huge conference table and a room of like fifteen people. Albert got up to start pitching and just died. He turned to me and I stammered. There was flop sweat. It was a disaster. It's not anyone's fault. As we were going through, it just wasn't working too well. We all hit those kinds of things.

Bernie Orenstein We had written a show and sold it. It was called *Coastocoast*. We shot the pilot and it was an expensive show. Fred Silverman was made the head of NBC while we were shooting it. Our show was about an airline that went from L.A. to New York. We felt it was pretty good. We didn't complete the music or editing or anything like that when Fred said, "No. I don't want to do that show. I want to do *Supertrain*." Which was basically the same show on a train. So he cancelled our show before we ever got on the air. It was a stupid move. *Supertrain* was awful.

7

Gold Is What You're Always Going to Get: Working with Actors

It has often been said that the success of a sitcom is almost completely in the writing and acting. In fact, casting is so important that sometimes a breakout character can change the intended direction of a series.

Jack Elinson   They figured Andy Griffith was very funny, he's a comedian on Broadway. But then as we were casting, we figured we have to have someone for Griffith to talk to, to bounce things off. They came up with the idea of Don Knotts and then right away Andy said to everybody, "He's going to get the laughs. Not me." He became the funny character. Andy still had plenty of comedy. It was terrific. They were the tops of comedy teams.

Fred Freeman   Andy was not threatened at all. Like Mary Tyler Moore. She was a great straight woman for the people around her. Compare that to a comedian like Joey Bishop who'd get upset if someone else got the laugh. That gets you in trouble. It was great to have a star who was secure enough to realize that. Like Jack Benny was a straight man. Andy Griffith was terrific. He knew who he was. Andy would sit in on story meetings. He was respectful and easy to work with. The smart ones appreciate good writing. Sometimes if they get involved, it can hurt if they're dictating what we're going to do. It's crazy. But if you have someone who has good taste, like Elizabeth Montgomery, when they said something wasn't going to work for them, we'd ask them what they wanted to do or asked them if they wanted to try something else. It's collaborative. There's no getting around it.

Arnold Margolin   Of course, the genius of the show that Andy discovered right at the beginning was that with Don Knotts in the cast, all

7. Gold Is What You're Always Going to Get

he had to do was be the straight man in the show, not the comic. I loved Andy. He was a very funny actor. The character that he evolved into was entertaining but very shrewd and very smart the way he saw himself as a lead in a TV series. He made it work. He understood, which a lot of actors wouldn't. If he hadn't been a comedy actor to begin with, okay. But here he was, somebody who broke into the business and made his fame as a comedy actor, and suddenly he wasn't getting the laughs but he understood what he had there.

Sam Bobrick I loved Andy Griffith and Don Knotts because they were such a great comedy team. They always made your script better. Most of the actors out there made it worse. The shows were nice. They were small little dramas with comedy in it. When I got on the show, it had been running for a couple of years already and Don was a hit already. The show was a big hit. I was happy to be writing for them because Don was so great. And Andy was a great straight man. Andy started out as a comic but they brought Don into the show and Andy became the straight man. He told a lot of people that you don't have to be the funniest person in the world to be a star of a hit series. Just surround yourself with the right people and you got yourself a hit. What was great was that Andy and Don remained great friends. They loved each other and it showed. And Andy was a gentleman, a total gentleman.

Fred Freeman If you're a comedy writer, you're in church praying every day that you get Don Knotts or someone like that. They're very funny. They know their craft. Good actors who've been in a show two or three years know the character better than you do. When we ran *Empty Nest* with Richard Mulligan, we came in about the third year for our retirement money — basically — I respected the actors when they would say something. You should honor that, I think, because they've been there for three years doing the same character. So they know it. It's important to respect the actors that have been in the show and know their character. You may not agree with them but they're the ones with their ass on the line out there. You have to respect them when they say they wouldn't say that. Sometimes you find a way to compromise even though sometimes it's frustrating and infuriating when they don't understand the joke and everyone else does. You can't force someone to say it.

Ed Scharlach Henry Winkler, Fonzie, was magical in front of a live audience. The first year he was this mystical guy and he's charismatic and he has this power over the other kids and he doesn't have to talk. They were smart to expand his part. He was really brilliant and that partnership with Richie really made the subsequent series.

David Lloyd *Frasier* is supposed to be a story about a guy and his father. His father the cop, he's a psychiatrist. They're sort of an *Odd Couple* thing. And somebody said to them, "You know there's an actor on one of Norman Lear's shows [*The Powers That Be*] who looks like Kelsey. He's got the high forehead. He's kind of elegant talking." They looked at him and said this is great and he's wonderful. I think David is a miracle. I adore David Hyde-Pierce. They just said, "He's very good. He'll be good." They didn't know what a great physical comic he is. That just came when they started doing stuff and said, "My God, he's funny!" The stuff he would do on that show. They didn't know that when they cast him.

Saul Turteltaub For *What's Happening!!*, we couldn't find a guy who would be a tall, good-looking athlete like a basketball player. We kept looking and looking. The day before ABC had to have the answer for the casting, I was getting my shoes shined at NBC. While I was sitting in the chair, this short, heavy guy walks over to me and says, "I hear you're looking for a tall athlete. That's me. I'm good. I can do it." I let him come up to the office and read the part. It was a million-to one-shot. He read it and he was no actor at all but there was just something so funny about the way he read it and his look compared to the guy we were looking for. So, on the spot, we made up his character. Bernie named him Rerun because every year he had to repeat school in the summer. We brought him to ABC and they were all expecting Sidney Poitier to walk in for this part and in came Fred Berry. They looked at us like we were crazy. He read it and they had the same reaction that we did and they said, "Go ahead. Do it."

Fred Freeman Sometimes Park Overall would have no idea what the joke was about and still get a laugh. Even when she did it wrong, she would get a laugh.

David Lloyd On *Taxi*, when they found Danny DeVito, they went crazy over him. They'd written this guy as kind of a rough-edged character, but then when Danny DeVito came in and read it, they just flipped.

Saul Turteltaub LaWanda Page was funny and there was a funny dynamic between her and Redd. The audience would go crazy every time he insulted her. Then she would get mad and swing her purse at him and they seemed to love that. She was important. She was also a great lady. She was wonderful.

7. Gold Is What You're Always Going to Get

Bernie Orenstein   She and Redd were dear friends. He was the one who got her on the show.

Arnold Margolin   I thought *Growing Pains* would be a hit, mostly because the cast was good and Kirk Cameron was definitely a star. The whole emphasis of the show changed after the pilot because he just popped on the screen. He blew everybody else away. So that's the direction the show went after that. It wasn't planned to go that way but he just was so good.

Jack Elinson   We really liked Jackée a lot on *227*. I remember telling her after half a season, "You've got big stuff happening after this one's finished." She was great. She gave it a lot of fun.

David Lloyd   It was fun on *Rhoda* if you could write for Nancy Walker. God, I think she was wonderful! I went in to pitch a pilot at some point. Some network idiot, for one of the parts he said, "Who do you see here?" And I said, "Oh, Nancy Walker would be good for it." He said, "Oh, I don't know, Nancy Walker, you always know what you're going to get from her." I said, "Gold is what you're always going to get from her! Gold!" She was wonderful.

Austin Kalish   Nancy Walker was a wonderful talent.

Irma Kalish   Yes, we loved Nancy. We had seen her on Broadway and she was very good.

Austin Kalish   She was very good and they wouldn't let her do things as well as she could on *Family Affair* because she would have taken it over. They had to pull back and hold her back.

Allan Burns   Julie Kavner is marvelous. Not just in that show. She was another one of Dave Davis' finds. He saw her in a play.

David Lloyd   Julie Kavner was terrific, too. A terrific actress.

Austin Kalish   Jimmie Walker helped make *Good Times*. He didn't like doing "Dy-no-mite!" We used to get letters from black people saying, "Get that guy off the show. He's offensive to black people."

Irma Kalish   Jimmie Walker was fine. We knew he had a hard time because a lot of people made fun of him.

Jack Elinson   You had Jimmie Walker. He was a real comedian. You could be just as funny black as white. Funny is funny. The fact that we could say things then that we couldn't say before gave us more choices. It helped us. We always knew we were going to be funny with him. Jimmie Walker was afraid of John Amos because he would always push Jimmie around on the stage. If the scene called for a hug from the father, he grabbed him and almost killed him. Jimmie came up to the office and said, "He's going to kill me, that man. He's going to kill me for sure. Look at my neck." He was a tough guy. He was a football player, Amos was.

A lead performer can not only make the series a hit with the audience but the star also helps set the tone for everyone that works on the series.

Paul Wayne There was nobody better than John Ritter. Nobody kinder. Nobody sweeter. I left the show and a couple of years later they asked me to write an episode for it. They invited me to come watch the show as it was being done. There was a mistake or something and they had to stop. And while they were stopped he went to the front and said to the audience, "I'd like you to meet the writer of this piece," and he had me stand up. That's John Ritter. He was just a big-hearted person. A wonderful, wonderful man. I'm very, very sorry, very sad to see him gone. Just stunned. Anything you'd ask him to do, he'd do it. He'd just work his heart out. And appreciated your talent. I don't remember him fighting us on a single thing. Imagine stopping the show, knowing that I was sitting there watching and introducing me to the audience. That was just an unnecessary but lovely thing to do. He was just loaded with talent. And he was terribly funny. He just knew. His sense of timing was just so precise and so impeccable. Just a lovely person and a great, great talent. Just a huge loss. Huge loss. I can't say enough about him.

Lila Garrett Dick Van Dyke can do anything. I did a Dick Van Dyke pilot. He was so brilliant. He does a pantomime bit that is one of the most brilliant things I've ever seen in my life. He is so talented. He takes your breath away. It was a wonderful show. I'm very, very proud of it. Years later, when he did that serious show, I felt it was a waste.

Bill Persky It was easy to write for him because you would try and find situations that would give him an opportunity to be physical. He played the best drunk, who could stop being drunk in an instant and then go back into it. Carl wrote that show where he was hypnotized to get drunk when the phone rang and then when it rang again he wouldn't be drunk. It was hysterical the kind of things he did.

Bernie Orenstein I loved Dick Van Dyke very much. Carl Reiner and Dick were very supportive of the two of us. Dick was a great comedian and he worked very hard. I have nothing but great things to say about him. He was lovely to us. He was respectful to us. By then he was a superstar. He was just a great guy to work with. A great actor and comedian.

7. Gold Is What You're Always Going to Get

He didn't take it lightly. He worked every weekend. When other people were not there he would walk through the set and try to think of bits that he could do. He was terrific. I had great respect for him.

Carl Kleinschmitt It was wonderful because besides being a good actor and a dancer and all that he is a wonderful physical comedian. In "Obnoxious, Offensive Egomaniac, Etc." the dialogue is secondary to the physical things that he does. We carefully wrote down the specific movements that we had in mind. And darned if he didn't go out and do it to a tee. He's just a marvelous physical comedian. We were very careful in all the physical aspects of Rob breaking into this office and he just did it the way it was written and made it come to life.

Fred Freeman He's amazing. He's terrific.

Sam Denoff It was like working at Disneyland. There was never any terror on the set. There was no nicer man than Dick Van Dyke.

Ed Scharlach He's brilliant to this day. He's still very entertaining in his eighties. It was fun to write for him. He was one of my idols.

Rick Mittleman With Dick, and Mary Tyler Moore both, what you see is what you get. Very nice people. Very decent. Very easy to work with, although when you're a freelance writer, sometimes you're six to eight weeks ahead of the show in terms of the actual filming of it.

Saul Turteltaub Dick would always add to the show, to the comedy. On the weekend, he would work on how to expand the comedy of something. He would come in Monday with physical moves. He was wonderful.

Ed Scharlach Robin Williams was very, very funny but the moments I was most proud of and most touched by was when Robin was dramatic and could make you cry. To be able to write those moments was really thrilling. Robin is a trained actor at Julliard and he really brought our material alive. He's a very creative mind. During rehearsals, he'd bring in suggestions. You're doing stories with other actors so there's not a lot of ad libbing you can do but he would find little things to throw in or use a funny voice or a funny accent. He'd try it in rehearsal to see if we liked it. If we did, we kept it in the script. Otherwise, he did the script as it was written. Once in a while he'd throw in a little nuance in front of the live audience and if it worked we'd leave it in. If it didn't, if there was no laugh, he would flub the next line so they'd have to redo the scene as written. And the audience there thought he was ad libbing and it would get a huge laugh. It didn't matter as long as the show was good. He was wonderful.

Jack Elinson Andy Griffith was just a clever guy. He was a smart,

smart guy. He was also a very nice man. Andy had that real nice way with words that a Jewish guy from the Bronx would never put in there. It was in the script but I have to confess that it was Andy's words. I'm a different person. I'm not a country guy. And yet I was able to do fine. It wasn't like I couldn't work on a show like that because I didn't talk like that.

Arnold Margolin Andy Griffith was definitely involved. Not all the time but he would come in and he was great because he would say, "Aunt Bee can't do that." Or something was not Floyd the Barber's thing and he needed to do something else. He knew the actors well enough to know what their strengths and weaknesses were and that was a big help.

Bill Persky I adore Jane Curtin and Susan Saint James. They are still among my closest friends. They are very different but they are both total pros. Really funny. Jane Curtin is one of the funniest actresses you will ever come across. Her mind is so quick. Susan is so adorably funny. They were a great combination. We never had a bad day on *Kate & Allie*. Everybody loved coming to work.

Jerry Mayer Charlotte Rae was good. She finally left the show on her own. She was a good performer. Always got the laugh. She would do something like have an expression when she didn't like something and it would get a big laugh. She had done a lot of Broadway. She was a pro. Good to work with. She could sing, too. She's a very talented lady. She was a lot like Paul Lynde. They both went to Northwestern. I was at a thing for Mitzi Gaynor last weekend and a little old lady with white hair gets on the elevator and she looks about four feet tall. It was Charlotte Rae. We gave each other a hug. That was fun.

Austin Kalish Charlotte was marvelous.

Carl Kleinschmitt I think Alan Alda was born to be Hawkeye. He's just a wonderful actor and a wonderful writer and director. He's a very talented man. I think he's the best. I also think he's a nice guy.

Jack Elinson Danny Thomas was sort of playing himself because in real life he was a guy that when the season was over would go to Las Vegas and he was very, very big there. He was terrific on *The Danny Thomas Show*. We never dreamed it would go that far, 11 years. He was just a good actor. A lot of comedians are okay but they really can't do the dramatic part. We could really go dramatic, which we did very often. He was one of the great ones. He wasn't just a guy who was funny, who had a show. So what we ended up doing was just about what his real life was like. And Rusty Hamer was a really good kid actor.

7. Gold Is What You're Always Going to Get

*The importance of casting can best be demonstrated with the deepest sitcom cast of all time—*The Mary Tyler Moore Show. *Assembling multiple Emmy winners Mary Tyler Moore, Ed Asner, Valerie Harper, Cloris Leachman, Betty White and Ted Knight, along with multiple Emmy nominee Georgia Engel and the underrated Gavin McLeod, was one of the keys to the show's immense popularity and acclaim.*

Allan Burns When we went to do the pilot, it would usually be Ethel Winant's job to assign a casting director to the show. And she decided to cast the show with us because she loved it and she wanted to make sure it was cast really carefully. She wanted to find actors who you don't see every day. She didn't want to go through the casting lists of the people you see all the time in comedy. We said, "Absolutely." And she just worked her tail off to find us interesting people. It was hard to cast. The first person we cast was Gavin McLeod, who came in to read for Lou. The first words out of his mouth were, "I'm wrong for this, I want to play Murray." We said, "Humor us. Please do Lou Grant for us." He did. It was okay but it was not very good. Then we let him do Murray. He was not the first person in the room but by the time he got there, we said, "You're it. Absolutely." He had played heavies mostly. He was damn good with those bitchy, pithy lines. We had originally conceived of this character as being gay. Because Jim had worked with a guy named Richard, which was the character's original name, who was gay and he had a pair of figure skates in his bottom drawer and every day at lunch time when it was cold, he would go out and skate at Rockefeller Center. So we had that picture of him. Murray never had skates. But we always felt the skates were there. For us they were. Although we had him married and gave him kids.

There were few easy parts to cast in the series. In fact, two actors primarily known for drama at the time were among the choices.

Allan Burns We cast the show for more than a month, which is unusual. But we were freed up by the fact that we were not in pilot season. Actors were available, so we read a lot of people. Cloris was very early on. Ethel suggested her and we said, "But isn't she the woman who played the mother on *Lassie*?" But she said, "Believe me. She's this character. You just have to take it on faith." She came in and read and knocked it out of the park. She's so crazy and wonderful. She's still incredible. We had a hell of a time casting Lou. We wanted somebody like Shelley Berman in that part.

We threatened to do it with him but we were talked out of it. We heard he was a very difficult guy. But we couldn't find anybody. Until Grant called and he said, "Dick Crenna tells me there's a guy who he thinks is right for this. I gave him a script and he thinks Ed Asner would be great for this." We said, "He's a dramatic actor." He came in to read and he didn't read well. He left. About five or ten minutes later our assistant called and said, "Ed Asner is back." He wasn't good. We wondered what this was about. He storms in our office and says, "I was really shitty. You didn't tell me. Tell me the truth. I wasn't any good. Right?" We told him, "Right." He asked what we wanted and we told him who we thought this guy was. He says, "Let me come back tomorrow." So he did. And he pretty much nailed it. He had just that right combination of gruff and loveable and we felt he was a guy who knew how to run a newsroom. And he was funny. One of Mary's duties was to come in when we had settled on actors to come in and read with them. She came in and they read together. I felt the hairs go up on the back of my neck. And I looked at Jim and Jim looked at me. And Mary said, "Well, I guess we keep looking," after he left. We said, "Mary, you weren't watching. You were in the scene. There was magic with what happened with you two." It was just terrific.

Just as unusual, two complete unknowns were tapped for two other key roles.

Allan Burns We read every good-looking guy in Hollywood who could be an anchorman, who had any comedy chops at all. We had settled almost on John Aniston. He was good. We had pictured the character as being a potential love interest for Mary and John Aniston fit that bill. He was the best we had tested. But something was telling us that it was not quite right. He was good but he was not really *funny* funny. Dave Davis, who was our producer, came in one day and said, "I just saw a guy in a play in a local production. His name is Ted Knight. People were screaming with laughter." Ted came in and he had the white hair and couldn't be a love interest for Mary. He was clearly about 50. He just read fabulously. He was so funny. And we brought poor Ted back about four times because we couldn't get past the idea that we would get a guy who was young enough but still had the chops to do the comedy. Each time he came in he was wearing this kind of old fashioned looking green blazer. It was so ugly. We kept thinking, is it us or is it the blazer? The last time he came in, and this was a guy who was a struggling actor because he never had any major parts, and he was wearing a natty blue blazer. He had clearly bought it for this. Partly, we were so touched that he had done that, but also because he was so funny we couldn't fight it any longer because this guy was so good. And he had that extra quality of the arrogance that you never believed he was that confident about himself. He just lacked confidence as the character and you saw all the way through the bluster. And you loved him for it. So he was our guy. There was a show where Mary makes Ted take a vacation. She realizes something. He's never taken a vacation. She tells Ted he has to take some time off and he doesn't want to. He doesn't want to because he's afraid that if he's replaced by someone else, that someone else is going to be better than he is. And he's going to be out of work. And exactly that happens. And they realize he's pretended to take a vacation to Mexico and they're getting postcards that don't have any pictures of Mexico on them. Mary realizes he's in town and watching this other guy be good. That's so sad. It just explained so much about him, what a pathetic, sad little man he was. We began to humanize him in these ways. Then, of course, Georgia Engel coming in — this sweet, innocent, wacky woman — who loves him desperately just gave him a side that nobody ever saw.

David Lloyd   Ted was the go-to guy. A couple of people said that at his funeral. That he made it easy in some ways. Because if you were stuck for how to get out of a scene, ah, bring Ted in. Two lines. We'll get our laugh, the scene's over. You knew you could get a laugh with Ted and that's a wonderful safety valve to have. You push your story along and you've had whatever interaction and development with the characters you need. Now where's the laugh to get off it? I know, bring Ted in. And we did that shamelessly in that show. You always have to have a dumb guy. Dumb is funny. Every show wants to have a dumb guy. On *Cheers*, Coach was a character I hadn't seen before. The guy who's taken one too many fastballs in the head in his playing days. A dumb guy who's also very skewed — his mind is half gone. That's a character that's fun to write for.

Allan Burns   The last person to get cast was Valerie. There were a number of really good actresses that came in to read for that. But there was never one we could quite push the button on. And Ethel remembered going to a thing where actors did scenes for casting directors. Apparently Valerie had come in on one of those. Ethel could not remember her name. She couldn't find her and she looked and looked and looked. They finally found her. I don't remember how. She came in and she did something that actors are not supposed to do, which is to come in character with the clothes. The scene had to do with her washing windows and Valerie comes in with a bucket and a mop and all this stuff and we thought, "Oh, God. This is awful." And then she started to do the scene and Jim and I looked at each other like, "Good God, where has she been?"

Of course, one performer was a given before casting even began.

Allan Burns   I'm saying a lot about how talented everyone was in the show but nobody was ever more funny than Mary Tyler Moore. For somebody as attractive as she is to be that funny is really unusual. She's got a comedy funny bone that just constantly surprised us. We always kind of knew what she would do but she would do that plus a lot more. She cried better than anybody in the history of television. We were the luckiest guys in the world to have those people to work with. The audience just loved her. There was something so appealing about her. She was so feminine and yet so funny at the same time. Mary had an extra little zip of something.

David Lloyd   It was Jim Brooks who said, "Mary is so good, it's very hard to spot when she's a little off." Jim Brooks could spot little things and work with the actors.

Bill Persky   On *Dick Van Dyke*, Mary got some great opportunities to do more than set things up for Dick. She grew into it. She's famous for her crying. She learned from Carl. She didn't know how to cry in a scene so Carl told her, "Then try not to." That's where she got her fighting the crying. That became her signature crying. You couldn't be around Dick and Carl without it affecting your timing and learning what subtlety was and where the jokes were and to not overplay them. She went on from there and was a consummate comedienne. Everyone was always looking for a beautiful, funny lady. Mary was the combination of sexy and funny. She played against it. Her humor came in large part from never realizing how terrific she was.

It's one thing to find the right original cast, but long-running series also often need lightning to strike twice. While The Mary Tyler Moore Show *found Georgia Engel and Betty White to replace Valerie Harper and Cloris Leachman, the producers of* Cheers *found it necessary to replace one of their leads when Shelley Long left the show. Their success helped the show run six more seasons, one more than Long's tenure with the series.*

7. Gold Is What You're Always Going to Get

Allan Burns Georgia Engel was in *The House of Blue Leaves*. It's a wonderful play, it's the strangest play, so funny. She plays a starlet. She wears a hearing aid. And the batteries on her hearing aid go out. She's in a scene with three nuns. And she begins talking to these nuns in this Georgia voice and you know by the look on her face that she can't hear a word. She's got to carry on a conversation with three nuns without benefit of hearing. I don't ever remember tears in my eyes from laughing so hard at anything. I saw her in that play. And Treva Silverman also saw the play. We knew we had to use her. So Treva made up this character at a goodbye party for Rhoda. It was a very short scene. She had about four lines. We walked out to see the run-through and Mary grabs us and says, "Get her." Mary has a great eye for talent and wanting to spread the laughter around. Very generous about that. Boy, was Georgia good. And she's still good. She hasn't changed a bit. I ran into Wendie Malick a couple of weeks ago and she says to me, "Georgia Engel was on the show [*Hot in Cleveland*] this week and she's really like that." I said, "Yes, she's really like that." She is that character. Wow! What a talent. She's the most innocent person you've ever met. She's a devoutly religious Christian Scientist. Never married. That somebody can have a life in show business and come out the end of it not being touched by any of this stuff is amazing. She's probably heard it all but it goes right past her.

David Lloyd With *Cheers*, they got the right guy in Ted Danson. And Ted was clearly good. And Shelley Long, even though she was a tremendous pain in the ass to work with, was quite wonderful in the part. When Shelley left, Les Charles thought it would have been okay to end the show after five years but said he'd be damned if he was going to let her dictate when the show ends. With Kirstie Alley, they didn't know what she could do comically. The Charles brothers quoted Jim Brooks. Jim always said, "Hire the best actor, if in doubt about the comedy. The comedy will come." I'm not sure that's true in every case but it sounded good. So they read some people, they read a lot of people, obviously. And Kirstie impressed them but they didn't know what she could do that was funny. She was good and she had a smart mouth on her and they knew she could nail Sam, which she did in her opening episode. She cries in a very funny way. She cries and she whines. And she could be very funny doing that. That's just something they discovered. At least they knew she could be tough and could zing Sam. One of the things that they found out was that being hurt, being vulnerable, being unhappy, being *audibly* unhappy, she could be very, very funny. They didn't know that when they cast her.

Allan Burns   The character was written as a "Betty White type." Betty and Allen Ludden, her husband, were best friends with Mary and Grant. They used to come to the show and sit in the audience and laugh and go out to dinner with Mary and Grant afterwards. There was an episode that Ed. Weinberger, who was by now our producer, had written the script about the woman at the station who was the Happy Homemaker having an affair with Phyllis' husband. It was a hysterical script. Ed. was trying to cast it. Ethel would make comments and suggestions. She said, "Here's a wild idea. How about Betty White?" We said that to Ed. But he said, "What if she isn't any good?" And then it gets really sticky if she comes in and reads for the part. We can't make her read for the part, we'd have to cast her and that's taking a long shot. That could be awful. We bit the bullet. We didn't have anybody else. The reading around the table was very funny. We went down for a run-through the second day and Mary pulls us over and says, "You're not going to believe how funny she is. I don't believe it. I didn't know she was *that* funny. She's one of my best friends and I didn't have an inkling. She's a funny lady in real life.'" She could get the quip off, as she still does. She's very quick. She said, "You've got to find a way to get her in the show on a regular basis."

Like The Mary Tyler Moore Show, Bewitched *had a remarkably large, eclectic and talented cast that was well-liked by the series' writers.*

Rick Mittleman   I think Elizabeth Montgomery was terrific. She was perfect.

Paul Wayne   It was a lovely cast. I thought Dick York was terrific. I thought he was a wonderful Darrin. He got his first experience on Broadway. He was in *Inherit the Wind*. I loved working with Dick.

Jerry Mayer   Darrin changed. We were sorry to see Dick York go because he was more of a funny guy than Dick Sargent. But they were both nice guys. Agnes Moorehead was friendly. Elizabeth was very friendly. David White was a good actor. They were all friendly and would tell you that you write great. I got very friendly with Sandy Gould. She was very complimentary. We became very close friends. She had a great career. We were very close. I spoke at her funeral. She lived out in the Valley and she was friends with Cary Grant. He'd come over for lunch. I never got so

7. Gold Is What You're Always Going to Get

successful that I didn't get excited when I met important people. You never get blasé about meeting your giants.

Lila Garrett We used to have story conferences at Bill and Elizabeth's house. So I got to know Elizabeth that way. I never got to know Dick York. There was no evidence of his problems in his performance. I though he was brilliant. When he left the show, it was not the same show. The show never got over his leaving.

Fred Freeman Paul Lynde was hysterical. Paul Lynde always made us laugh. Geez. And Elizabeth was a lovely person who died too young.

Lila Garrett I loved him. We got to know him. Paul was genuinely a funny man with impeccable taste. Sweet and just hilarious.

Jerry Mayer Marion Lorne was a wonderful comedy actress. She was great. I loved her. She was in *Mister Peepers* and I always thought she was great. You'd always want to use her. She'd always get a laugh, even with moderate material. She was great.

Lila Garrett Agnes Moorehead was a hell of an actress.

While some amount of luck is involved in great casting, it's even luckier if the cast works well with the writers. David Lloyd's first long-term sitcom experience on The Mary Tyler Moore Show *was a happy one, which he — and other writers — soon learned would not always be the case.*

David Lloyd It was wonderful. There was no us and them, which very often besets a sitcom. Us, the writers, versus them, the actors. Or us, the actors, versus them, the writers. There was none of that on the *Mary* show. And, of course, they were wonderful people and we saw a lot of each other socially. And it was lovely. But I didn't know because it's the first sitcom I'd been on. I thought this was the way it was always going to be. And people said, "Oh, no. You're going to find out how lucky you are." And they were right. I had something of that experience finally with *Frasier*, but not until then did I. I mean, there was a lot of hostility, for example on *Taxi*, but I'm not mentioning any particular show. Not as happy a group. Not as much fun to be with. Judd Hirsch, when he finally won an Emmy, got up and thanked Herb Gardner and Paddy Chayefsky. What the hell kind of gratitude is that?

Jack Elinson I was lucky in not having bastards as the stars of shows. We used to get guys coming in saying, "I wish I didn't write this show. Those sons of bitches." I never got hit on the head that way. Stars themselves were all nice people. Because a lot of times you get a star that's a monster, like a Joey Bishop. Everybody knew about Joey Bishop.

Fred Freeman   Joey was a very limited talent to me. This was crazy. Joey played two people in one episode. It was him and someone that was his double. We were in watching dailies. At the end of the show, Joey would always turn to the camera and say, "Son of a gun." That was his signature thing. At the end of the show the two Joeys are talking to each other and the Joey who is the double says, "Son of a gun." And Joey said to us, "You can't go out on him. You've got to go out on me." We all looked at each other like we thought we were going out on you. He got furious.

Sam Denoff   He said, "The other guy is getting all the laughs."

Fred Freeman   He was just nasty. Garry Marshall helped him for a long time and then he got mad at Garry. Danny Thomas was a smart businessman. I remember one day he called us in because we were having trouble with Bishop and he said, "Look. I know he's crazy but we've got to get through this. It's a lot of money that we're talking about here."

Carl Kleinschmitt   He was also a very funny man. He could be very funny. He had a bright, quick mind. He could come up with lines on his own that were very clever. But in the human being department he was a little lacking.

Jack Elinson   Marla Gibbs on *227*, she was tough. She wasn't mad or anything but she wanted to do a lot of changes. She used to piss us off. While they were reading the first draft downstairs, we're upstairs. And we get pages from downstairs and there are new jokes from her without telling us. We don't mind people saying, "We had a thought. What do you think?" She just decided to write it and that's the way it was going to be. She was pretty cocky. I guess of all the stars, she was probably the one I loved the least.

Irma Kalish   Marla Gibbs really resented me. She was a good actress, though. She was fond of saying, "You're white. You wouldn't understand."

I Love Lucy *offers a perfect example of all the right elements coming together in a hit show. Possessing the soul of a clown, Lucille Ball was obviously the catalyst. However, she also had a perfect supporting cast, a top-notch technical crew, a very talented and experienced producer in Jess Oppenheimer and writers who understood her talents perfectly. Combining these elements with Ball's incredible focus and work ethic, she peaked as a performer — outshining*

7. Gold Is What You're Always Going to Get

everything she had done in radio and films and would do in subsequent television series.

Bob Schiller It was a pleasure to work on *I Love Lucy*. You write it, she'll do it. Not only will she do it the way you imagined it, she'll do it better than you imagined it. That's a bonus for a writer. Makes you almost believe that you wrote it. Lucy was indestructible until she got too old to play an ingénue. She played an ingénue in her sixties on her later shows.

Madelyn Davis You could see how funny she was with the audience in radio and also she had done some things in movies. She did *Miss Grant Takes Richmond* with Bill Holden and *Fancy Pants* with Bob Hope. We knew that she could do physical comedy. We had no idea how marvelous, of course, she was. The whole thing, I don't want to say it was an accident, but it all evolved and everything came together and it was an incredible thing that it all worked like that.

Bob Carroll, Jr. We were all at the right place at the right time.

Madelyn Davis We knew how to write for her and she was better than we had ever dreamed. And, the Mertzes worked. We wanted Gale Gordon and Bea Benaderet for the Mertzes because we worked with them on radio and they were both marvelous. But they both had contracts on other shows. They were not available and we started looking around. So it was all just serendipity. Not that Gale and Bea wouldn't have been wonderful but Vivian and Bill were perfect. They were more earthy. Gale always looked like a banker no matter what with a little moustache and the suits and all. He couldn't have ever played the guy who fixed the plumbing. So everything kind of just worked out now that you look back. We realized how great Lucy was so we started thinking about her that way. Right from the beginning we started doing physical stuff. When you're doing a show like that, you usually pick up all the qualities that the performer has. You see them do something funny, maybe talking around the table and you say, "Ah! We can use that." So you just soak up everything and use it for their character. Whenever she told a story, of course, she was marvelous. So we could see how she would act it out. She said that they were going to raise chickens and then they made the chickens pets and they couldn't kill them, so she said. "We have the oldest chickens in the Valley." And she got up and walked around like an old chicken. Well, we said, "A-ha!" And we didn't use it for ages but later we had her when they raised chickens out in Connecticut, we had her lead the little chickens and we used that. In person, when she did things, she acted them out. She never said real funny things, never made jokes. But physically, her face and her body were just marvelous.

Bob Schiller Lucy was never anything less than beautiful and feminine, even with a pie in her face. Remarkable talent.

Norman Lear revolutionized television comedy with mature themes and realistic, thoroughly flawed characters. After just a year and a half in sitcoms, Lear had three top-five shows in All in the Family, Sanford and Son *and* Maude. *Although the writing on his early hits was outstanding, it certainly didn't hurt that he cast three of the most legendary comedic talents in the history of television for the leads in those series.*

Bob Schiller Bea Arthur was brilliant. As good verbally as Lucy was with physical comedy. She just accepted the writing and she had infinite trust in Norman and the rest of us. Carroll O'Connor knew the Archie Bunker character better than anyone else. He knew the character a lot better than Norman knew it. Norman is from Boston and Carroll O'Connor was a real New Yorker. Actors really rarely in sitcoms ad lib. One that he did in the "Cousin Liz" episode, he is told that Cousin Liz is a "les" by Edith. And he's shocked. And he walks, storms into the living room and takes her partner and shakes her and says, "Why don't you people just stop?" And he walks back to Edith and says, "I think I straightened her out." He liked to think he was a writer. It's easy to add lines or subtract lines once it's written. Nobody likes to admit that they have writers. They like to create the illusion that they're the clever ones.

Paul Wayne Spectacular cast. There were a lot of things that Carroll O'Connor brought to it that weren't on the page. I remember talking to another one of the writers and he said when Mike Stivic was impotent, Archie was trying to tell somebody about his problem and he said, "He's stuck in neutral." That was Carroll's idea. That was his line. So he had a lot of stuff on his own.

Lila Garrett The cast was absolutely brilliant on *All in the Family*. I don't know how they found Carroll O'Connor. He was not that big of an actor when he got that part but he nailed it like nobody else could. And so did Jean Stapleton. You absolutely believed every single second that they were married and every single second of that marriage. And you also believed the children.

7. Gold Is What You're Always Going to Get

Jerry Mayer   They were great. All of them were great.

Austin Kalish   Jean Stapleton was wonderful. Carroll was a force. People were afraid of him. Norman was afraid of him, too. The staff was afraid of him. We finished a show and we looked into a room and there were 14 people sitting in a room, the whole behind-the-scenes staff. We said, "What are you doing? You're doing nothing." They said, "We're waiting for Carroll to have a thought." Fourteen people were waiting for Carroll to have an inspiration.

Saul Turteltaub   We worked well with Redd Foxx. We got along very well with him. We liked each other. Redd Foxx was a genius. What people never realized was that Redd Foxx was a great actor. He was so funny and a great comedian but he was a terrific actor. He was only 55 years old when he was playing that old man. He didn't walk like that. He made up that walk. He could do the comedy as well as anyone. He could act sorry or sad or whatever he was given. He was just wonderful.

Bernie Orenstein   We admired Redd from day one. He was very nice to us. He would not let anyone say anything derogatory toward us. We liked him a lot. He was about the funniest person I ever met. He would make it better than we wrote it. He was a lot younger than the character in the show. He was playing a guy about 70 when he was in his early fifties. He was very sharp. He knew a lot about humor and performing. He was great.

Rick Mittleman   Redd Foxx was a terrific performer. He has a lot of years experience performing. You turn a camera on, he goes to work. The relationship between father and son, I think you can't help but get a little bit of your own background into relationships like that. The shows turned out very well. I was very happy with the ones I did.

Writing television comedy often provided the opportunity to work with larger-than-life stars—some a pleasure, some, not so much.

Irma Kalish   *Anna and the King* was a nice show to write because Yul Brynner was a very nice guy. Really great guy. When we were filming, the Olympics were going on and the Israeli athletes were killed and he asked for a moment of silence.

Jerry Mayer   I wanted to write a *M*A*S*H*, obviously. Everyone did. I talked to Gene Reynolds, who was producing. Very nice guy. I wanted a meeting. But he said what they needed more than another *M*A*S*H* writer was someone to write for *Anna and the King*. It was with

Yul Brynner. He said, "If you do a good job on that, we'll have you come in and pitch stories for *M*A*S*H*." The producer was Bill Idelson. So I went in and I pitched a story where they're hunting tigers and the King is carried in a contraption and has his rifle. They make a mistake and drop him and the gun falls and he cuts his leg. They go in to the doctor and the doctor has to give him a shot. And he is so afraid of the shot that he faints. And now they have to hush up that the King fainted over getting a shot. Bill Idelson thought it was very funny because it showed that everyone has a weak spot. So Yul Brynner read it and said, "Who is this Jerry Mayer?" He couldn't believe I was making the King look like a coward. He didn't see the humor in it at all. And they told him he comes out in the end looking great. They did it and I had never met Yul Brynner. So Bill Idelson said, "He's kind of pissed at you, even though he's doing the script. So if you want to come and watch, stay in the shadows. You can't meet him this time." I came and watched and people were laughing. Then I wrote a second one and it was much better for him and he kind of forgave me.

Bob Schiller   I always used to say *The Red Skelton Show* was a wonderful job for any writer with no pride in his work. We would write a good script. The scripts were funny going in. He would fly in on Monday afternoon and see the script for the first time and do a run-through Monday night for the people at CBS. Filthy. He'd throw in dirty jokes and then retire to his apartment on Wilshire, get out his file and put in all old jokes. He had absolutely no sense of story. He was in the top 10 for years doing this. It was hard to believe anybody would take a perfectly good script and screw it up. There was a television columnist on the *L.A. Times* named Hal Humphrey and he interviewed us and we were talking about *The Red Skelton Show* and my partner said, "Working for Skelton is like going to junior high. It's good for three years." So Skelton apparently read the thing. We watched the show and the run-through was like 17 minutes over with the laughs. So Seymour Berns, the producer, says to Weiskopf, "You should have given Humphrey an interview every week. Skelton said, "I'll show those bastards. I'll read it exactly as they wrote it." He was wrong. We were right. But he stayed on the air for a long time. Skelton was nuts.

Rick Mittleman   There were about eight writers and every writer was asked to do about ten monologue jokes a week. Eighty jokes every week. He would look at them and maybe, if we were lucky, pick one or two. Then he would go out to his Rolls and he would get a portable file

7. Gold Is What You're Always Going to Get

of jokes out of the trunk. He was so insecure that he knew those jokes would work because he used them before and people laughed. That was Red Skelton. Very insecure. He'd do something wonderful. He was probably one of the best physical comedians ever. And when he was finished he was so insecure that he would have his producer, a wonderful gentleman by the name of Cecil Barker, standing next to the cameras and the minute the red light went off, Skelton would come running over to him and say, "How was I?" He was that insecure. This is what I would hear from people who were on the set. I didn't even meet Red Skelton. We got on the elevator at CBS Studio Center and that's the only time I got that close to him. He didn't want writers near him. He was from the old school and he was worried. He was quite a head case, really. He would have loved not to have writer credits. He wanted it to be "Written by Red Skelton" but the Writers Guild wouldn't permit that, of course. So we had to stay away. We couldn't even go to the show.

Fred Freeman I always regarded Gleason as one of the few people I met who was one of the old-time stars. He was bigger than life — physically and figuratively. I thought he was a genius because we'd put stuff together and we'd be in his dressing room a couple of hours before show time and he'd look at everything and he'd say, "This is shit. I can't do this." So we'd all look at each other like what are we going to do. He would go out there, pick the stuff he wanted to do and pulled it off. He was amazing like that. The show itself, quite honestly, was not particularly good. I happened to get in a very small elevator when he was in there. And the elevator got stuck. I tried to make small talk and he was like, "Just shut up, pal." He was a great talent.

Ed Scharlach I wrote a few years on *The Dean Martin Show*. He was probably the most naturally funny comedy performer, or one of them, that ever lived. He was not good when he had to rehearse things. He was brilliant when he was spontaneous. They would rehearse the show all week long with a stand-in for him. On Sunday he would come in and watch as they ran through the sketches. He had been learning the songs in his car or the golf course. So he knew the songs. They'd stage it in a simple way and he'd master it in one day. He'd get more out of the comedy than if he'd been there all week. He'd bring another element to it that was so wonderful. He was so charming and great with audiences. It was a little risqué for television in those days, which was fun to write for. That was one of the golden dream shows that I was associated with. Everything that you imagined was even more wonderful and funny when Dean actually did it. It was very thrilling.

Saul Turteltaub With Carol Burnett, she would work on the comedy. When you gave her a script you knew it was going to be better than when you gave it to her.

Sam Denoff We were doing a television adaptation of *The Man Who Came to Dinner*. Orson Welles was starring and we had Don Knotts playing the doctor. When we do the table read and Don Knotts starts to speak we hear this rumble from Orson's end of the table. And it keeps getting louder and pretty soon it's this eruption of laughter. He had never heard Don Knotts speak before. He'd been in Europe when *Andy Griffith* was on. And it was that way the whole time. He'd laugh every time Don Knotts opened his mouth.

Guest roles offered the opportunity to work with seasoned actors and up-and-comers alike.

Jerry Mayer In one episode of *The Facts of Life*, Charlotte's husband comes back. And looking through the actors in the big book with all the pictures, there was Robert Alda. I said, "This is the guy." Because when I went to military school in 1948 he was in *Rhapsody in Blue* and Gershwin was always a big hero of mine and there was Robert Alda playing Gershwin and now he's going to play Charlotte's ex-husband. I told him how I loved that movie. That was the height of his career. That was a lot of fun. Meeting your heroes and being on a level where they admire your talent. In another show I wrote for *The Facts of Life*, I wrote something where Natalie's grandmother came to the school to visit. It was a grandmother that was from Russia and Natalie was a little ashamed of her. In the show, she bonds with her. I said, "Let's get Molly Picon." They flew her in from New York. That was nice to have the power to make them understand that it might cost an extra thousand dollars but we should do it. We also had an episode of *The Bob Newhart Show* where they were interviewing secretaries, Teri Garr came in and I said, "She is great. She is going to have a great future." She didn't have a big part but she just glowed.

8

Like a Marriage: Collaborators

Writing a sitcom is a collaborative process. In addition to collaborating with producers, directors, actors and executives, most sitcom writers collaborated with each other, working in pairs.

Elroy Schwartz They wanted two writers. You went out looking for a partner because they wanted partners.

Fred Freeman It's like a marriage. You spend more time than you do with your wife.

Jack Elinson It's harder to write by yourself, much harder. I didn't write that many shows by myself.

Bob Schiller Bob Weiskopf, who I miss terribly, we worked together almost 50 years. When I met him, I said, "Hello." He said, "That's what you think." So I knew I'd found a partner. I knew we'd mesh. I always say the way to become a comedy writer is to think crooked, learn to type and find a funny partner. So I said, "I can type and you're a funny person, so let's team up." We were pretty much the same. It was not a thing where one did one thing and one did another. We were very, very similar in our tastes. There are so many things that were the same. Once when I thought I was drowning, his entire life passed before my eyes.

Bernie Orenstein I teach now at Long Island University about the history of television and one of my classes is totally about Weiskopf and Schiller. One of the unsung comedy writing teams of television. They're wonderful, the two Bobs. I always looked up to them. They were absolutely terrific writers. I would learn from them even in some cases where I was their boss.

Bob Schiller Weiskopf was a grump. He was a curmudgeon. He had written for Fred Allen and he loved that kind of sour humor. He hated everything—and particularly actors. He felt that actors were put on Earth just to screw up his lines. He once said to Carroll O'Connor, "Goddammit! You're not reading the line right!" And Carroll, who was always amused by him, said, "Bob, the problem with you is you're too sensitive." Weiskopf said, "If I were insensitive, I would have become an actor." Another time, we were walking back after a first read. It was our script and the actors had dogged it. They read it without any inflection. You can't do that with comedy. You have to act it. We're walking back to our offices, knowing we'll be up all night rewriting. Weiskopf says, "Bastards. Expletive, expletive, expletive." I said, "Bob, have a little compassion. They were up until 4:00 this morning, doing pickups. They're tired." He said, "Screw 'em. They're actors. Let them act not tired."

Carl Kleinschmitt I was introduced to Dale McRaven by Garry Marshall. Garry is a great guy for putting people together, for forming partnerships. He's a very collaborative kind of individual. He thought we could help each other more than trying to make it on our own. Dale and I both, strangely enough, had written sample scripts for *McHale's Navy* and given them to an agent Garry had introduced us to. I think Dale McRaven and I complemented each other. For me, comedy is about not going at something head-on. It's about the oblique. If you can see things from a slightly different point of view, that's more comedy than hitting it on the nose. Dale's humor is even more oblique than mine at times. Dale is not a guy you sit in a room with and say, "Oh, that's very funny." But he has a very kind of sly and clever outlook on life. A different outlook on life. To me, that's comedy. I don't want to listen to the same things everyone else says. I think comedy writers have a way of looking at things from a different angle than most people do. Dale and I broke up around 1969. It was the beginning of the Age of Aquarius and Dale decided he was going to be a hippie and I hadn't quite reached that point. So it was easier for me to work alone. We've remained friends. We just had dinner the other night.

Paul Wayne On *The Smothers Brothers* and *Sonny and Cher*, we used to revolve partners to see who would make the best partners. So I got to work with Steve Martin a lot. He was remarkable. He was very giving, remarkably giving. He knew where your talents were and appreciated your talents. He was a terribly, terribly nice human being. He was here every week playing chess with me and doing magic tricks with my children.

Lila Garrett Mort Lachman and I worked magnificently together. It was a thing of beauty. When he got the sound of a show, he did wonderful things.

8. Like a Marriage

In their long careers, it was often necessary for successful writers to find chemistry with a new partner.

Jack Elinson I know people think that with two writers one does nothing but construction and the other does the jokes but that's not the way that I ever found it with other writers. Just be funny. Find a good story first and find great scenes. If you're funny, you'll be funny alone. If you have a partner, you have two funny people. Charles Stewart was a very good writer. Norman Paul was terrific. He had written for *Burns and Allen*. He was just a funny guy, good with stories; he was kind of a nutty guy. He was a little wild. But what a great nut. I thought Norman Paul was great.

Ed Scharlach Tom Tenowich is a brilliant comedy writer. His sensibility was unusual and he had this phenomenal sense of humor, so we would come up with imaginative and funny things that stretched our comedy writing in a lot of ways.

Sam Bobrick Ron Clark is a great guy. A lot of fun. What he gave me was confidence. I don't think I had the confidence that I needed. When I worked with Billy Idelson, he was very, very positive about everything, what he wanted. He'd say what was going to work. He'd say what's not going to work. And I didn't have that much of a say. A little bit but I would say Billy was 70 percent the writer and I was 30 percent. I was very cautious about everything. In fact, when I had an idea I would kind of whisper it to Billy. He was an older guy and I was younger. As we went, I got more and more confident but I remember the first few scripts it took awhile. But I was very good with ideas so that's where I think it worked out well. I was coming to the end of the partnership with Billy Idelson. We just felt we were drifting, writing differently. I felt one way about his writing, he felt one way about my writing. It wasn't working out as much. He wanted to continue on half-hours. I loved variety shows. I went on *The Smothers Brothers Show.* That was a lot of fun. I started writing a lot of variety shows. Ron and I also had the same comedy rhythms. And writing became very, very easy for us working together. When you're writing with someone, you think one way yourself and another way when the two of you are writing. It was working okay but sometimes you want to go a little bit deeper than the two of you. By yourself you can go a little bit deeper into what things are. We went off by ourselves and we both did pretty well. But we remained friends. A lot of teams break up and they don't remain friends.

Fred Freeman Sometimes you learn a certain discipline from someone. I had never written jokes a lot. Garry Marshall was good at jokes. Garry made me write jokes. I learned how to write jokes. Every step of the way, if you're paying attention, you learn something else.

I obviously had a sense of humor of some kind. But it's like a trade. Garry and I were good partners because we were almost opposites in ways. We got along great and we still do. We still talk about once a week. We're still pretty close friends. Larry Cohen and I were both in an Army Reserve unit. We had similar points of view. We both liked satiric things. After we teamed up, our first assignment was *Gilligan's Island.*

Allan Burns Chris Hayward and I had a falling out. We got a chance to write a movie based on a book. We went and pitched our approach to it and got the job. Right after we left the office of the producer and we're about ready to get in our cars and Chris suddenly says, "I don't want to do it." We just got a movie offer. I said, "Why?" He said, "I don't have to tell you. I don't want to do it." What the hell? I said, "I think you owe me an explanation why." He said, "No. I don't. I don't want to do it. I'm going to go back and do *Get Smart.*" So I said, "Okay. But I don't think we can work together after this." He said, "Fine." I'm making him the heavy in this but I never had an answer. Chris went back and produced another year of *Get Smart*, did it very successfully and did a great job. I wrote the script. And as most screenplays are wont to do, it didn't get made. I was sacred to death to do it alone, but I did. Movies don't get made. Maybe that's why Chris didn't want to do it. He wanted the security of a series. I don't like to be negative about it because we became friendly again later. I don't want to besmirch his memory. He was a very funny man. He was just plain funny.

Arnold Margolin Allan and Chris were a great team. I first met them because they created *My Mother the Car*. Chris was a very witty, sarcastic writer. Allan was much more of the mold of what we were. He was a good writer — literate and funny. Obviously, his best work was on *Mary Tyler Moore*. We really enjoyed them. We spent a lot of time together. There was no jealousy or rivalry.

Allan Burns While I was panicking about writing a screenplay and what I was going to do, I got a call from Jim Brooks, who was a friend. We met though other writer friends. Chris and I gave Jim his first shot. He was writing documentaries for David Wolper. He had come out of the local CBS station in New York. He had the misfortune of the first thing

8. Like a Marriage

that he ever wrote being on *My Mother the Car*. That was his first script. He's done well enough since. He called me and said, "I wrote this pilot and I got together with Gene Reynolds. It was based on an idea Gene had. It's called *Room 222* and I'd like you to see it." I told him I'd moved on from television. I still had hopes my screenplay would get made. He was proud of it and he wanted me to see it and he had some other writers in to look at it. It was absolutely wonderful. I asked where I could line up. I wanted to write that show. I did freelance writing on *Room 222* and then Jim had a pilot. Jim was working on that and they asked me if I would produce the last seven or eight episodes of *Room 222* that first year. And I did. Through that relationship, Jim and I got to know Grant Tinker at Fox. He was a big fan of the show. Jim Brooks is the best writer I've ever worked with. We had some wonderful writers on *Mary Tyler Moore*—David, Bob, Ed., Stan — but nobody's as good as Jim. He just never settles for anything but the best. It used to provoke me because I would say, "We've got it here." And he would say, "No, we can do better." I'm not telling anybody anything they don't already know, but look what he's done since — *Taxi, The Simpsons,* and he's still on that, *The Tracey Ullman Show,* which was full of wonderful, brilliant, inventive things with a brilliant actress. He was aggravating. We fought. Not a lot, but we did fight. A writing team fights. That's part of the deal. I've never seen anybody who was right more than he was. He never settled for anything but the best.

Classic sitcom writers had the perfect place to learn — in the room with experienced writers and producers who gave them valuable lessons in the trade.

Rick Mittleman You would sit at their knees, so to speak, and they would nurture younger writers. Mort Lachman, Milt Josefsberg, Larry Gelbart, Carl Reiner. A lot of poor writing you see is because people don't have experience and don't learn from the real masters.

Jerry Mayer Being around a lot of creative people, everyone's learning what works and what doesn't work. Marty Ragaway on *The Facts of Life* said something that I'll always remember. He said, "Never tell a joke on the way to a joke." Where you're telling a joke that has a good payoff and you think of something funny on the way, don't do that. Because it takes away from the eventual big laugh. It's wisdom. That's how the mentoring is done. Someone makes a good suggestion that makes sense and you listen to them.

Carl Kleinschmitt Fred Fox and his partner, Izzy Elinson, had written for Burns and Allen. They had worlds of experience. They were working on the same shows as Dale and I when we were neophytes. I don't know if that happens today that you get to meet legends. Fred stuttered. When you first met Fred he would give you his phone number. And he would say, "If nobody answers, it's me." They were funny people. That was how we learned. We worked with older, wiser and, many times, more talented people than ourselves. I grew up with radio. I was 10 or 12 before television came in. I think that's a generational difference. I *hear* comedy while many other people *see* it.

Irma Kalish   In those days, you paid your dues. You were getting your education.

Austin Kalish   It was like a college for writers. You learned.

David Lloyd   I didn't really learn how to do a decent script until I got to *The Mary Tyler Moore Show*. Jim Brooks, the resident genius, gave a short course. For a long time, when I was pitching a story, I would just sit down and keep him talking. The thing was, he wanted to talk with me and go home. And I'd say, "Just one more thing," and get him to talk some more. And I would write down everything he said and I'd incorporate everything he suggested into the script. And then when he read it later he would laugh and say, "This is wonderful stuff." Jim is concerned with character. He spews dialogue off the top of his head. He would spew stuff which didn't have jokes as such; it was just wonderful character stuff. Because I knew I could put jokes in it. I had been training to do that for 13 years. So I could pop the jokes in. But learning how to do the character stuff, I learned so much from him and from Allan. Jim is just such a larger-than-life character that it's unfair to Allan. I think Allan has suffered under that, of being sort of the silent partner there. But Allan is very creative and very nice and funny. He was good, too. I'm afraid that's going to be on his tombstone. He was good, too. Allan's terrific. He kept us tasteful and classy. Because Jim would go overboard and Allan would bring him back. Allan is a very nice, generous, classy individual, like Grant Tinker, which is what made that whole experience wonderful.

Jerry Mayer   I admire Jim Brooks tremendously.

Ed Scharlach   He's brilliant. Nearly everything he has touched has been well thought out and brilliant and successful. After all these years he still keeps his hands in *The Simpsons*. He's got his Oscars and he's got his Emmys. Some of the most brilliant shows in television history and in movie history. When he first came to town, he sat and watched Peggy and

I write a script. So I think that two-hour experience, of course, propelled him into the success he's had.

Bill Persky   The first script he wrote for *That Girl*—that was the only script we got that we never changed a word.

David Lloyd   A mantra of Jim if somebody was pitching something, he'd sort of frown and say, "I've seen it." And, that killed that. In other words, we're not going to do that because he'd seen it. He'd say, "We've got to find a different way, a way to switch it. We'll go a different way." And that was a good lesson to learn. This is probably the only criticism I'll ever make of Jim Brooks, is that somewhere, I think maybe the fourth season of *Taxi*, with Jim and Latka we left Earth behind. I think it was Jim who suggested that Jim be a psychic and Latka have multiple personalities. Okay! All right! They weren't weird enough? It wasn't a weird enough show without doing that?

Sam Denoff   Carl Reiner had very strict rules. He always said that the best comedy comes from telling the truth. Something may be funny, but that doesn't mean it could happen. He would say, "You're two of the most neurotic, crazy people I know. Don't have Rob do something you wouldn't do. Don't have him doing something stupid." We never had people climbing out on windowsills. If we were going to have them do crazy things, we had to make it a dream. When Carl didn't like something, he would write "RR" on the script. Rotten writing.

Bill Persky   Carl Reiner was dying because he was doing all the work by himself. He had some outside writers but they were just giving him something to fix. He liked the way we wrote. He had a very specific approach. The way we wrote fit in. Carl loved the idea of writing the truth and seeing what was funny about it rather than trying to write jokes. I think that there's a little bit of Carl Reiner in everybody who ever worked for me. When you are influenced by somebody, you make it your own but it still has that element of Carl for me. Then the way I ran my shows, it's in the DNA of probably 50 writers out there. There's a little trace of Carl in a lot of people's work.

Carl Kleinschmitt   What I learned from that whole experience, and I appreciate in hindsight now, is that Carl Reiner as well as Sheldon Leonard, who was running the Thomas-Leonard empire—I learned that there are some people in the business who are decent and honest. I went from there into the rest of my career that there weren't many people like that. Both of them were gentlemen. From Carl Reiner what you get is that it is not always about a punch line, it's about people interacting, characters interacting. It's not just ciphers making jokes; it's people being unique characters. That was a good lesson. Carl Reiner liked to take jokes out. He didn't like jokes, per se. He liked the attitudes.

Bernie Orenstein He'd always say, "The joke won't work if it's not based in truth." He was very helpful. Carl is a comedy maven. He knows what he's talking about. And a nice guy.

Sam Bobrick Sheldon Leonard brought people in to run shows and he trusted them.

Bill Persky He had a style of working that became part of my approach to things. What I got from Sheldon was that he would never say something was wrong. He would say, "I think we could do something a little different or better here." And Carl was that way, too. No one ever said, "This is lousy." I never said that to anybody I ever worked with. I got a positive approach to working with people from them. There was only one time Sheldon didn't do that. You could always tell during the reading whether Sheldon was happy or not because he would take very deep, prolonged breaths when he didn't like something or something wasn't working. There was one particular day when he never stopped with those breaths. When the reading was over, he said, "This is a disaster." That's the only time I ever really heard him say anything negative.

Fred Freeman Sheldon was very sweet. A nice man. It was such a pleasure to work for decent people. But even if you worked for a prick, if you have your eyes open, you're going to learn something if they are good in certain areas. You find some very angry, hostile people who are good at comedy.

Sam Denoff Sheldon Leonard was the greatest executive producer ever.

Jack Elinson He was as good as any writer. He knew the sort of things that were wrong or right. He was very into the scripts. Each script before it got done, Sheldon had his say in it. We made our changes. Danny, when he had time, came up with thoughts himself. They left it basically to the writers. Sheldon never sat down and rewrote a script. Sheldon was a strong man so the network people didn't start up with him.

Carl Kleinschmitt There were legendary people, like Milt Josefsberg, who wrote for Jack Benny on the radio. When I first got a peek at the business, there were really legendary radio writers who had moved into television. For me it was like being a kid in the candy store. These guys knew what they were doing. At that time you could learn from somebody who had a great deal of experience. They were very generous.

Fred Freeman Milt Josefsberg had great stories. I loved to hear the stories about Bob Hope and Jack Benny. He claimed credit for the famous Jack Benny joke about your money or your life. It's always nice being around people that are experienced because sometimes they can tell you what won't work and how to make it work. That's where you learn.

Sam Denoff Milt Josefsberg gave us a big break on *The Joey Bishop Show*. He was really a kindly man and so helpful when we were just beginning. It was an education to work for someone who was truly experienced.

Bill Persky Milt was a sweetheart of a guy. He was a gentle, gentle soul and Joey Bishop almost killed him. You couldn't have had a worse person for Milt Josefsberg to work for because he took everything so personally. He was a real gentleman and very funny. Very kind. He would never criticize. He was very supportive and he came up with great jokes.

Bob Schiller Milt Josefsberg had one eye. And Milt used to work with Mort Lachman on *All in the Family*. Mort was the head writer. And Weiskopf once threw a telephone. Weiskopf was inept manually. He couldn't figure out the hold button on a telephone. He was constantly cutting off people wanting to talk to him. So, his phone rings one day and he says, "It's for you." He doesn't know what to do with the hold button. I said, "Push the hold button." He says, "Here, you do it!" And he throws it at me and missed me by that much. And I said, "That's it." And I walked into Mort and said, "I can't work with him any more." And he's sitting there with Milt. He said, "All right. I'll work with Bob. And you work with Milt." I said, "Yeah, but you owe me one eye."

Arnold Margolin We learned some things that first year from a man named Chuck Stewart. He was very patient with us. There were three shows we were on and we learned something on every one of them. None of the shows were very good and none of them survived the first season. On *My Mother the Car* we learned from Rod Amateau. Another one was *O.K. Crackerby* with Burl Ives and that was the one that Chuck Stewart was producing. He came out of the Danny Thomas school that was doing *Andy Griffith* and he taught us things. And then we were doing *The Smothers Brothers Show*. This was before their variety show. This was a sitcom where Tommy played an angel. We had as our producer a man named Fred de Cordova, who went on to produce *The Tonight Show* for many years with Johnny Carson. We learned a little bit from all of them. In our second season, we spent one day with Garry Marshall and Jerry Belson. They had a show called *Hey, Landlord* and they gave us an episode. Jim and I wrote a first draft. We were very proud of it and we turned it in and they called us in and said, "Boys, this is not going to work. You guys are good but you don't understand how this needs to go." They basically sat down with us for one day and went over that script line for line and it finally dawned on us that good comedy comes out of reality. It's just taking the things that happen to real people in real life and finding the fun in them. That was all we needed. Our careers really took off from that point. It was an interesting epiphany.

Carl Kleinschmitt   Garry Marshall is a good teacher. And he's patient and a generous man. He helped us and he helped Arnold Margolin and Jim Parker and he helped his partner, Jerry Belson. Further on, when he had *Happy Days* and *Mork & Mindy* and *Laverne & Shirley*, he started a lot of other writers in the business. Garry is a wonderful team player. Jerry Belson was always crazy and we miss him greatly. They were very funny as a writing team. They did well with pretty much whatever they did. Belson had a dark sense of humor but goofy. Jerry spoke to a comedy writing class and his opening line was "I've got mine, screw you." Jerry, in his own way, was one of the funniest people I've ever encountered. He could do dumb things that were absolutely funny but he also had a very smart mind and a quick wit. And he had a depth just beyond jokes. He always made me laugh.

Arnold Margolin   Jerry had a very dark sense of humor. He and Garry, who has a totally opposite sense of humor, made a very interesting team.

Ed Scharlach   Their meetings were always great. So smart and so funny. Really great in terms of putting stories together. They complemented each other. Jerry was naturally funny with a dark sense of humor. An offbeat sense of humor. He found a way to make things a little different from the world we know. Garry was a wonderful writer and very, very hard working and ambitious.

David Lloyd   I adored the Charles Brothers. I had worked with them on *Phyllis*, *Bob Newhart* and *Taxi*. Glen and Les Charles ran a very tight room on *Cheers*. I think, the first season, there were a number of rewrite nights where I was home in time for dinner, which is very rare. They kept things moving along. We had a very small staff the first year. They were so invested in it, it was theirs and they were damn sure it was

8. Like a Marriage

going to work. I'm very happy, I was very lucky to be on those shows. It's so much harder to write a successful pilot and get it on than to get someone else's successful pilot and attach yourself to it and then write episodes once the characters are established and we know what their relationships are. I had a very easy road of it because I had been lucky enough to land on several good shows run by good people who knew exactly where they wanted to go with the show. And I could just get in there and be a hired gun.

Sam Bobrick Aaron Ruben was my first producer and I would say that he was the best producer I ever worked for because he told you what he wanted, you gave it to him and he said, "Thanks." Ninety percent of your script would be up there. I admired Aaron Ruben a lot. I thought he was great.

Saul Turteltaub Aaron Ruben was a brilliant writer.

Carl Kleinschmitt Aaron Ruben was a gentleman. He was very helpful, very nice. Not the funniest guy in the world. Kind of a serious guy. But he knew what he wanted to do with *Gomer Pyle* and apparently it worked. Aaron was very nice and very businesslike. And very good at what he did. He was excellent with story and character.

Fred Freeman Aaron was very nice. Aaron was very good. Of course, sometimes he made us crazy but they were more concerned with character, which is right. That's where I learned a lot.

Jack Elinson They didn't have a producer on *Andy Griffith* when we started. Aaron came in. He was very nice. We had some scripts written for him. That was very helpful. He was there for five or six years and he worked his ass off. He was always behind the door. I would say he was a huge influence. He really did quite a job.

Bernie Orenstein Aaron Ruben made *Sanford and Son* what it was. When we came in, the relationships among the characters were already established. As were the kinds of stories and the style. That credit goes to him.

Rick Mittleman I had nothing but good luck with Aaron. We would sit together, just the two of us. He had a terrific story mind. I never had any problems. He seemed to like what I did, with a minimal rewrite. He did all the rewriting. In those days, there weren't big staffs. *Gomer Pyle* was Aaron Ruben. Period. There wasn't even another producer who worked with writers. He did all the work. And that's when they were doing thirty plus shows a year.

Allan Burns Leonard Stern is kind of a legend. I've said to his widow a million times, "Leonard saved our lives." I don't know how but in some of this stuff we had written he saw something that he liked. Leonard was a great producer and a terrific writer and a great mentor, a great teacher. I learned about character. Everything I'd written up to that point was sort of jokey and one-dimensional.

Lila Garrett Leonard Stern was an inspirational man. He was a marvelous man. He was very opinionated and very specific about what he wanted. You could see that on *Get Smart.* The characters were very, very specific. He's one of the people that I most enjoyed working with.

Sam Bobrick Leonard was a very nice man. He had the greatest vocabulary in the world. I never knew what the hell he was talking about. He used words that weren't even in the dictionary. Terrific guy. He did *The Honeymooners.*

Irma Kalish Leonard Stern was a very good friend of ours. He liked our writing but he always had to change something. He hated to let something go out of his hands.

Austin Kalish We did a pilot for him. It was called *Parker and Son.*

Irma Kalish It was a good concept. It was about a guy who had a family with older children and then had another baby. It was about an older man getting along with his young son.

Austin Kalish So we worked with him and finished our script. Then he wanted some changes. So we went in and worked with him on changes. We wrote the final, final, final script. No more changes.

Irma Kalish The network wanted to get it.

Austin Kalish This was nighttime when we finished it. That was it for everybody. It was the perfect script for this point. So we said we'd take it to the post office at the airport, because that was the only one that was open. He said, "No, I'll take it. That's out of your way." I said, "We've gotta take it because if you take it, on the way, you'll make a change." So we took it to the airport.

David Lloyd It was great working with my son, Chris, on *Frasier.* I was very impressed by him. He knew what he was doing. I was very proud. When he first wanted to be a writer. I was doing a pilot for Witt-Thomas called *Moscow Bureau.* I took him along to the run through. When we were stuck for a joke, he pitched one. I put it in the script and told them. Then he wrote funny letters to Paul Junger Witt and Tony Thomas and they hired him as a trainee. He was with them for a number of years and wrote for *The Golden Girls.*

8. Like a Marriage

Fred Freeman   I liked Norman Lear a lot. He was very good to work with. We were warned when we did the screenplay for *Start the Revolution Without Me* that Norman and Bud Yorkin would change everything. They didn't touch a word. Norman was very respectful of the script. We were flattered.

Jack Elinson   He was a very smart guy. He could find things that we couldn't find. As we went on and on, he came around less because he was getting so many shows. How many shows can one person oversee? When he was peeking in on *Good Times*, he had a lot to say. On *One Day at a Time*, it was great, he just left us alone, period. I don't think he was that crazy about the show. He figured if that's what they want, give it to them.

Bob Schiller   Norman was great. Norman was a pioneer. He'd try anything. He was around a lot. He was at all of the run-throughs and the shows and the pickups. We'd all sit in a room together to get a story. And oftentimes, Norman was still there. He was pretty good with stories. Not a good joke writer.

Lila Garrett   Norman was a very good friend of mine. It was wonderful to work with him because he was one of the few people who wore his politics on his sleeve and survived it. Not only survived it but prevailed. He never lied about who he was. He never pretended. Yet he was able to succeed brilliantly. So I think of all the heroes of my era, he would be the number one.

Austin Kalish   Working with him at the beginning, it was great.

Irma Kalish   He knew us from earlier. He was very big on women's rights. And very big on having black writers.

Fred Freeman   Sherwood Schwartz was a terrific producer because he would say, "I like this. I don't like this. That's good. That's not good." It's a pleasure to work with someone who doesn't say, "I don't know, it doesn't work for me. Try something else." You learn from someone who you may not have their taste but you learn how to adjust to do what they want because it's their show. That's an important lesson.

Elroy Schwartz   Sherwood was not a good brother. There's something I never understood. I don't understand it to this day. If you asked the industry, of the writers that Sherwood worked with, they would all tell you he was a great guy. The two writers he screwed were his two brothers. I don't have any answer for that one. If there was a pat on the back to give, he gave it to himself. I didn't admire Sherwood at all. I don't think

Sherwood was a good writer. There wasn't any depth to his characters. The Skipper was Skipper. You don't know where he came from to this day. You know nothing about his upbringing or his parents. Or Gilligan's. You just accepted them as bigger than life caricatures. *The Brady Bunch*—you don't know where the mother and father came from. There's no structure to them. I don't think Sherwood was a good writer.

Rick Mittleman It was a pleasure to work with Larry Gelbart. He was a very nice, decent guy. Not at all insecure. He was one of the best in the business. He treated people very well. And he was extremely talented. I remember seeing *Something Happened on the Way to the Forum* on Broadway and he co-wrote that. And he was very young and had a Broadway show. He was just good. He did *Caesar's Hour* and he was always one of the best in the business. Very soft-spoken and quiet and funny.

Bob Schiller Larry Gelbart is a superb writer. When I first me him on *Duffy's Tavern*, he was a 16-year-old child.

Carl Kleinschmitt The reason *M*A*S*H* was so good was Larry Gelbart. He was, bar none, the smartest and quickest in terms of thoughts coming out and jokes coming out of any person I've ever worked with. He'd been working in the business since he was in high school. His father was a barber and passed some of his jokes to Danny Thomas. He was a brilliant writer and a hell of a funny guy to be around.

Fred Freeman Marvin Marx had written *The Honeymooners* and he was a very funny guy. I quit *The Joey Bishop Show*—we had gotten in a big fight—Garry and I and I think two other writers were in the room and I said something like, "I don't agree with that. I don't think that works." And Joey said, "If you don't like it, you can get out of here." So after a year of Joey, I said, "You know, I think I will." I told Garry he could stay. Garry, who was very firm-headed, stayed. So Garry and I broke up then. Marvin Marx quit about a month or two later. Then he took me back to New York for *The Jackie Gleason American Scene Magazine*, which was sketch comedy. I went there for four or five months. Marvin was funny. He used to do a Gleason imitation because he was rotund. He could do all the mannerisms and everything. He was very talented. He followed Gleason to Miami. Marvin died one of those weird deaths when he was in Miami. I never heard of anyone dying this way. A pigeon shit in his ear and it got to his brain and killed him. I had never heard of that before. That's what I was told. I've heard that from a few people so I assume it's true. But he was very funny. I liked Marvin a lot.

8. Like a Marriage

Paul Wayne   Danny Arnold was a genius. Danny was just marvelous. I loved working with Danny. Working with Danny was just a revelation. He was so talented. Very gifted. He could conduct a story meeting and a call to his bookie simultaneously and be brilliant at both. His sole purpose was to draw out the very best in whatever kernel of competence he could discern in lesser talents. "Here's a better idea," he'd say to one of yours and damned if it wasn't. You'd jot it down and the telephone would ring, he'd pick it up and spend 10 minutes with his bookie. He'd hang up, he'd say, "Where were we?" You'd tell him his terrific idea; he'd bang his fist on his desk and say, "Wait! Wait! I've got a better idea." And damned if he didn't top his own sensational idea. Then he'd get an even better one.

Carl Kleinschmitt   Danny Arnold was nuts. In a good way. He was very hyper. One day I was pitching stories to him in his office and we're eating lunch and he thought he was having a stroke. It turned out the straw from his drink had gone up his nose. Another time he told me he was driving in his car with his wife and his wife was talking and unconsciously he reached for the radio and kept trying to turn the volume down.

Bill Persky   It was like working in the midst of a hurricane. Danny was brilliant but he was very didactic and very opinionated and his opinions were very good. He was a real force. He did some great, great stuff. He was right more than he was wrong. We were less in the middle of *That Girl* the two years he was there. If we had tried to have a battle of wills, it would have gotten in the way of things. He was doing terrific and Marlo trusted him.

Fred Freeman   We worked with Danny Arnold on *Bewitched*. I know when he did *Barney Miller* I heard he made his writers crazy. It was a good show. As crazy as Danny was, he was talented. But the writers were there all night half the time. It's your living but you want to have a life.

Arnold Margolin   It was maddening. He was a lovely guy but he drove us crazy. He drove everybody crazy. He just had that reputation. He had to do it himself.

Lila Garrett   When we talk about genius, we have to include Danny Arnold. He was very opinionated. He never really liked what other people wrote. But he did like other people. And I learned a lot from Danny Arnold. I was a script editor for him on *Barney Miller* for about 10 minutes because I left that job to write my own movie of the week and he let me out of my contract and I was very grateful for that. Time spent with Danny Arnold was like spending your time in a master class. There was never a time when you didn't learn about comedy from him. He just saw the humor in everything and the irony in everything. He was very open and communicative. Very opinionated and critical but never cruel. It was a real gift.

Rick Mittleman Danny was probably one of the most difficult of all. He was extremely enthusiastic and very proud of his work. He demanded a lot of writers. He had a temper. I remember once he said, "Come with me." We were going to have a story conference and we went over to Glen Glenn Sound to see some of the dailies. There's a scene where a character comes through a gate and he doesn't like the squeak of the gate. So we spent I don't know how much time working on the squeak of the gate and I've got a story to work out and we're listening to a gate squeaking. That was Danny.

Sam Denoff Danny just couldn't believe that anyone else might have an idea that was better than his. He just had to do it his way. It could be something as simple as one frame of film.

Bob Schiller I'm sorry that Jess Oppenheimer isn't here to share in the acclaim for *I Love Lucy*. He was a brilliant producer. Jess knew vaudeville. They used a lot of vaudeville things that Jess knew. Like, "Slowly I turned." Everything went through Jess' voice.

Bob Carroll, Jr. We learned a lot from him.

Paul Wayne Mickey Ross and Bernie West were just absolutely brilliant and lifelong friends. Mickey was my friend until the day he died. He and Bernie West were my mentors. Bernie was a great joke teller. He loved to laugh and tell jokes. He had a great style and a great sense of comedy, rhythm and timing. Mickey, on the other hand, was exactly like me. He was 10 years older and had 10 years ahead of me on all those studies that I studied. We found so many things in common. He loved most of the stuff that I loved. I would mention something that I had read and he knew it. An opera, a symphony. He knew it all. I just worshipped him. There was a great deal that he taught me. He was one of those guys that didn't take notes, he just remembered. When he was giving notes, he'd do everything from memory. I would never write a word without Mickey's input. I do remember from time to time sounding like an idiot. There was a *Three's Company* that got so confusing and it got so loaded with people running around. We just forgot about who was where and who was going where and who was coming from where. And I had said the most stupid thing that you could possibly conceive. It embarrasses me to think about

8. Like a Marriage

it now. I said, "Isn't there a hell of a lot of traffic going on?" And Mickey said, "Isn't that what we want?" It's what's funny. Going in and out of doors and people going and confusion and traffic and bumping into each other. That's what it's all about. We had lunch every Friday until he died. Three days after our last lunch, he died. I still miss him.

Elroy Schwartz   I don't know how Ed Hartmann did what he did. I'd come in and start pitching ideas. Let's say I came in with 10 storylines that were one or two sentences. After I finished with ten of them, he'd say, "Let's go back to number three." And then he would practically dictate an outline. He was working on an outline in his head while I was pitching the other stories. So I'd take notes and go home and write the script. The whole thing took me four days.

Allan Burns   Treva Silverman had worked with us on *Room 222*. She was a friend of both Jim and mine. I have just always loved her work. Talk about a strange and wonderful mind. Hers is just unique. She was the first writer we hired on *Mary Tyler Moore*. She just connected with the show and the character of Rhoda and what it is like to be a single, Jewish woman. Treva just pushed us in the right directions about Rhoda. And the sense of humor that Rhoda had was something that nobody ever wrote better than Treva. She wasn't the fastest writer in the world but it was always worth waiting for. Very unusual mind. Treva once said she was walking in Manhattan the night of the great blackout and she said she thought it was her fault somehow. She was the only woman who was ever on staff. We had other good women writers who freelanced — Charlotte Brown, Sue Silver, a number of good female writers.

Elroy Schwartz   My brother, Al, was probably one of the most prolific jokes writers in the United States. Al was a great joke writer. He wouldn't know a story if he tripped over one. He was a very nice, gentle man. He had more cheeks to turn. At one time he was king of the comedy writers. He was a pleasure to work with. We worked well together.

Allan Burns   Jay Sandrich found Ed. Weinberger for us. Dave Davis was our producer and one of our really good writers with Lorenzo Music the first and second season when they came up with *The Bob Newhart Show*. We knew we were going to lose them. Jay was doing work on other shows, among them *The Bill Cosby Show* where Cosby was a gym teacher. He said this guy is really good, an unusual talent, very funny. He's gruff and curmudgeonly but he's wonderful. He brought us a screenplay that Ed. had written and it was just wonderful. It never got produced. I don't know why. We knew we had to meet him and hire him because he was just too good. He and Stan Daniels got the foibles of the characters. They got inside them. Just terrific writers. We were really fortunate who our staff was.

David Lloyd Joe Keenan is wonderful. He writes great farce. He is better at it than I am and he can figure out 19 ways to get the entrances and exits and make it all logical.

Paul Wayne David Lloyd was wonderful. Very funny man.

Bob Schiller Susan Harris is a wonderful writer. She's superb.

Fred Freeman Susan's very prolific and very good. I think she paid a price for it physically.

As writers gained experience, they paid the favor forward and helped young writers learn.

Jack Elinson *a.k.a. Pablo* was a good show. That was nice to have a Mexican family. It was different. We only got six shows. One of the writers on it was a guy who's now a big shot in the movies — Paul Haggis. He's a big smash now.

Jerry Mayer Paul was a writer on *The Facts of Life*. But he went along to write a lot of hour shows. Obviously, he was a very good writer from the beginning.

Bob Schiller We gave a lot of people their first break — Charlie Hauck, Elliot Schoenman. They all mentioned that at the Weiskopf tribute. Thad Mumford, a lot of them. Since we broke in and somebody helped us, we were always conscious of the fact that somebody is wanting to break in and it's our obligation to help them. And I was happy to see they all acknowledged it.

Arnold Margolin My biggest success in television was the number of writers I was somehow involved in helping them get started in the business. I do have a good eye. That was one of the great things about *Love, American Style*. It gave me the opportunity to give a lot of new writers jobs. Dennis Klein went on to do shows for Garry Shandling. He's a very good writer. Lorenzo Music and Dave Davis wrote on *Love, American Style*. I gave Susan Harris her first comedy writing job. I had known Susan before she was a writer. I thought she had a good sense of humor. I don't think I'd seen anything she'd written. I thought she was smart and witty and she came up with a good story. She showed me that she knew where the fun was. She turned out to be great. As we all know. And turned out to have

8. Like a Marriage

a hell of a career. That was the good thing about that show. You could hire new writers to do an eight-minute show and if they screwed it up, you didn't get hurt too badly. Neal Marlens, who ended up creating *The Wonder Years*, wrote me a very funny letter when I produced *Private Benjamin* and I helped him get an agent.

Madelyn Davis   On *Alice*, we had Vic Rauseo and Linda Morris, who went on to *Frasier* and won some Emmys.

Bob Carroll, Jr.   And Mark and Mark.

Madelyn Davis   Solomon and Egan.

Bob Carroll, Jr.   They respected us.

Madelyn Davis   We didn't make them work all night or all weekend. I think that's why they liked us.

Not every writer needed a collaborator. Some found they could accomplish more on their own.

Carl Kleinschmitt   I never had a problem working by myself. You miss the input of a partner. But I liked the idea of being a writer where you sat down and wrote. Or messed around for several weeks and sat down and wrote it and handed it in the next day. I liked writing at the time. It worked okay.

Paul Wayne   Sometimes it was nice to go off on my own because no one was telling me what to do. Sometimes you would go crazy thinking you knew something was funny and you knew it was right but no one else did and you didn't understand why everyone else didn't see it your way. It happens to everybody, no matter how much experience you have. They're just as certain about their ability to tell what's funny as you are. So you try it. Try it at another angle. And another angle. But don't obsess about it.

Elroy Schwartz   I realized Rocky had his way of writing and I had mine. So we split up. Sherwood insisted on having two writers on episodes of *Gilligan's Island*. A script had gotten in trouble and he wanted it rewritten. So I did a rewrite on a script over a weekend. He gave me the problem on Friday and I gave him a script on Monday. And they shot it starting on Wednesday. I called and said, "Can I get an assignment?" He said, "Who are you working with?" I said, "I just wrote that damn script by myself over a weekend. Why do I need a partner?" And he agreed for me to work by myself. I wrote 13 *Gilligan*s and became script editor at the end. That was my start of working alone.

Arnold Margolin Jim Parker hated producing. He couldn't do it anymore. I spent three years producing and directing. I hated the thought of writing alone. I hadn't written anything alone. After Jim and I split up, I was really terrified of doing that. I was going to supervise a team of writers on a pilot and they couldn't do it. I was stuck having to write it. I called Jim and told him he had to help me write it. He told me I could do it. I only did it because he said he would help me write the second draft. That was like Dumbo's feather. It gave me the courage to do it. I wrote the first draft. But he thought it was great and said I didn't need him.

9

The End of It: Retiring

Experience was once highly regarded in television. In 1979 the entire writing staff of All in the Family *was in their sixties. Now it is increasingly difficult for older writers to land jobs. Although many classic writers retired of their own volition, others left the business due to ageism.*

Ed Scharlach   Coming in, ageism was the fact that most writers were in their forties and we were in our early twenties. We were looked upon as these young, green, inexperienced writers. These days it's the other way around. The writers that work in these large rooms until late at night are young. There are some wonderfully talented people but once they're around 40, they're replaced by the new ones. Ironically, around 40 is when their craft and skill start to kick in and could probably make a better show. I was lucky enough to keep working constantly until my mid-sixties. I feel blessed because a lot of people I know didn't.

Jack Elinson   It's very scary. It's run by all the kids now. If you're the producer and you're young, who are you going to get to write? More kids. You're not going to bring an old guy in. Never in a million years could a 60-, 70-year-old guy come in with an idea for a show. They'd throw him out the door. Even forties and fifties is not considered young enough. It's ironic because a lot of the youngsters learned from watching television.

Irma Kalish   I think we lasted beyond what some others did through ageism in the industry. We were still working way past 40.

Saul Turteltaub   Our careers ended in 1998. I was 66 and Bernie was 67. We still felt, as I do now at 80, that I could go in and produce a show. You don't feel any different, you don't think any different. You still have the same mind. We went in for a couple of jobs and we didn't even get an interview. That was the end of it. We were in our late sixties. Guys in their fifties were getting turned down. It was ageism without question.

Bernie Orenstein   I'm just finishing my second novel so apparently

I can write. But there is a feeling of being uncomfortable about being around writers who have already heard the joke that you're trying to sell. I've been on shows where young writers will want to do some story and I'll say, "I did that 20 years ago. I can't do that again." I think they are missing the boat by not hiring certain more experienced writers to work on some of the shows. They think old is old-fashioned. It's a shame. That is not to say that the young writers are not excellent. There are some really good young writers.

Rick Mittleman   I had a good enough reputation that I kept working well into my sixties. What happens is that there is a changing of the guard. I never directly felt the impact but I felt it indirectly. Younger people come in and like to surround themselves with friends and associates in their own age bracket. They don't want writing lessons from old timers. It's just the nature of things. I had no bitterness. It was rampant. No one just ever told me I was too old.

Sam Bobrick   When I wanted to go back, no one knew me any more. I was an old-fashioned writer. I was in my sixties. I was very lucky that I had a long career.

Fred Freeman   Sometimes things pass you by. Some people adjust to it and some people don't.

Arnold Margolin   It's there. It's a reality. In comedy it clobbers you probably before it does in drama. I think it's just a fact of life. I think it exists among writers who run shows and network executives and the studios. It's a matter of socialization. Nobody likes to give notes to their Grandpa. I think it's just a natural order of things. I had a great career. I worked for 40 years in Hollywood. That's a long time to be steadily employed doing anything. I think I had a longer career than most people employed today. They just don't keep them around as long. I'm grateful that I got into it when I did. It was a great time to be in the business.

Carl Kleinschmitt   I think it's not so much ageism as such, it's the fact that the people who run the business are of a different generation and are much more comfortable working with their peers.

Sam Bobrick   I feel sorry for someone who's a writer and stops because he can't get work. I think it does something to you. Unless you've got all the money in the world and you just want to enjoy it. I enjoy writing. I think you need something to do.

Lila Garrett   I didn't get out of television. Television got out of me. By the time I stopped working in television, except for an occasional script

9. The End of It

here and there, I was about 60. I did feel age prejudice. I felt it very strongly. More than I felt prejudice against women.

Elroy Schwartz The tough thing has been, since around 1980, when I finished with *General Hospital*, I went to Irv Schechter and said, "What now?" And he said, "Nothing. You're too old." I had just turned 60. He said, "You won't get an agent. You won't get any assignments." I didn't believe him but he was right. Ageism came into the industry then. I kept hitting my head against the wall, trying to get an agent, trying to keep in the business and I wasn't able to. I'm a much better writer than I was 40 years ago. Much better. I know that. I'm comfortable with that. I enjoy writing.

Some former television comedy writers have beaten ageism by writing fiction or memoirs and teaching comedy writing. Others found second careers as playwrights.

Sam Bobrick What happened to me was I was teamed with Ron Clark and we were writing the *Kraft Music Hall* in New York. Ron and I had a great time together. We were hired for the summer show and they'd do a show every 10 days. We used to write two of them in a day because they were so easy. While we were there we wondered what we should do in New York. So we decided to write a play. And we wrote this play called *Norman, Is That You?* It lasted on Broadway for just a couple of weeks. The critics killed us, mostly for being television writers. New York critics hated television writers at that time. We thought we had the biggest hit ever because the audience was roaring. The reviews were just atrocious. I remember picking up the newspaper and reading about a guy who brutally murdered some woman in Carnegie Hall, stabbed her and threw her down the elevator shaft and then I read our reviews and I realized that they were nicer to that guy than they were to us. Once I wrote a play, I was hooked. I just loved writing plays. I love going off and doing something different and not being regimented with the same half-hour. Most of the time, I worked for very nice people and I did have a good time writing for TV. I just didn't feel satisfied writing for TV. I would say my heart was in the theatre. My partner and I had four failures on the Broadway theatre but still on the east coast, we were playwrights. One time when we were in the air, I said, "If our plane goes down east of the Mississippi, we die as playwrights. But if it goes down west of the Mississippi, we die as gag writers."

Paul Wayne I got interested in my roots. I started writing plays.

Jerry Mayer I had been writing for some time and earning a good living. By now I was 53 or 54 and when you get to be a certain age, with some exceptions, you kind of get edged out as the young people come in. So I started writing plays. That's all I do now. I've written eight plays. It doesn't pay like television but it's more gratifying because you don't have people telling you what you can and can't do.

In spite of a few regrets, I found classic sitcom writers to be a happy lot. Not only did they give audiences an immense amount of pleasure, they enjoyed the ride themselves.

Jerry Mayer It's a lot of fun. It's a lot of hard work. It's endless. We used to hit a brick wall and stay up until three or four in the morning. Not see your wife and kids for a week when you have a tough show. It's fun and it's for younger folks, I think.

Sam Bobrick At least you're laughing while you're working.

Lila Garrett It's fun to laugh with someone all day.

Irma Kalish I couldn't imagine getting up in the morning and doing anything else. It was always fun to get up and go to work, whether it was to write or go to the set.

Saul Turteltaub It was very successful. I'm basically a family person. I'm married and have two children. I would go to work, come home and have dinner with my wife and kids. Life as a comedy writer was good because I was doing what I wanted to do. That was terrific. This was doing something that was fun. There was a little bit of fame involved. It makes you feel good, of course.

Bernie Orenstein I had the experience of working with some of the most talented, wonderful people — writers, performers and producers. And I made a life for myself in an industry I loved.

I do get a kick out of things like when we were going up an elevator and a young person said, "Are you Turteltaub and Orenstein?" We said, "Yes." He said, "You guys are a legend." Well, that's worth a lot.

Carl Kleinschmitt It's better than a regular job. It was fun. It was a pretty good run.

Index

Numbers in **_bold italics_** indicate pages with photographs.

ABC 20, 106, 122, 125, 128, 135, 149–150, 154, 168
Adams, Don 70–71, 85, 140
Addams, Charles 130
The Addams Family 11, 13
African-American writers 31, 112, 199
ageism 1, 207–209
a.k.a. Pablo 204
Albert, Eddie 164
Alberto-Culver 145
Albertson, Jack 110
Alda, Alan 22, 68, 172
Alda, Robert 186
The Aldrich Family 35
Aletter, Frank 135
Alexander, Jason 139–140
Alice 4, 7, 13, 51, 58, 124, 150, 205
All in the Family 1, 9, 10, 11, 40, 42, 54–55, 60–61, 64, 68, 79–81, 85–86, 88–89, 106, 118, 134, 182–183, 195, 207
Allen, Fred 187
Allen, Gracie 161, 192
Allen, Marty 21
Allen, Steve 18, 21, 24, 28
Alley, Kirstie 177–178
All's Fair 132
Amateau, Rod 152, 195
Amen 5, 129
American Graffiti 123
Amory, Cleveland 149
Amos, John 112, 169–170
Amos 'n' Andy 19
Amsterdam, Morey 67–68
Anderson, Louie 146
Andrews, Julie 6
The Andy Griffith Show 6, 10, 12, 15, 29, 37, 48, 59, 60, 64, 71–74, 82, 97, 105, 110, 166–167, 171–172, 186, 195, 197
Angell, David 82
animation writing 16, 22, 28–29, 130, 152
Aniston, John 174
The Ann Sothern Show 5, 72, 102, 104

Anna and the King 183–184
Apple Pie 12, 148
Archie Bunker's Place 5, 106
Arden, Eve 132, 164
Arnaz, Desi 35, 64, 66, 102, 104, 156
Arnie 13, 77, 155–156
Arnold, Danny 89, 127, 161, 201–202
Arthur, Beatrice 79, 182
ASCAP 123
Asher, William 69–70, 179
Asner, Ed 78, 90, 173, 174
The Associates 149
Astaire, Fred 63, 134
Aubrey, James 115–116
Auntie Mame 156

Baby, I'm Back 59, 133
Bachelor Father 13
Baddeley, Hermione 132
Baer, Art 129
Baker, Cecil 185
Baker, Herbert 56
Baker, Joby 41, 157–158
Bakula, Scott 8, 138–139
Ball, Lucille 2, 18, 20, 46–47, 60, 64–66, 67, 87, 88, 102–103, 104, 141, 180–182
Ballard, Kaye 132
Barefoot in the Park 125
Barney Miller 11, 113, 161, 201
Batman 126
Beetle Bailey 22
Belson, Jerry **_15_**, 26, 45–46, 74, 83, 108, 123, 126, 196
Benaderet, Bea 181
Benjamin, Richard 159–161
Benny, Jack 166, 194, 195
The Benny Goodman Story 21
Benson 10
Berle, Milton 19
Berman, Shelley 173
Bernardi, Herschel 77, 155–156
Berns, Seymour 184

Index

Berry, Fred 112, 168
Bessell, Ted 125–127, 165
Best of the West 152
The Betty White Show 142–143
The Beverly Hillbillies 117, 161
Bewitched 10, 11, 12, 13, 25, 27, 41, 48, 55, 59, 60, 61, 66, 68–70, 100, 145, 178–179, 201
Big Eddie 134
The Bill Cosby Show 203
The Bill Dana Show 140
Billy Budd 105
Bishop, Joey 23, 27, 31, 37, 66, 93, 108, 180, 195, 200
Bloodworth-Thomason, Linda 34
The Bob Cummings Show 5
The Bob Newhart Show 5, 9, 11, 60, 78, 186, 196, 203
Bobby Parker and Company 165
Bobrick, Julie 146
Bobrick, Sam *10*–11, 20–21, 29, 37, 39, 43, 53, 54, 55–56, 57, 62, 69–70, 71–73, 85, 105–106, 113–114, 144, 146, 158, 163, 167, 189, 194, 197, 198, 208, 209, 210
Bochco, Steven 156
Bolger, Ray 20
Boone, Pat 30
Booth, Shirley 144
Borgnine, Ernest 119
Bosley, Tom 123
The Boys 145, 163
The Brady Bunch 13, 200
The Brady Bunch Hour 153
Brennan, Eileen 150–151
Brennan, Walter 76, 111
Brezhnev, Leonid 136
The Brian Keith Show 32, 146
Bridget Loves Bernie 151
Brill, Marty 104
Broadway 11, 38, 49, 61, 92, 94, 110, 140, 141, 154, 155, 166, 169, 172, 178, 200, 209
Broadway Danny Rose 162
Broadway Open House 25
Brogan, Jimmy 156–157
Brooks, Albert 165
Brooks, James L. 8, 36–37, 74–78, 90–93, 98, 142, 148, 149, 163, 176, 177, 190–191, 192–193, 203
Brooks, Mel 70, 150
Brown, Charlotte 107, 203
Brunner, Bob 150
Brynner, Yul 183–184
Buckley, William 132
Bull, Sheldon 154
Bullock, Jimmy 109

The Bullwinkle Show 7
Bupkis 6
Burditt, George 10, 43, 85
Burnett, Carol 8, 56, 186
Burns, Allan 7–*8*, 21, 28–29, 43–44, 49, 70–71, 74–78, 90–93, 98, 108–109, 130–131, 135–136, 138–139, 145–146, 147–148, 152–153, 158–161, 163, 169, 173–177, 178, 190–191, 192, 197–198, 203–204
Burns, George 161, 192
Burrows, James 91
Burton, Richard 103

Caesar, Sid 6
Caesar's Hour 67, 200
Cameron, Kirk 169
Camp, Hamilton 159
Candid Camera 8, 23
Captain Crunch 7
Captain Kangaroo 21
Captain Nice 150
Carey, Ron 134
The Carol Burnett Show 5, 56, 63
Carrey, Jim 8, 136
Carroll, Bob, Jr. 1, *3*–4, 20, 31–33, 35–36, 39, 46–47, 49, 51, 57, 64–66, 87, 102, 103, 132, 151, 181, 202, 205
Carsey, Marcy 128
Carsey-Werner Productions 154
Carson, Johnny 22, 24, 30, 195
Carter Country 111
Carvey, Dana 138
Cassidy, Jack 159, 161
Cat on a Hot Tin Roof 84
Catch-22 150
Caucus of Television Writers and Producers 160
Cavett, Dick 24
CBS 20, 53, 64, 66, 74–77, 90, 91–92, 96, 97, 103, 115–116, 133, 134, 135, 137, 138, 140, 145, 146, 148, 156, 159, 161, 163, 184, 190
Chaplin, Charles 103
Charles, Glen 98, 141, 177, 196
Charles, Les 98, 141, 177, 196
Chayefsky, Paddy 179
Cheers 5, 81–82, 98, 109, 129, 139, 141, 175, 176, 177–178, 196
Chekhov, Anton 94
Chicken Soup 154
Chico and the Man 16, 109–110, 111
CHiPs 13
Clark, Ron 11, 146, 163, 189, 209
Clooney, George 115, 139–140
Coastocoast 165

Index

Coca, Imogene 6
Cohen, Lawrence J. 12–13, 42, 72, 74, 116, 132, 162, 190
Cohn, Mindy 114
Colby, Barbara 141
Cole, Carol 140
The Colgate Comedy Hour 9, 19
Colodny, Les 130
Conried, Hans 116
The Continuing Story of the Shameful Secrets of Hastings Corners 163–164
Conway, Tim 119, 163
Cooley High 111
Cornell, Lydia 109–110
Cosby 8, 50, 102, 104
Cosby, Bill 6, 11, 104, 203
The Cosby Show 104, 124, 154
Cosell, Howard 108
The Courtship of Eddie's Father 11, 13, 14, 122
Crane, Harry 26, 27, 108, 126
Crenna, Richard 18, 111, 132, 174
Crosby, Bing 63
Cullen, Bill 22
Curtin, Jane 124, 145, 172
Cyrano de Bergerac 40

Daly, Tim 110
Dana, Bill 140
Danes, Claire 158
Daniels, Stan 141, 142, 149, 162, 191, 204
Dann, Michael 74–76
The Danny Kaye Show 26
The Danny Thomas Show (sitcom) 5, 12, 29, 31, 48, 51, 82, 172
The Danny Thomas Show (variety series) 20
Dano, Linda 134
Danson, Ted 81–82, 177
Davenport, Bill 1
Davis, David 26, 77, 169, 174, 203, 204
Davis, Madelyn 1, *3*–4, 18, 20, 31–34, 35, 36, 39, 46–48, 49, 50, 51, 57, 58, 64–66, 87, 102, 103, 124, 132, 151, 181–182, 205
Dawber, Pam 108, 141
The Dean Martin Show 16, 106, 185–186
Death of a Salesman 84
The Debbie Reynolds Show 103
December Bride 19
de Cordova, Fred 195
DeLuise, Dom 151–152
Denoff, Sam 6–*7*, 23, 24–25, 30, 40, 45, 59, 62, 64, 66–68, 74, 93, 94, 95, 108, 124–125, 126, 128, 151, 156, 157–158, 163, 171, 180, 186, 193, 194, 195, 202
Designing Women 34
Desilu Cahuenga Studios 41, 67

DeVito, Danny 168
DeWood, Mitch 21
The Dick Cavett Show 30
The Dick Van Dyke Show 6, 12, 13, 14, 27, 37, 38–39, 47, 48, 60, 61, 64, 66–68, 74, 93–95, 108, 124–125, 157, 158, 170–171, 176
Diller, Barry 122
Diller, Phyllis 25, 135
directing 6–7, 12, 29, 32, 52, 55, 58, 59, 91, 128, 152, 164, 206
Disney 114, 134, 158
Doc 48, 147
The Donna Reed Show 13, 24
Don't Call Us 162–163
The Doris Day Show 6, 13, 14, 16, 115
Double or Nothing 22
dramatic series writing 13, 16, 208
Drescher, Fran 158
Dru, Joanne 156
DuBois, Ja'net 113
The Duck Factory 135–136
Duckman 16
Duffy's Tavern 17, 19, 129, 200
Dugan, Dennis 133
Duncan, Sandy 134–135
Dussault, Nancy 104, 109

The Ed Wynn Show 20
Egan, Mark 205
Eisenhower & Lutz 138
Elias, Michael 11
Elinson, Iz 17, 20, 191–192
Elinson, Jack 1, 5–*6*, 17, 20, 29, 38, 39–40, 42, 48, 51, 52–53, 55, 64, 71, 73, 82, 97, 105, 110–111, 112, 114, 115, 123, 125, 140, 152, 156, 166, 169–170, 171–172, 179–180, 187, 189, 194, 198, 199, 204, 207
Elliott, Peggy 16, 27, 44, 126, 160, 192
Ellison, Bob 55, 142–143, 191
Emmy award 5, 6, 7, 8, 23–24, 56, 81, 92, 99, 149–150, 160, 173, 179, 192, 205
Empire 12, 132–133
Empty Nest 13, 16, 108–109, 167, 168
Engel, Georgia 93, 173, 175, 176–177
Engel, Peter 113–114
Entertainment Weekly 4
E/R 139–140
Everybody Loves Raymond 53

F Troop 9, 118–119
The Facts of Life 6, 9, 11, 114–115, 172, 186, 191, 204
Family Affair 9, 13, 120–121, 169
A Family for Joe 137

213

Index

Fancy Pants 181
Fedderson, Don 121
Feldon, Barbara 71
Ferrell, Conchata 139
Fields, Kim 133
Finley, Patte 148
1st & Ten 14, 129
First Impressions 12, 136–137
The Flintstones 11, 13
The Flip Wilson Show 5, 56
The Flying Nun 9, 10, 13, 40, 121–122
Flynn, Joe 119
FM 138–139
Fonda, Henry 121, 136
Fonda, Jane 106–107, 132
Fontaine, Frank 21
Forsythe, John 76, 121
Foster, Phil 23
Four Star Television 144–145
Fox, Charles 123
Fox, Fred 1, 191–192
Foxx, Redd 81, 85, 101, 140, 168–169, 183
Frasier 5, 77, 82, 99, 107, 139, 168, 179, 198, 205
Frawley, William 181
Freeman, Fred *12*–13, 22–23, 31, 37, 40, 42, 48, 55, 56, 58, 59, 61, 66, 69, 72, 74, 85–86, 94, 97, 108–109, 116–118, 132–133, 135, 136–137, 162, 163–164, 165, 166, 167, 168, 171, 179, 180, 185, 187, 190, 194, 195, 197, 199, 200, 201, 204, 208
Freeman, Kathleen 151–152
French, Victor 111
Frey, Leonard 152
Friedman, Paul 70
Fritzell, Jim 97
From a Bird's Eye View 148
Funny Face 123, 134–135
Funt, Allen 23

game show writing 7, 13, 20–21, 22, 29
Ganzel, Teresa 136
Garagiola, Joe 25
Gardner, Ed 18
Gardner, Herb 179
Garland, Judy 63
Garr, Teri 186
Garrett, Brad 137
Garrett, Lila 11–*12*, 22, 30–31, 32, 34, 38, 52, 55, 59, 61, 68–71, 79–80, 85, 102–103, 116–117, 121, 133, 161–162, 170, 179, 182, 188, 198, 199, 201–202, 208–209, 210
The Garry Moore Show 20
Gary, Carol 154
Gaynor, Mitzi 11, 172

Gelbart, Larry 1, 96, 149–150, 191, 200
General Hospital 209
The George Burns and Gracie Allen Show 19, 189
Gerber, Roy 83
Gershwin, George 186
Get Smart 8, 11, 13, 70–71, 85, 113, 150, 190, 198
The Ghost & Mrs. Muir 151
Gibbs, Marla 180
Gilford, Jack 136, 148, 162
Gilligan's Island 9, 12, 13, 31, 48, 59, 103, 115–118, 190, 200, 205
Gleason, Jackie 8, 32, 185, 200
Glen Glenn Sound 202
Gless, Sharon 156
Gobel, George 21
Goldberg, Whoopi 82
The Goldbergs 35
The Golden Girls 198
Gomer Pyle, U.S.M.C. 6, 11, 13, 14, 67, 105–106, 111, 197
The Good Life 12, 132
Good Morning, Miss Bliss 11, 114
Good Morning, World 41, 157–158
Good Times 6, 9, 14, 112–113, 133, 169–170, 199
Gordon, Gale 102, 181
Gorme, Eydie 21
Gould, Elliot 139
Gould, Harold 123, 125
Gould, Sandra 178
The Graduate 150
Grady 140
Grammer, Kelsey 82, 168
Grant, Cary 178
Green Acres 13, 27, 161
Greenbaum, Everett 97
Greenberg, Jeff 82
Griffith, Andy 29, 71, 73, 166–167, 171–172
Groh, David 107–108
Growing Pains 16, 169
Guestward, Ho! 156
Gunn, Moses 113
Gunsmoke 118

Haas, Ed 130–131
Hackett, Buddy 28
Haggis, Paul 204
Hagman, Larry 132
Hamer, Rusty 172
Happy Days 16, 110, 123, 167–168, 196
Harper, Valerie 78, 90, 107, 173, 175–176
Harris, Susan 46, 204
Harry and Maggie 164
Harry and the Hendersons 6

Index

Hartman, Lisa 141
Hartmann, Edmund 31–32, 120–121, 203
Hauck, Charlie 204
Hawn, Goldie 6, 157–158
Hays, Robert 138–139
Hayward, Chris 7–8, 43–44, 70, 130–131, 159–160, 190
HBO 14, 88, 129
He & She 8, 16, 70, 158–161
Hecht, Ken 150
Hee Haw 76
Hemphill, Shirley 111, 112
Hemsley, Sherman 129
Henry, Buck 70, 150
Henry VIII 162
Hepburn, Katharine 136
Here's Lucy 4, 102, 103
Hey, Landlord 56, 196
Hillerman, John 142–143
Hirsch, Judd 99, 179
Hitler, Adolf 164
The Hogan Family 9
Holden, William 181
Holliday, Kene 111
The Hollywood Palace 8, 30, 63
The Hollywood Squares 144
The Honeymooners 198, 200
Hope, Bob 16, 18–19, 79, 181, 195
Horn, Alan 164
Hot in Cleveland 177
The House of Blue Leaves 177
Houseman, John 149
Howard, Ron 71
Hughes, Barnard 147
Humphrey, Hal 184
Hurst, Lew 36
Hyde-Pierce, David 82, 168
Hyde-White, Wilfrid 149

I Dream of Jeannie 9
I Love Lucy 1, 4, 5, 18, 29, 31, 34, 35, 39, 46–47, 49, 57, 60, 64–66, 79, 87, 180–182, 202
I Spy 13, 67
Idelson, Bill 10–11, 29, 43, 184, 189
In the Heat of the Night 111
Inherit the Wind 178
It Takes a Thief 13
It's a Long Way to Tipperary 93
It's About Time 153
It's Garry Shandling's Show 6
Ives, Burl 195

Jackée 169
The Jackie Gleason American Scene Magazine 12, 185, 200

Jackson, Janet 113
Jacobi, Lou 101
Jacobs, Seaman 1
Jake and the Fatman 13
Jay Ward Productions 7, 28–29, 130
Jewison, Norman 23
Joelson, Ben 128–129
The Joey Bishop Show 6, 12, 14, 26, 30, 67, 108, 180, 195, 200
Johnson, Georgann 164
The Jonathan Winters Show 129
Jones, Anissa 120–121
Jones, Henry 141
Josefsberg, Milt 1, 191, 194–195
The Judy Garland Show 30
Julian, Arthur 1, 129

Kahn, Bernie 11
Kahn, Madeline 146
Kalish, Austin 1, *9*, 19–20, 31–34, 42–43, 44, 47, 49, 54, 58, 59, 80, 88–89, 109–110, 112–113, 116, 118–119, 120–122, 146, 156–157, 164, 169, 172, 183, 192, 198, 199, 205
Kalish, Irma *9*, 19, 31–34, 42–43, 44, 47, 49, 52, 54, 79, 80, 81, 88–89, 109–110, 112–113, 115, 118, 120–121, 122, 146–147, 156–157, 164, 169, 180, 183, 192, 198, 199, 207, 210
Kanter, Hal 21
Kaplan, Gabe 143
Karen 149–150
Kate & Allie 7, 8, 58, 124, 145, 172
The Kate Smith Hour 19
Katon, Rosanne 140
Kaufman, Andy 25, 162
Kaufman, George S. 164
Kavner, Julie 169
Keaton, Buster 100
Keenan, Joe 204
Keith, Brian 32, 121, 146
Kennedy, John F. 27
King, Mabel 111–112
King, Perry 133
King Features 22
Kiss Me, Kate 141
Klein, Dennis 204
Kleinschmitt, Carl 14–*15*, 26, 27–28, 37, 45–46, 47, 50, 51, 52, 53–54, 59, 60, 67, 68, 83–84, 93, 95, 105–106, 108, 122, 123, 127, 128, 129, 134–135, 148–150, 153, 158, 161, 171, 172, 180, 188, 191–192, 193–195, 196, 197, 200, 201, 205, 208, 210
Klugman, Jack 83–84, 100, 143
Knight, Ted 109, 173, 174–175

215

Index

Knotts, Don 11, 29, 71–73, 76, 97, 164, 166–167, 186
Koock, Guich 143
The Kraft Music Hall 209
Krazy Kat 22
Krinski, Sandy 12

Lachman, Mort 11, 188, 191, 195
Landesberg, Steve 148
Lane, Nathan 138
Lange, Hope 104
Larroquette, John 101
Lassie 173
Laverne & Shirley 148, 196
Lawrence, Steve 21
Leachman, Cloris 30, 90, 141–142, 173, 176
Lear, Norman 5, 21, 37, 54–55, 78–81, 82, 85–86, 88, 89, 111, 112, 123, 133, 148, 164, 168, 182, 199
Leeds, Howard 1
Leonard, Frances 148
Leonard, Jack E. 28
Leonard, Sheldon 29, 39, 48, 51, 67, 71–72, 82, 134, 148, 158, 193–194
Lester, Jerry 25
Lewis, Jerry 9, 19–20, 21
Lewis, Shari 8, 21–22, 23
Lewis, Juliette 137
Lewis & Clark 143
Liebmann, Norm 130–131
The Life of Riley 19
Life with Bonnie 6
Lillie, Beatrice 135
Linden, Hal 164
The Little People 32
A Little Romance 8
Living in Paradise 164
Lloyd, Christopher 198
Lloyd, David 4–5, 24, 30, 36–37, 41, 47, 48, 49, 51, 54, 55, 57, 64, 76–77, 81–82, 90–91, 98–99, 107, 110, 129, 134, 141–143, 147, 148, 149, 152, 162–163, 165, 168, 169, 175, 176, 177–178, 179, 191, 192, 193, 196–197, 198, 204
Long, Shelley 81, 176, 177
Lorne, Marion 179
Los Angeles Times 184
Lotsa Luck! 151–152
Lou Grant 5, 8, 48, 78, 150
Louise, Tina 116, 117
Love, American Style 8, 11, 14, 16, 52, 122–123, 128, 159, 204
The Love Boat 13, 14, 128–129
Lowry, Judith 141
The Lucille Ball-Desi Arnaz Show 4, 5, 66, 87, 104

The Lucy Show 4, 5, 11, 13, 102–103
Ludden, Allen 178
Lynde, Paul 135, 144, 172, 179
Lyons, Leonard 18

MacGyver 13
MacMurray, Fred 121
Macnee, Patrick 133
Magnum, P.I. 143
Mahoney, John 82
Make Room for Daddy 5
Malick, Wendie 177
Mama 35
The Man Who Came to Dinner 186
Margolin, Arnold 14, *15*–16, 25–26, 44, 45–46, 50, 51, 52, 56, 59, 60, 71–73, 77–78, 97, 122–123, 126, 127, 128, 138, 144, 145, 150–151, 153, 154–155, 159–161, 164, 166–167, 169, 172, 190, 195–196, 201, 204–205, 206, 208
Marie, Rose 67
Marlens, Neal 205
Mars, Kenneth 159
Marshall, Garry 12, *15*, 22–23, 26, 27–28, 31, 32, 45–46, 56, 74, 83, 108, 123, 126, 180, 188, 190, 196, 200
Marshall, Penny 148
Martin, Dean 9, 19–20, 186
Martin, Millicent 148
Martin, Steve 147, 188
The Mary Tyler Moore Show 4–5, 8, 11, 13, 16, 30, 36–37, 48, 55, 57, 64, 67, 74–78, 79, 85, 90–93, 98, 141, 142, 148, 161, 173–177, 178, 179, 190, 191, 192, 203
Marx, Marvin 200
Marx Brothers 84
*M*A*S*H* 11, 13, 14, 41, 60, 68, 78, 80, 91, 96–97, 135, 140, 142, 149, 150, 155, 172, 183–184, 200
Mason, Jackie 154
Matlock 13
Matthews, DeLane 139
Maude 5, 9, 11, 37, 65, 79, 85, 88, 96, 182
Mayberry R.F.D. 13, 73
Mayer, Jerry *11*, 25, 28, 39, 41, 42, 46, 52, 54, 55, 60, 68, 69–70, 77, 78, 80, 90, 91, 96, 114–115, 128–129, 141, 151, 172, 178–179, 183–184, 186, 191, 192, 204, 210
Mayo, Whitman 85, 140
McDonnell, Mary 139
McGavin, Darren 165
McHale's Navy 6, 11, 13, 25, 30, 119, 130, 188
McKeon, Nancy 114
The McLean Stevenson Show 154–155
McLeod, Gavin 78, 173

Index

McRaven, Dale 14, *15*, 26, 28, 45–46, 67, 93–94, 108, 137, 28, 142, 188, 192
Me and the Chimp 163
Meader, Vaughn 27
Merman, Ethel 63
MGM 55
Miller, Tom 134
The Million Dollar Duck 134
Mills, Alley 149
Mills, Donna 132
Miss Grant Takes Richmond 181
Mister Peepers 164, 179
Mr. Sunshine 134
Mitchum, Robert 137
Mittleman, Rick *13*, 23–24, 36, 38–39, 40, 41, 46, 48, 50, 53, 58, 61–62, 63, 67, 69, 71, 81, 82–83, 85, 95, 96–97, 99–100, 105, 111, 119, 126, 151, 155–156, 158, 162, 171, 178, 183, 184–185, 191, 197, 200, 202, 208
The Mod Squad 76
Modern Family 80
Monday Night Football 108
The Monkees 8, 29–30
The Montefuscos 133–134
Montgomery, Elizabeth 69–70, 166–167, 178–179
Moore, Garry 20
Moore, Mary Tyler 6, 74–78, 90, 92, 93, 99, 146, 148, 155, 157, 166, 171, 173, 174, 176, 177, 178
Moorehead, Agnes 178–179
Morison, Patricia 141
Mork & Mindy 16, 99, 106–107, 149, 171, 196
Morris, Linda 205
Morrow, Karen 141
Morton, Joe 140
Moscow Bureau 198
Mostel, Zero 136
The Mothers-In-Law 4, 132
Mozart, Wolfgang Amadeus 41
MTM Enterprises 74, 78, 139, 142
Mulligan, Richard 109, 167
Mumford, Thad 204
The Munsters 7, 130–131, 153
The Munsters Today 14
Murder, She Wrote 13
Murphy Brown 149
Murray, Warren S. 104
Music, Lorenzo 203, 204
My Favorite Husband 4, 18, 35–36
My Favorite Martian 9, 11, 13, 30, 119, 145
My Mother the Car 26, 77, 152–153, 191, 195
My Three Sons 9, 13, 31–32, 121
My World and Welcome to It 158, 161–162

NAACP 81
Nabors, Jim 105–106
The Nanny 158
National Institute of Health 88
NBC 21, 81, 113–114, 134, 137, 139, 143–144, 148, 152, 153, 155, 164, 165, 168
Nelson, Haywood 141
Nettleton, Lois 146
The New Dick Van Dyke Show 6–7, 8, 16, 102, 103–104, 170–171
The New Yorker 41, 130
Newhart, Bob 78
Nicholas, Denise 133
Nicholl, Don 80
Nichols, Mike 150
Nielsen, Leslie 96
A Night at the Opera 84
Night Court 139
Nixon, Richard 150
No Time for Sergeants 105
Norman, Is That You? 209
Not Until Today 165
Nye, Louis 21

Occasional Wife 12, 135
O'Connor, Carroll 182–183, 187
The Odd Couple 13, 14, 16, 61, 82–84, 99–100, 143, 150, 153, 168
Oh Madeline 146–147
O.K. Crackerby 153, 195
On Golden Pond 136
On Our Own 163
On the Buses 151
One Big Family 57, 144
one-camera sitcom 60–62, 69, 83–84, 111, 123, 126, 135–136, 151
One Day at a Time 6, 13, 123–124, 199
One of the Boys 137–138
Oppenheimer, Jess 20, 29, 35, 39, 49, 64, 180, 202
Orenstein, Bernie 8–*9*, 23, 29–30, 39, 44–45, 47, 50, 51, 52, 56, 61, 63, 81, 101, 103, 104, 111–112, 122, 124, 126, 138, 139–140, 143, 144, 154, 163, 165, 168, 169, 170–171, 183, 187, 194, 197, 207–208, 210
Orion 137
Orkin, Harvey 20
Our Miss Brooks 19
Out of the Blue 156–157
Overall, Park 168

Paar, Jack 23, 24, 108
Page, LaWanda 168–169
Paley, William 118
The Paper Chase 149

Index

Paramount Pictures 122, 123, 134, 139, 142, 165
Parker, Jim **15**–16, 26, 44, 45–46, 159–160, 196, 206
Parker, Lew 125
Parker and Son 198
Pataki, Michael 148
Patterson, Lorna 150–151
The Patty Duke Show 9
Paul, Norman 5, 189
The Paul Lynde Show 144
Paul Sand in Friends and Lovers 147–148, 163
Persky, Bill 6–7, 24–25, 36, 45, 50, 57, 58, 59, 60, 62, 64, 66–67, 68, 74, 93–95, 104, 108, 119, 124, 125, 126–127, 133–134, 140, 142, 145–146, 157–158, 163, 165, 170, 172, 176, 193, 194, 195, 201
Pete and Gladys 5, 141
Peters, Bernadette 132
Petticoat Junction 11, 13, 82, 121, 161
Phyllis 48, 141–142, 196
Picon, Molly 186
pilot 7, 12, 16, 31, 48, 76, 83, 85, 90, 116, 122, 123, 124, 125, 127, 128, 132, 135, 138, 139, 140, 142, 144, 145, 151–152, 162–165, 169, 170, 191, 197, 198, 206
Pincus, Irving 110–111
Pinky and the Brain 16
Platt, Edward 71
Playboy 25
playwriting 4, 11, 55, 62, 80, 116, 144, 209–210
Poitier, Sidney 168
Police Woman 13
Poston, Tom 21, 108, 164
Powell, Dick 144
The Powers That Be 168
Prentiss, Paula 159–161
Price, Arthur 75
Prinze, Freddie 110
Private Benjamin 16, 150–151, 205
Private Secretary 104
Procter & Gamble 157
producing 4, 6, 7, 8, 9, 11, 12, 13, 16, 23, 30, 31, 32–33, 37, 38, 43, 50, 51–54, 55, 56, 58, 59, 67, 69–70, 71–72, 77, 78, 81, 83, 86, 89, 98, 103, 107, 109, 114, 119, 120, 122, 123, 124, 125, 126, 129, 141, 146, 147, 150, 152, 155–156, 176, 178, 180, 183–184, 194, 195, 197, 198, 199, 206
Promised Land 16
The Pruitts of Southampton 12, 135
Putnam, George 91

Quantum Leap 16, 138
Quincy 143

radio 1, 5, 13, 17–19, 35–36, 47, 64, 181, 187, 191–192, 194
Rae, Charlotte 114, 172, 186
Ragaway, Martin 191
Randall, Bob 58
Randall, Tony 83–84, 100, 164
The Ransom Sherman Show 18
Rapp, Joel 11
Rauseo, Vic 205
The Real McCoys 6, 110–111
The Red Skleton Show 5, 13, 23–24, 102, 184–185
Redgrave, Lynn 154
Regalbuto, Joe 149
Reiner, Carl 37, 67–68, 74, 93, 95, 103–104, 108, 119, 157, 171, 176, 191, 193–194
Reiner, Estelle 67
Reiner, Rob 61, 80
Remington Steele 13
rewriting 49, 52, 54–60, 74, 85, 90, 92, 96, 97, 98, 99, 108, 119, 120, 122, 127, 129, 142, 143, 148, 151, 156, 180, 184–185, 188, 198, 205
Reynolds, Gene 91, 96, 149–150, 191
Rhapsody in Blue 186
Rhine, Larry 1
Rhoda 5, 8, 48, 98, 108–109, 169
Rhodes, Michael 156
Richardson, Patricia 8, 139
Rifkin, Ron 157
Ringwald, Molly 114
Ritter, John 170
Rivers, Joan 23
Rocky & His Friends 28
Rolle, Esther 112
Room 222 8, 16, 74, 149, 191, 203
Rooney, Mickey 63, 89, 138
Rose, Jane 141
Rose, Mickey 11
Rose, Si 119
Roseanne 154
Rosenthal, Phil 53
Ross, Bob 71
Ross, Michael 80, 202–203
Ruben, Aaron 1, 67, 73, 81, 105, 197
Run, Buddy, Run 156
Ryan, Meg 138

Saint James, Susan 124, 172
Samuel French 11
Sand, Paul 147–148
Sandrich, Jay 91, 92, 93, 164, 203
Sanford and Son 8, 10, 13, 81, 85, 101, 109, 111, 134, 144, 151–152, 168–169, 182–183, 197
Sanford Arms 141

218

Index

Sargent, Dick 178
Saved by the Bell 11, 114
Schaal, Richard 141
Scharlach, Ed *16*, 26, 36, 38, 44, 51, 58–59, 61, 63, 83–84, 99, 100, 106, 110, 115, 122–123, 126, 127, 128, 143–144, 150, 151, 155, 158, 160, 167–168, 171, 185–186, 189, 192–193, 196, 207
Schechter, Irv 209
Schell, Ronnie 41, 158
Schiller, Bob 1, *5*, 17, 20, 29, 36, 37, 48, 49, 54, 56, 58, 62, 64–66, 79, 80, 87, 88, 102, 104, 106, 132, 141, 156, 164, 181, 182, 184, 188–189, 195, 200, 202, 204
Schoenman, Elliot 204
Schramm, David 110
Schreiber, Avery 152
Schuck, John 156
Schwartz, Al 13, 18–19, 203
Schwartz, Elroy 9, 13–*14*, 18–19, 22, 31, 39, 42, 43, 46, 48, 56, 60, 115–116, 118, 119, 120–121, 153, 187, 199–200, 203, 205, 209
Schwartz, Sherwood 13, 18, 32, 59, 115–117, 153, 199–200, 205
Scott, Bill 29
screenplay writing 8, 10, 12, 16, 40, 49, 56, 150, 191, 199
Sedgwick Hawk-Styles 135
Seinfeld 78, 139
Seinfeld, Jerry 25
Shalhoub, Tony 110
Shandling, Garry 204
Shapiro, George 20–21, 25
Shayne, Alan 124
Sheldon, Jack 156
Shephard, Harvey 133, 140
Short, Martin 149
Show Business 22
Shriner, Herb 19
Silver, Susan 203
Silverman, Fred 76–77, 108, 111, 135, 148, 163, 165
Silverman, Treva 30, 177, 203
Simmons, Ed 23
Simon, Danny 82–83
Simon, Neil 82–83, 100
Simon & Simon 13
The Simpsons 191, 192
Sinatra, Frank 26
The Six Million Dollar Man 13–14
The $64,000 Question 22
Skelton, Red 184–185
Slade, Bernard 27, 69, 151
The Smith Family 121
Smothers, Dick 144–145

Smothers, Tom 144–145
The Smothers Brothers Comedy Hour 10, 11, 57, 145, 189
The Smothers Brothers Show 144–145, 153, 188, 195
Snuffy Smith 22
Solomon, Mark 205
Something Happened on the Way to the Forum 200
Sommers, Jay 121
The Sonny and Cher Comedy Hour 10, 188
Sothern, Ann 66, 104, 153
South Pacific 118
Spelling, Aaron 144–145
Spencer, Danielle 111
Stamos, John 143
Stander, Arthur 18
Stander, Lionel 18
Stapleton, Jean 88, 182–183
Start the Revolution Without Me 12, 199
Stephens, John 121
Stern, Leonard 70–71, 158–160, 197–198
The Steve Allen Show 25, 119
Stevenson, McLean 154–155
Stewart, Charles 5, 37, 64, 189, 195
Struthers, Sally 55, 80
Studio City 40
Sultan, Arne 70–71, 135, 158–160
Summer and Smoke 84
Supertrain 165
Sutton, Frank 105
Swift, David 155

Tabitha 141
Talbot, Nita 135
Tambor, Jeffrey 134
Tarses, Jay 136
Tartikoff, Brandon 113–114, 124, 137, 139
Taxi 5, 98–99, 142, 149, 168, 179, 191, 193, 196
Taylor, Elizabeth 103
Tenowich, Tom 16, 99, 106, 189
That Girl 6, 8, 9, 10, 13, 14, 15, 16, 30, 66, 103, 123, 124–128, 157, 193, 201
That Was the Week That Was 8
Thigpen, Lynne 139
This Week in Nemtin 163
Thomas, Danny 6, 39, 57, 62, 73, 82, 87, 105, 115, 125, 144, 158, 172, 180, 193, 195, 200
Thomas, Marlo 123, 125–128, 201
Thomas, Terre 126
Thomas, Tony 109, 198
three-camera sitcom 58–59, 60–62, 83–84, 111, 123, 127, 135, 136, 148
The Three Musketeers 38

219

Index

Three's Company 10, 40, 84, 109, 170, 202–203
Thurber, James 158, 162
Time 4
Tinker, Grant 74–75, 78, 92, 114, 135, 139, 146, 153, 155, 163, 165, 174, 178, 191, 192
To Rome with Love 76, 121
The Tonight Show 12, 21, 22, 23, 24, 25, 108, 195
The Tony Randall Show 48
Too Close for Comfort 9, 109–110
A Touch of Grace 144
TOY Productions 111
The Tracey Ullman Show 191
Travolta, John 143
Turnabout 156
Turner, Lloyd 130
Turteltaub, Saul *8*–9, 21–22, 23, 30, 39, 44–45, 50, 52, 63, 81, 101, 103–104, 111–112, 124, 137–138, 139–140, 141, 143, 154, 168, 171, 183, 186, 197, 207, 210
TV Guide 93, 100, 149
TV movie writing 12, 16, 52, 122, 137, 201
Twentieth Century Fox 92, 155, 191
227 6, 9, 169, 180

Universal Studios 130–131
Urich, Robert 141

Valentine, Karen 149–150
Vance, Vivian 64–66, 102, 156, 181
Van Dyke, Dick 6, 39, 67, 74, 94, 95, 103–104, 108, 146, 155, 170–171, 176
Van Dyke, Jerry 152
The Van Dyke Show 146
variety shows 5, 10, 11, 19, 20, 29, 62–63, 76, 102, 145, 153, 184–186, 189, 195
vaudeville 202
The Virginian 13

Wait Til Your Father Gets Home 152
Walker, Jimmie 169–170
Walker, Nancy 92, 169
Ward, Jay 29, 136
Warner Brothers 118, 124
Watkins, Carlene 152
Wayne, David 132
Wayne, John 65
Wayne, Paul *10*, 27, 38, 40–41, 43, 50, 54, 58, 60–61, 62, 68–69, 84, 85, 89, 100, 127–128, 147, 161, 170, 178, 182, 188, 201, 202–203, 204, 205
Weber, Steven 110

Weinberger, Ed. 30, 36–37, 98–99, 129, 141, 142, 147, 149, 162, 178, 191, 203
Weiskopf, Bob 1, *5*, 29, 49, 64, 79, 80, 164, 184, 188–189, 195, 204
Welch, Raquel 106–107
Welcome Back, Kotter 7, 10, 13, 14, 143
Welles, Orson 186
Wells, Dawn 116
Werner, Tom 128
West, Bernie 80, 202
Weston, Jack 163
What's Happening!! 8, 13, 111–112, 168
White, Betty 77, 142–143, 173, 176, 178
White, David 178
Who Do You Trust? 22
Who's the Boss? 7
Wickes, Mary 147
William Morris Agency 20, 25
Williams, Andy 21
Williams, Cara 141
Williams, Robin 99, 106–107, 156, 171
Williams, William B. 24, 157
Wilson, Demond 133
Wilson, Elizabeth 147
Wilson, Flip 56
Winant, Ethel 76–77, 173, 175, 178
Winchell, Walter 5, 17, 18
Wings 5, 82, 109–110, 139
Winkler, Henry 123, 167–168
Winters, Jonathan 11
Witt, Paul Junger 109, 198
WNEW 24–25, 94, 157
Wolper, David 190
Women in Film 33
women writers 4, 11–12, 22, 31–34, 114, 163, 203, 209
The Wonder Years 205
The Wonderful World of Disney 134
Wood, Robert 74, 76
Woollcott, Alexander 41
Working It Out 145–146
Wright Brothers 79
Writers Guild 33, 43, 130–131, 185
Writers Guild Award 10–11, 14, 29, 71, 85, 93–94, 96, 97, 99, 100, 161, 162

York, Dick 178, 179
Yorkin, Bud 81, 111, 199
You Again? 143
You Asked for It 23
Youngman, Henny 19
Your Show of Shows 48, 67
YouTube 161

www.ingramcontent.com/pod-product-compliance
Ingram Content Group UK Ltd.
Pitfield, Milton Keynes, MK11 3LW, UK
UKHW041954140426
5217IPUK00015B/791